The Development of Commercial Law in Sweden and Finland (Early Modern Period – Nineteenth Century)

Legal History Library

VOLUME 40

The titles published in this series are listed at *brill.com/lhl*

The Development of Commercial Law in Sweden and Finland (Early Modern Period–Nineteenth Century)

Edited by

Katja Tikka

BRILL
NIJHOFF

LEIDEN | BOSTON

Cover illustration: A map of Sweden (Finland), Norway and Denmark from the year 1638. Made by Hendrik Hondius, Amsterdam. The National Library of Finland.

Library of Congress Cataloging-in-Publication Data

Names: Tikka, Katja, editor.
Title: The development of commercial law in Sweden and Finland (early modern period-nineteenth century) / edited by Katja Tikka.
Description: Leiden, The Netherlands : Koninklijke Brill NV, [2020] | Series: Legal history library ; volume 40 | Includes bibliographical references and index. | Summary: "The Development of Commercial Law in Sweden and Finland provides a broad perspective on recent research into the history of North European commercial law in a comparative and international framework. The book brings together themes that have previously been considered largely from a national perspective. Despite Sweden's and Finland's peripheral locations in Europe, global legal phenomena occurred there as well. These countries were at the crossroads of cultures and commercial interests, allowing us to re-examine them as lively laboratories for commercial laws and practices rather than dismissing them as a negligible periphery. The importance of trade and international transactions cannot be disclaimed, but the book also emphasizes the resilient nature of commercial law"-- Provided by publisher.
Identifiers: LCCN 2020023480 (print) | LCCN 2020023481 (ebook) | ISBN 9789004393196 (hardback) | ISBN 9789004436046 (ebook)
Subjects: LCSH: Commercial law--Sweden. | Commercial law--Finland.
Classification: LCC KJE2045 .D48 2020 (print) | LCC KJE2045 (ebook) | DDC 346.48507--dc23
LC record available at https://lccn.loc.gov/2020023480
LC ebook record available at https://lccn.loc.gov/2020023481

Typeface for the Latin, Greek, and Cyrillic scripts: "Brill". See and download: brill.com/brill-typeface.

ISSN 1874-1793
ISBN 978-90-04-39319-6 (hardback)
ISBN 978-90-04-43604-6 (e-book)

This book is printed on acid-free paper and produced in a sustainable manner.

Contents

Contents

Illustrations

Notes on Contributors

Dave De ruysscher
(M.A., LL.M., Ph.D.) is legal historian and lawyer. He researches themes regarding the history of commercial and private law until the present day. In 2016, he was awarded an ERC Starting Grant, on the theme of collateral rights and insolvency (early modern period–19th century). He is a member of the Young Academy of Belgium and associate professor at Tilburg University. His latest key peer-reviewed publications are De ruysscher, D. and Puttevils, J., "The Art of Compromise. Legislative Deliberation on Marine Insurance Institutions in Antwerp (c. 1550–c. 1570)" in *BMGN-Low Countries Historical Review* 130/3 (2015), 25–49; De ruysscher, D., "Antwerp 1490–1590: Insurance and Speculation" in A.B. Leonard (ed.), *Marine Insurance: Origins and Institutions, 1300–1850* (London: Palgrave MacMillan, 2015).

Stefania Gialdroni
is Assistant Professor of Medieval and Modern Legal History at the Law Department of the Roma Tre University. She obtained the Italian National Qualification as Associate Professor in 2018. She holds a Ph.D. in legal history both from the University of Milan-Bicocca and the École des Hautes Études en Sciences Sociales (EHESS). As a Ph.D. student, she spent one year at the Max-Planck-Institut für europäische Rechtsgeschichte in Frankfurt a. M., one year at the London School of Economics and two years at the EHESS in Paris (Doctorate in European Legal Cultures: Marie Curie, 6th framework program). As a post-doc research fellow, she worked at the Roma Tre University, Arcadia University (The College of Global Studies, Rome Center), the University of Palermo and the University of Helsinki. She has published a number of articles on the history of commercial law and on law and the humanities. She is the author of *East India Company. Una storia giuridica (1600–1708)* (Bologna: Il Mulino, 2011).

Ulla Ijäs
(Dr. Phil.) teaches Finnish history as a post doctoral researcher at the University of Turku. Currently, she is working in the Finnish Academy project *Agents of Enlightenment. Changing the Minds in Eighteenth-Century Northern Europe.* Her research interests are urban elites and economic and social history prior to the Industrial Revolution. In her latest research articles, she has focused on the urban elite family strategies. Her latest publications are "Marriage and Education in the Eighteenth- and the Nineteenth-century Provincial Towns in the

Northern Baltic" in U. Aatsinki et al. (eds.), *Families, Values, and the Transfer of Knowledge in Northern Societies, 1500–2000* (New York: Routledge, 2018) and "Marie Hackman – The Female Manager in the Family Firm Hackman & Co" in Heinonen, J. and Vainio-Korhonen, K. (eds.), *Women in Business Families: From Past to Present* (New York: Routledge, 2018).

Marko Lamberg
is Professor of Nordic history and history of the communities. Lamberg took his Ph.D. degree at the University of Jyväskylä, Finland, in 2000. His dissertation dealt with town councils and urban culture in late medieval Stockholm, Malmö and Bergen. Since then he has treated several aspects of Nordic social and cultural history, mainly in medieval and early modern contexts. Some of his latest articles written in English can be found in the following books, "Religiosity and Readiness for the Reformation among Late Medieval Burghers in Stockholm, c. 1420–1570" in Toivo, Raisa Maria and Katajala-Peltomaa, Sari (eds.), *Lived Religion and the Long Reformation in Northern Europe c. 1300–1700* (Leiden-Boston: Brill, 2016) and "Mutual Testaments in Late Medieval Stockholm, c. 1420–1520" in Korpiola, Mia and Lahtinen, Anu (eds.) *Planning for Death. Wills and Death-Related Property Arrangements in Europe, 1200–1600.* (Leiden-Boston: Brill, 2018). Currently Lamberg works as a collegium researcher at Turku Institute for Advanced Studies.

Heikki Pihlajamäki
is Professor of Comparative Legal History at the University of Helsinki, Finland. His research focuses on the legal history of the early modern period and encompasses Europe and the Americas. Within legal history, Pihlajamäki's main subject areas include procedural law, criminal law, legal sources, and legal profession. His recent publications include The Oxford Handbook of European Legal History ed. with Dubber, M. and Godfrey, M. (Oxford: Oxford University Press, 2018) and "Merging Comparative Law and Legal History – Towards an Integrated Discipline" in *The American Journal of Comparative Law*, Vol. 66:4 (2018) 733–750.

Jussi Sallila
(LL.D.) serves as editor of the Law section of the Helsinki Term Bank for the Arts and Sciences attached to the Finnish Lawyers' Association. He obtained his doctorate from the University of Helsinki in 2016. During his doctoral studies, he also spent a year at the Max Planck Institute for European Legal History in Frankfurt am Main as a Marie Curie Fellow. He has also worked as project coordinator and post-doctoral researcher in the Academy of Finland research

project *The Making of Commercial Law: Common Practices and National Legal Rules from the Early Modern to the Modern Period*. His research interests include the history of bankruptcy law, commercial law and the intellectual history of legal scholarship.

Katja Tikka
defended her doctoral dissertation *Laivojen tuomaa lakia* [Shipping Legal Norms: Swedish Trading Companies in the Seventeenth Century] in 2020 at the University of Helsinki. In 2013, she began working as research assistant in Heikki Pihlajamäki's project *The Making of Commercial Law: Common Practices and National Legal Rules from the Early Modern to the Modern Period*, and in 2015, she became a doctoral student in the same project. During her doctoral studies, she was also visiting scholar at the Max Planck Institute for European Legal History in Frankfurt. Tikka's interests lie in the first Swedish (and Finnish) trading companies: in their role in state-building and their importance for commerce and for introducing new company models to Sweden from abroad. She has also studied the earliest Swedish marine insurances from the seventeenth century and has published an article on the topic.

CHAPTER 1

Introduction: A Swedish-Finnish Viewpoint

Katja Tikka and Jussi Sallila

1 The Project Behind the Book

This volume deals with the history of commercial law in Sweden and Finland.[1] It has its origins in a research project which charted the development of commercial law in Europe and the wider world in the Early Modern period and the "long nineteenth century." The project was strongly interdisciplinary and comparative.[2] It aimed at contributing to the international debate on the character of the European *lex mercatoria* from the sixteenth century to the start of the First World War. The viewpoint of this volume is Swedish-Finnish and brings together themes previously considered largely from a national perspective. It is time to place Swedish and Finnish commercial law into the international context. Despite Sweden's peripheral location in Europe, global legal phenomena occurred there, too.

The book provides a broad temporal perspective on recent research into North European commercial law in a comparative and international framework. As an ensemble, it offers a novel and unique approach to this branch of research into legal history.

It remains to be seen whether this and other recent volumes on the history of commercial law will eventually lead to a consolidation of "standard" histories of European (or Western or global) commercial law, similar to the history of European private law with its established canonical textbooks. The persistence of older narratives of the commercial law of the past, especially the narrative concerning the allegedly pan-European *lex mercatoria*, underline the need for reappraisal.

1 As Finland was part of the Swedish realm until 1809, the two countries share a common legal past. Even in later periods, as an autonomous part of the Russian Empire and as an independent state since 1917, Finland has developed its legal system in close connection with neighbouring Sweden.

2 The international project "The Making of Commercial Law: Common Practices and National Legal Rules from the Early Modern to the Modern Period" was funded by the Academy of Finland and the Finnish Cultural Foundation.

 | DOI:10.1163/9789004436046_002

2 The History of Commercial Law: A View from the Periphery

Scholars working on sources from the European heartland – France, England – dominate new research on commercial law or areas located in the great commercial axis extending from the Low Countries to northern Italy. From a North European perspective, this new research provides fresh insights that can be used in framing further studies on developments in Sweden and Finland. At the same time, it must be acknowledged that scholars from the heartland investigate commercial law in a context fundamentally different from that of more peripheral countries. The contrast between centre and periphery is more than apparent to a Finnish scholar based in Helsinki, a city where the oldest remaining building dates from 1757. With its medieval old town and baroque palaces, Stockholm is closer to the European norm and has indeed served as a European influence on the northern periphery. In this book, the common legal history of Sweden and Finland (until 1809) is analysed by Finnish historians and legal historians as well as "outsiders" from the heartland countries.[3]

Historical sources have strongly guided the research themes. The fact is that the available material is scanty and fragmental, which favours newer topics and research questions. However, combining contemporary scholarly literature and statutory material with court records, some conclusions can be drawn. The perspective of the "marginal man" is not unusual. In an appraisal of private-law focused literature on European legal history, Heikki Pihlajamäki has stressed that "in these histories it is always the European heartland that sets the standard. You either follow the standard more or less in time, and you follow the development in the heartlands more or less completely," adding that "[t]he standard of European legal history is (…) learned law, the *ius commune*, Roman law and canon law. Being 'standard' means that the legal history of the peripheries is constantly measured against the centre." According to Pihlajamäki, this heartland-centred research agenda is fruitful as it allows the "peripherals" to look at their legal past through comparative glasses.[4]

As far as commercial law is concerned, the main difference between the heartland and the periphery has less to do with learned law, considering that commercial law was at best a marginal object of inquiry in the learned tradition. Instead, the main difference relates to the operative context of commercial law: for example, the scale of commercial transactions, the degree of specialization, and the position in commercial networks. In a recent article on the early modern development of customary law in Antwerp, Van Hofstraeten notes that experts such as merchants played an important role in devising

3 See the entire books Müller 2011; Gustafsson 2006.

4 Pihlajamäki 2014, p. 121–132.

articles on commercial law and that the role of European commercial law jurisprudence is very small.[5] In other respects, reformers compiling new editions of local customs took many influences from a variety of non-customary elements, such as Roman law and legislation.[6] The title of Van Hofstraeten's article refers to Antwerp's position as a "commercial metropolis," and it is in such an environment that the expert role of merchants is to be expected. Antwerp was, after all, one of the "world cities" dominating the European "world-economy" in the sequence reconstructed by Braudel. In analysing the commercial law of medieval Bruges (for Braudel, a world market but not quite a world city) Lambert emphasizes that Bruges realized "higher volumes of trade and attracted more merchants from a wider range of regions than any other place north of the Alps."[7]

In a comparative perspective, Sweden and Finland were mainly rural societies with small towns, which, admittedly, had trade relations and traditions from the Hanseatic period. Even so, contacts were thin and often depended on personal relationships between merchants. Local markets served less by way of specialization, serving the world economy as peripheries producing raw materials such as copper, timber, and tar. It is true that in the seventeenth century, when military conquests made Sweden a great European power, attempts were made to develop Stockholm as a great commercial centre in the Baltic region. However, Sweden's dominant status in the Baltic Sea did not lead to control of the Russian and Eastern trade that the empire-builders had hoped for. In addition, the colonial plans of Sweden did not lead to lasting results, unlike the policies of Western Europe. Therefore, colonies played a much smaller role in the development of commercial law in Sweden.[8]

Since the nineteenth century, both Sweden and Finland have become prosperous countries, a development enabled by multiform evolution: in transport, communication technology, and industrial production. Nevertheless, according to Michael Roberts – a magisterial foreign observer of Swedish history – Sweden has always been a rural country, and its urban society predominantly that of a small country town.[9] The same can be said even more emphatically of Finland.

5 Van Hofstraeten 2016, p. 288–301, 293.
6 Van Hofstraeten 2016, p. 288.
7 Van Hofstraeten 2017, p. 92–96.
8 Rössner 2011, p. 35–38; see the entire book Johnson 1915.
9 See the introduction in Karonen et al 2017; Roberts 1967, p. 4.

3 Sweden and Finland as European Peripheral Countries

In order to understand the basic features of the history of Swedish commercial law, it is essential to place it in the broader social context. The political scenery of Sweden and Finland has always been different from the southern parts of Europe. Despite the existence of the Crown, the estates had their voice in national decisions. Particularly since the eighteenth century in sessions of parliament, the four estates together discussed and voted in parliamentary meetings. The lowest of these estates were peasants, the others being burghers, the clergy, and the nobility. Of course, the system was not democratic, yet the northern way of thinking about equality can still be perceived.

From a comparative perspective, the northern location of the country is the dominant characteristic that explains many of the differences in social and economic development. The population density of Sweden and Finland has always been low, and long distances have posed challenges for administrative control of the territory.[10]

Through the connections of maritime trade, many important cultural influences have been absorbed in Sweden and Finland, though this has often happened slowly. Naturally, adoption of foreign influences has been a selective process, and developments have not always followed the Central European pattern. In this book, the chapter by Dave De ruysscher cites examples of legal transplants in early modern Swedish trading companies. The general debate about the topic has concerned the substance of the term: whether legal systems or written law were adopted. De ruysscher's chapter offers a novel insight into Swedish company law.[11]

When comparing Sweden with central European areas, or even lands on the southern shores of the Baltic Sea, development of the social structure has been divergent. After the relatively late Christianization of Northern Europe, the Church came to possess a strong economic and political position in medieval Sweden. By contrast, feudalism never achieved the same broad dimensions as in Central Europe, as the peasantry maintained its independent position in Swedish estate society. The power of the King was not very strong in the medieval period. However, through his Law of the Realm (governing rural areas) and Town Law, King Magnus Eriksson (r. 1319–1364) managed to unify the law of Sweden in the mid-fourteenth century.[12]

---

10 Lappalainen 2017, p. 113–139; Lappalainen 2014, p. 195–197.
11 Watson 2000, p. 638–686; Kahn-Freund 1974, p. 1–27; De ruysscher 2017, p. 158–161.
12 Hechscher 1954, p. 36–38.

FIGURE 1 Map showing the most important cities, towns and their distances in early modern Sweden.

The relative poverty of Sweden was reflected in the small number of towns and its undeveloped urban culture, especially in Finland where only six towns existed in the Middle Ages. The towns mostly supplied the rural trade, selling products from farmers such as butter, dried fish, and furs, keeping business slow and small in scale. Foreign influences in urban culture were brought largely by German merchant families, who controlled foreign trade.[13] In this book, Marko Lamberg's focus of study is on foreign influences in Sweden. He highlights that immigration brought foreign influences to Stockholm during the turn of the medieval age to the early modern period. Current research on the topic has concentrated on Low German influence, despite evidence of other effects too, such as Dutch and English. Lamberg's chapter brings to this debate the immigrants' legal traditions and prejudices. His point of view elevates the topic to a new and unexplored level.[14]

The sixteenth century was a period of transformation in Sweden, triggered by the religious and administrative reforms of King Gustav I Vasa (r. 1523–1561). Supported by the peasants, he assumed royal power in 1523 and ended the Danish-dominated Scandinavian union monarchy. Some years later, he initiated the Reformation in the Swedish realm. With the help of confiscated Church property, he began to build the Swedish state according to models adopted from Central Europe. An important part of the bureaucratic state model was a conscious effort to direct economic activity on a large scale.[15]

Following Gustav I Vasa's reign, Sweden was almost continuously at war for a hundred years. During the reign of Gustav II Adolphus (r. 1611–1632), Sweden became a North European empire. The expansion opened new possibilities for commerce but required endless rearmament and additional taxation. Mercantilist policies were adopted in order to strengthen the Swedish economy and control by the authorities. Among other things, this led to the founding of the first modern Swedish trading companies with a strong contribution from Dutch entrepreneurs.[16]

Attempts were made to develop Stockholm as a great commercial centre of the Baltic Sea. However, as already noted above, Sweden's dominant status in the Baltic Sea did not lead to control of the Russian and Eastern trade that the empire-builders had hoped for. Partly because of its geographic position, Sweden also played a marginal role in the intercontinental sea trade. As a result, its colonies played a much smaller role in the development of commercial law in

13 Korpiola 2017, p. 288–290; Kallioinen 1981, p. 14–19; Lappalainen 2017, p. 189; Wubs-Mrozewicz 2004, p. 53–67.

14 Ahnlund 1929, p. 1–34; Gustafsson 2006, p. 45–54.

15 See the entire book Glete 1999; Aalto 2012, p. 19–20.

16 See also the entire books Gerner (ed.) 2014; Klein 1999; Israel 1990; Odhner 1865, p. 298–300.

Sweden. While the Swedish East India and West India companies did acquire greater significance in the eighteenth century, according to the assessment of Müller they are best analysed as offshore companies largely dependent on foreign capital and a minor influence on the Swedish economy and Swedish society. However, increasing demand for Swedish forest, iron and copper resources in the European-centred world economy made it possible to use trading companies as a means of controlling the export of these strategic resources.

Katja Tikka's chapter is closely connected with De ruysscher's part as a continuation of the trading companies. The chapter opens up the peripheral side by drawing the tar route from deep in the Finnish forests through local cities to Europe. After the first era of Swedish trading companies, Sweden had signed the peace treaty of Westphalia, which opened the door to Sweden's so-called "Era of Greatness." Tar and pitch rose to become one of the country's main products and development of the tar companies began. The topic has lately attracted interest among Finnish scholars, which hopefully will expand.[17] Tar companies provide a significant example of legal history because they played a notable role in developing Swedish commercial law. Previous research on the topic can be traced back for over sixty years.[18]

An important part of the seventeenth-century state-building process was concerned with law reforms. After the failure of earlier attempts, King Carl XI[19] (r. 1660–1697) set in motion a codification project that culminated with the Law of 1734 unifying rural and town law in Sweden. At this point, Sweden's great power status had already ended with the Great Northern War (1700–1721). Eighteenth-century Sweden was no longer merely a recipient of cultural influences, as its flourishing natural scientists gained worldwide fame, although in economic terms Sweden remained marginal and towns were relatively small.[20] After the Great Northern War, parts of Finland came under Russian rule, followed by new conquests in 1743 and then the whole of today's Finland in 1809. This has meant that development of Swedish legal tradition has proceeded in both Sweden and Finland as jurisdictions independent of each other. Since the nineteenth century, both Sweden and Finland have become prosperous countries, a development enabled – as we have seen – by evolutions in transport, communication technology, and industrial production.[21] The chapter by Ulla Ijäs opens previously unnoticed commercial practices in nineteenth-century Finland.

17 See the entire Dissertation Wirta 2018.
18 See the entire book Hallberg 1959.
19 In English also as King Charles XI.
20 Åström 1988, p. 31–35.
21 Roberts 1967, p. 4.

On the basis of earlier scholarship, we may conclude that commercial law played a relatively insignificant role in the development of Swedish and Finnish law. Jussi Sallila and Heikki Pihlajamäki clarify practices of teaching law. An example of older surveys is a 1944 article by Finnish legal scholar Gunnar Palmgren, then professor of commercial law at the Swedish School of Economics in Helsinki. In his view, the relatively marginal role of commercial law was mainly due to the relatively undeveloped economy, at least in earlier periods. Considering that commerce, shipping, and industry had not been clearly differentiated sectors of society, it was understandable that a special legal regime for commercial law was not seen as necessary or even desirable.[22] Although the Town Law, enacted by King Magnus Eriksson in the mid-fourteenth century, did include some rules concerning commerce and shipping, commercial law only became an area of conscious legislative policy in the seventeenth century, when Sweden became a great European power. During this period, a maritime code and legislation on bills of exchange were enacted.[23]

The Swedish Law of 1734 amalgamated the old medieval land law and the town law codes. The Commercial Section of the code included mainly norms of general private law, as well as regulation of economic activities of a public law character. Rules concerning partnerships, security, and loans, for example, were of course important in commercial contexts, but their applicability was not restricted to such cases. Maritime law and the law on bills of exchange were left out of the codification. In the following centuries, the legislation of both Sweden and Finland was built on this foundation.

4 Scientific Relevance

The volume begins with Marko Lamberg's analysis of tolerance towards legal customs and traditions in late medieval and early modern Stockholm circa 1475–1635. Lamberg analyses the consequences of immigration and asks how foreign influence changed the capital of Sweden from a commercial law standpoint. Trade as well as communal life were in principle regulated by the medieval town law written in the mid-fourteenth century. This was regarded as an entirely domestic law which together with the privileges and ordinances issued by latter-day governments formulated the basis of merchant business.[24] The core question is how the local Town Court approved external legal patterns

22 Palmgren 1944, p. 113.
23 See also p. 6.
24 Adding to the earlier mentioned literature, Lamberg's main source books in his chapter are: Kumlien 1953; Lamberg 2001; Trolle Önnerfors 2010.

in Stockholm. Lamberg shows that Swedish legislation was considered as the sole basis for all decisions of the court, and the law was constantly prioritized by the courts. The Swedish Crown allowed courts less and less discretion in their actions; even on the idealistic level the Town Courts sought decisions that foreigners could accept rather than merely subordinate themselves to. This policy had already been expressed in the medieval Town Law. Notwithstanding, entries in the court records changed considerably over the decades, so it is difficult to compare between different eras and different changes. At the end of the day, the connecting factor is that the Town Court of Stockholm nevertheless possessed a certain freedom of choice that on some occasions resulted in solutions that actually contradicted the written law. Lamberg's chapter explains the practical side of town courts' operations. This fills a gap in existing research and develps the viewpoint of this book on legal commercial actions during the Middle Ages. The chapter is an example of how medieval legislation in peripheral Sweden was affected by foreign influences.

Next, Dave De ruysscher covers chartered companies in Sweden and the Dutch Republic during ca.1600–1630, including examination of a case of legal transplantation through which Dutch commercial innovations were transferred to Swedish conditions. De ruysscher's principal contribution to this book is to observe Scandinavia and Sweden from the Dutch angle, thus providing a comparative context to Lamberg's and Tikka's texts. The conclusions are based on archive source materials. De ruysscher argues that rules of governance for the earliest chartered companies were national, whereas crafting these norms was an energetic and interactive process. Foreign company statutes strongly moulded the first Swedish company plans, but legal borrowing was concerned with parts of charters, practices and views, but not with transplants of charters as a whole – they were not simply replicated. Drafts of the first company statutes were mainly written in close cooperation with merchants and they involved elements from Dutch and English "Indian" Companies.[25] Additionally, De ruysscher asks whether the motives behind the foreign characteristics of organization were based on the cultural and political scene rather than business.[26] He concludes that several Dutch and some English ideas were inserted into Swedish company charters, though they were combined with local conditions and under the acknowledgement of the Swedish royal entourage. During the seventeenth century, Sweden was still largely inexperienced in terms of chartered companies, and the country served as a testing ground for new concepts. Some ideas were even implemented in Sweden

25 See the entire books Boulle 1981; Steensgaard 1982; Gelderblom 2013; Chaudhuri 1965.

26 Some of the latest and the main articles on the theme are Grell 2016; Gialdroni 2011; Müller 2005.

before they gained acceptance in the Netherlands. Many indications prove that progress was long lasting with regard to the core aspects of corporate organisation. The chapter by De ruysscher shows that Sweden was not connected with European evolution as closely as it might have. Nevertheless, the peripheral situation of Sweden did not prevent some modern reforms from taking place. The chapter thus challenges previous impressions of Swedish legal development.

Continuing some of De ruysscher's themes, Katja Tikka approaches the early development of the Swedish monopolist Tar Company in a local mercantilist context. The chapter includes important new research on a type of corporation which was completely new in Sweden. Tikka's chapter lends the book an important view on the lower-level formation of law, the more so as existing research in this field is decades old and does not study legal aspects. Tikka now brings novel findings to the field of Swedish company legislation around the years 1648–1680.[27] Satisfyingly, Nordic tar has recently aroused the interest of other researchers as well. Kaarle Wirta defended his dissertation "Dark Horses of Business" recently, at the end of 2018, at Leiden University.[28] Tikka's chapter further develops Wirta's conclusions. At the heart of Tikka's chapter is an explanation of the management of the company, how it related to previous Swedish trading companies, and to what extent the rules on the company resulted from foreign influence.

As a result, Tikka discovers that the legal character of the Tar Company exemplified changes in ideas and influences from many directions. The laws of the Netherlands, England and France all exerted an influence. However, because Sweden was politically more centralized, the impact of foreign law was mitigated and sieved through the conventional legislative models of the country. The tar companies never achieved the status of established institutions but remained a series of failures. Despite this, the tar companies can be seen as a necessary step in the development of Swedish company law.

Ulla Ijäs displays the Finnish timber trade and its legal practices in the nineteenth century. She proceeds from a grassroots level and focuses on the Hackman merchant house, a family company of German origin. Problematizing the concept of legal modernization, Ijäs tracks the changes which occurred when Swedish law was introduced in the region of Vyborg after it became part of the Grand Duchy of Finland. Her chapter focuses on the solutions that an international business environment on the European periphery found to the problem

---

27 See the entire books Waris approx. 1940; Hallberg 1959; Fyhrvall 1880. See also Lappalainen 2017, p. 113–139.

28 Dissertation of Wirta 2018.

of legal plurality.[29] Ijäs concludes that businesspeople trusted communal values, codes of conduct, and informal information channels more than legal texts and their interpretations. Valid information was a valuable asset for transnational traders, with the flow of information protected and assured in several ways, for instance by keeping records and by spreading information through institutional channels. The Hackmans were export merchants who followed the traditional family firm model, and they avoided distractions from protecting familiar methods. Ijäs's findings result from combining business history with legal history "from below."[30] Previous studies exist on central and northwest European as well as North American merchant houses and their legal evolution. However, because of the dissimilar economic and legal conditions, these studies are not fully applicable to the European northern periphery.[31]

Jussi Sallila's chapter is concerned with the teaching of commercial law at the Finnish university during the era of transition from Swedish to Russian rule. In a period with practically no publications on commercial law, lecture manuscripts provide insights into the state of knowledge among the jurists of the time. Sallila investigates the teaching of commercial law at university in Finland during the late eighteenth and early nineteenth centuries. He focuses mainly on lecture manuscripts, since handbooks or other legal literature did not include systematic treatment of commercial law.[32]

Sallila argues that although the characteristic features of the Swedish-Finnish legal tradition were not conducive to the emergence of commercial law as a specific field of law, the early nineteenth century enabled this development. His study shows that university teachers experienced difficulty in determining the scope of commercial law as a separate field of law. Despite the conservative tone of the lectures, Professor Nordström, however, was able to look in his teaching for ideas in countries with more sophisticated legal cultures. His followers were then already relying extensively on foreign legislation and literature.

Heikki Pihlajamäki presents developments in Finnish commercial law with the help of comparative legal history in an international context. His aim is to observe theoretical questions through nineteenth-century legal literature. Using international comparisons, Pihlajamäki's chapter describes and explains the birth of Finnish commercial law in the nineteenth century. Although Finnish commercial law scholarship was subject to foreign influence, reception was

29 Kallioinen 2012: Ulianova 2009; Müller 2004.
30 Harris 2011, p. 4–10; Cotterrell 2009, p. 19–36.
31 Flume 2015, p 45–83; De ruysscher 2012, p. 3–29.
32 Sallila's main literature includes: Scherner 1977; Kessler 2007.

by no means passive. Recent research on other themes and periods show similar results.[33]

Finally, Stefania Gialdroni summarizes Nordic evolution of commercial law. Her chapter weaves together five centuries and six scholars with different backgrounds.[34] Gialdroni connects local mercantile transactions – as seen through archival work and scholarship – to the international aspects of trade. Indeed, as she concludes, transoceanic trade carried legal influence from coast to coast, and from cities to peripheries.

Literature

Aalto, Seppo. 2012. *Sotakaupunki; Helsingin Vanhankaupungin historia 1550–1639* (Helsinki: Otava).

Ahnlund, Nils. 1929. "Svenskt och tyskt i Stockholms äldre historia" in *Historisk Tidskrift* 49, 1–34.

Åström, Sven-Erik. 1988. *From Tar to Timber, Studies in Northeast European Forest and Foreign Trade 1660–1860* (Helsinki: The Finnish Society of Sciences and Letters).

Boulle, Pierre H. 1981. *Companies and Trade. Essays on Overseas Trading Companies During the Ancien Régime* (Leiden: Leiden University Press).

Calasso, Francesco. 1949. *Gli ordinamenti giuridici del Rinascimento medievale* (2nd ed.; Milan: Giuffrè).

Chaudhuri, Kirti N. 1965. *The English East India Company. The Study of an Early Joint-Stock Company, 1600–1640* (London: Cass).

Cortese, Ennio. 2000. *Le grandi linee della storia giuridica medievale* (Rome: Il Cigno).

Cotterrell, Roger. 2009. "Spectres of Transnationalism: Changing Terrains of Sociology of Law" in *Journal of Law and Society* 36, no. 4, 19–36.

De ruysscher, Dave. 2012. "From Usages of Merchants to Default Rules: Practices of Trade, Ius Commune and Urban Law in Early Modern Antwerp" in *The Journal of Legal History,* 33, 1, 3–29.

De ruysscher, Dave. 2017. "Partnerships as Flexible and Open-Purpose Entities: Legal and Commercial Practice in Nineteenth-Century Antwerp (c.1830–1850)" in De ruysscher et al. (eds.).

De ruysscher, Dave. Cordes, Albrecht. Dauchy, Serge. and Pihlajamäki, Heikki. (eds.). 2017. *The Company in Law and Practice: Did Size Matter? (Middle Ages – Nineteenth Century)* (Leiden-Boston: Brill).

33 See the entire books Pihlajamäki 1997; Korpiola 2009; Trolle Önnerfors 2014.

34 Gialdrioni's conclusions are mainly based on Calasso 1949; Cortese 2000; De ruysscher et al 2017; Favali 2004; Goldschmidt 1891; Scialoja 1913; Mayenburg 2019; Sarti 2016.

Favali, Lyda. 2004. *Qirād islamico, commenda medievale e strategie culturali dell'Occidente* (Turin: Giappichelli).

Flume, Johannes W. 2015. "Law and Commerce: The Evolution of Codified Business Law in Europe" in *Comparative Legal History* vol. 2, 45–83.

Fyhrvall, Karl Oscar. 1880. *Svenska Handelslagstiftningens historia, Tjärhandelskompanierna* (Stockholm).

Gardberg, Carl, Jacob. 1981. "Kaupunkilaitos keskiajalla ja uuden ajan alussa" in *Suomen kaupunkilaitoksen historia* (Helsinki: Suomen kaupunkiliitto).

Gelderblom, Oscar and Jonker, Joost. 2013. "The Formative Years of the Modern Corporation. The Dutch East India Company VOC, 1602–1623" in *The Journal of Economic History* 73/4 , 1050–1076.

Gialdroni, Stefania. 2011. *East India Company. Una storia giuridica (1600–1708)* (Bologna: Il Mulino).

Gerner, Kristian (ed.). 2014. *The Swedes and the Dutch Were Made for Each Other. 400 years of Swedish-Dutch Relations* (Lund: Historiska Media).

Glete, Jan. 1999. *Warfare at Sea 1500–1650. Maritime Conflicts and the Transformation of Europe* (London: Routledge).

Goldschmidt, Levin. 1868–1891. *Handbuch des Handelsrechts* (Stuttgart).

Goldschmidt, Levin. 1891. *Universalgeschichte des Handelsrechts* (Stuttgart: Ferdinand Enke).

Grell, Ole Peter. 2016. "Dutch and English in the Baltic, North Sea and the Arctic" in Kouri, Erkki I. and Olesen, Jens E. (eds.), *The Cambridge History of Scandinavia.* vol. II: 1520–1870 (Cambridge: CUP).

Gustafsson, Sofia. 2006. "Svenska städer i medeltidens Europa. En komparativ studie av stads-organisation och politisk kultur" in *Stockholm Studies in History*, vol. 86, 45–54.

Hallberg, Annagreta. 1959. "Tjärexport och tjärhandelskompanier" in *Historiska och litteraturhistoriska studier* no 34 (Helsinki: Svenska litteratursällskapet i Finland).

Harris, Ron. 2011. *Industrializing English Law. Entrepreneurship and Business Organization 1720–1844* (Cambridge: Cambridge University Press).

Heckscher, Eli F. 1954. *An Economic History of Sweden* (Cambridge: Harvard University).

Israel, Jonathan I. 1990. *Dutch Primacy in World Trade, 1585–1740* (Oxford: Clarendon press).

Johnson, Amandus. 1915. *The Swedes on the Delaware 1638–1664* (Philadelphia: The Swedish Colonial Society).

Kahn-Freund, Otto. 1974. "On Uses and Misuses of Comparative Law" in *The Modern Law Review* vol 37, 1, 1–27.

Kallioinen, Mika. 2017. "Inter-Communal Institutions in Medieval Trade" in *The Economic History Review* 70, 1131–1152.

Kallioinen, Mika. 2012. *The Bonds of Trade. Economic Institutions in Pre-modern Northern Europe* (Cambridge: Scholars Publishing).

Karonen, P. and Hakanen, M. (eds.). 2017. *Personal Agency at the Swedish Age of Greatness 1560–1720* (Helsinki: Suomalaisen Kirjallisuuden Seura).

Kessler, Amalia. 2007. *Revolution in Commerce: The Parisian Merchant Court and the Rise of Commercial Society in Eighteen-Century France* (New Haven: Yale University Press).

Klein, Peter W. 1999. *De Trippen in de zeventiende eeuw. Een studie over het ondernemersgedrag op de Hollandse stapelmarkt* (London: Routledge).

Korpiola, Mia. 2009. *Between Betrothal and Bedding: Marriage Formation in Sweden 1200-1600* (Leiden-Boston: Brill).

Korpiola, Mia. 2018. "Svea Court of Appeal Records as a Source of Commercial Law: Founding Year of 1614" in Pihlajamäki, Heikki, Cordes, Albrecht, Dauchy, Serge and De ruysscher, Dave (eds.), *Understanding the Sources of Early Modern and Modern Law: Courts, Statutes, Contracts and Legal Scholarship* (Leiden-Boston: Brill).

Kumlien, Kjell. 1953. *Sverige och hanseaterna. Studier i svensk politik och utrikeshandel*, Kungl. Vitterhets-, historie- och antikvitetsakademiens handlingar 86 (Stockholm).

Lamberg, Marko. 2001. *Dannemännen i stadens råd. Rådmanskretsen i nordiska köpstäder under senmedeltiden* (Stockholm, Stockholmas stad).

Lappalainen, Mirkka. 2017. "Loyal Servants of the King and the Crown (1620–1680): Stewards and Governors in Sweden before the Age of Absolutism" in Karonen, Petri and Hakanen, Marko (eds.), *Personal Agency at the Swedish Age of Greatness 1560–1720* (Helsinki: Suomalaisen Kirjallisuuden Seura).

Lappalainen, Mirkka. 2014. *Pohjolan leijona; Kustaa II Aadolf ja Suomi 1611–1632* (Helsinki: Siltala).

Mayenburg, D. von. 2019. "'Wörter für Wucher': Ius commune and the 16th Century Debate on the Legitimacy of South German Trading Houses" in Gialdroni, Stefania (ed.), *Migrating Words, Migrating Merchants: Migrating Law* (Leiden-Boston: Brill).

Müller, Leos. 2004. *Consuls, Corsairs, and Commerce. The Swedish Consular Service and Long-distance Shipping, 1720–1815* (Uppsala: Uppsala Universitet).

Müller, Leos. 2005. "The Dutch Entrepreneurial Networks and Sweden in the Age of Greatness," in Brand, Hanno (ed.), *Trade, Diplomacy, and Cultural Exchange. Continuity and Change in the North Sea Area and the Baltic, c.1350–1750* (Hilversum: Verloren).

Müller, Leos. 2011. "Swedish Shipping Business between the Baltic Sea and the Atlantic World, 1650–1800" in Müller et al. (eds.).

Müller, Leos, Rössner, Philipp and Tamaki, Toshiaki (eds.). 2011. *The Rise of the Atlantic Economy and the North Sea/Baltic Trades, 1500–1800* (Stuttgart: Franz Steiner Verlag).

Odhner, C.T. 1865. *Sveriges inre historia under drottning Christina's förmyndare* (Stockholm: Norstedt).

Palmgren, Gunnar. 1944. "Utvecklingen av Finlands handelsrättsliga lagstiftning" in Pipping, Hugo (ed.) *Vårt näringsliv och kriget: spridda studier samlade av Ekonomiska Samfundet i Finland på femtionde årsdagen av dess instiftande och tillägnade professor J. V. Tallqvist* (Helsinki: Schildt).

Pihlajamäki, Heikki. 2014. "Comparative Contexts in Legal History: Are We All Comparatists now?" in Adams, Maurice and Heirbaut, Dirk (eds.) *The Method and Culture of Comparative Law: Essays in Honour of Mark van Hoecke* (UK: Hart Publishing).

Pihlajamäki, Heikki. 1997. *Evidence, Crime, and the Legal Profession: The Emergence of Free Evaluation of Evidence in Nineteenth-Century Finland* (Lund: Institutet för rättshistorisk forskning).

Roberts, Michael. 1967. *Essays in Swedish History* (London: Weidenfeld & Nicolson).

Rössner, Philipp Robinson. 2011. "A Shift from the Baltic to the Atlantic in Early Modern European Commerce and Economic Activity: Evidence from the Sound Toll Register and Scotland, c. 1660–1760" in Müller et al. (eds.).

Sarti, N. 2016. "Il medioevo dei diritti" in P. Alvazzi del Frate et al. (eds.), *Tempi del diritto. Età medievale, moderna, contemporanea* (Turin: Giappichelli).

Steensgaard, Niels. 1982. "The Dutch East India Company as an Institutional Innovation" in Aymard, M. (ed.) *Dutch Capitalism and World Capitalism. Capitalisme hollandaise et capitalisme mondial* (Cambridge: CUP).

Trolle Önnerfors, Elsa. 2010. *Justitia et Prudentia. Rättsbildning genom rättstillämpning – Svea hovrätt och testamentsmålen 1640–1690* (Lund: Juridiska fakulteten, Lunds universitet).

Ulianova, Galina. 2009. *Female Entrepreneurs in Nineteenth-Century Russia* (*Perspectives in Economic and Social History*) (London: Pickering & Chatto).

Van Hofstraeten, Bram. 2017. "Delving for Diversity in Early Modern Company Law: Mining Companies in Seventeenth-Century Liège" in De ruysscher et al. (eds.).

Van Hofstraeten, Bram. 2016. "Recording Customs in Early Modern Antwerp, a Commercial Metropolis" in *Rechtsgeschichte – Legal History Rg* 24, 288–301.

Waris, Heikki. approx. 1940. *Tervakauppakomppania vuosina 1648–1661* (Helsinki: University of Helsinki).

Watson, Alan. 2000. "Legal Transplants and European Private Law" in *Electronic Journal of Comparative Law*, vol 4.4 http://www.ejcl.org/ejcl/44/44-2.html.

Watson, Alan. 2013. "Walton, and the History of legal Transplants" in *Georgia Journal of International and Comparative Law*, Vol. 41, No. 3, 638–686.

Wirta, Kaarle. 2017. *"Dark Horses of Business": Overseas Entrepreneurship in Seventeenth-Century Nordic Trade in the Indian and Atlantic Oceans*, Dissertation (Leiden University).

Wubs-Mrozewicz, Justyna. 2014. "Interplay of Identities. German Settlers in Late Medieval Stockholm" in *Scandinavian Journal of History* 29, 53–67.

CHAPTER 2

"Unlawful Contracts and Foreign Subtlety" – (In)Tolerance towards External Legal Customs and Traditions in Late Medieval and Early Modern Stockholm, c. 1475–1635

Marko Lamberg

1 Introduction

Although Stockholm officially became the capital of the Swedish kingdom only in the seventeenth century, it had already become an important international harbour town and market place by the thirteenth century, the biggest of its kind in the Swedish kingdom.[1] Because Sweden belonged to the interest sphere of the Hanseatic merchants, it was natural that merchants and craftsmen speaking Low German dialects visited Stockholm and other towns and regions in the Swedish realm. Several of these visitors also settled down, at least temporarily.[2] From the early sixteenth century onwards, the local community of Stockholm as well as several other Swedish towns felt the growing influence and presence of other foreign groups, especially Dutch, English and Scottish burghers.[3]

These and other immigrant groups have been dealt with in several studies, but the main interest has been in their economic, cultural or societal significance. In particular, the role of the Germans has been given a lot of consideration in studies dealing with Stockholm in the fourteenth, fifteenth and sixteenth centuries. Nevertheless, there exists a gap in scholarly knowledge regarding the interaction between different legal practices. Formally, the justice system in Stockholm followed Swedish legislation, which consisted mainly of the Town Law (Sw. *Stadslagen*) issued in the middle of the fourteenth century and valid until 1734 as well as the local and royal ordinances completing it.[4] But

1 Dahlbäck 1987, p. 13–20, 50; Regner 2013, p. 20–26.

2 See the entire books Koppe 1933; Kumlien 1953.

3 Svanberg and Tyden 1990, p. 7–14.

4 A modern translation of the medieval Swedish Town Law with commentary has been published as *Magnus Erikssons stadslag i nusvensk tolkning* (Stockholm, 1966). The main part of the ordinances issued for Stockholm and other Swedish towns (till 1632) can be found in the

 | DOI:10.1163/9789004436046_003

since Stockholm was a multi-ethnic local community and a site of international commerce, different legal traditions met and even clashed with each other. For example, in 1486, a tavern-keeper of German origin answered in his mother tongue: "*Ja, dat ist en holmisk budh*" ("Yes, that is a Stockholmer regulation"), when a member of the town council had reminded him of the fact that he should not have any customers after the licit business hours.[5] Apparently, the immigrant hinted that he was not so fond of following local rules.

So far, studies of the presence of foreign legal practices in Stockholm have focused on the late medieval German influence, especially on the Swedish Town Law and on the forms of town administration in Stockholm and in other Swedish towns. Overall, urban life forms and practices in Sweden – urban administration, town plans, communal norms, et cetera – were to a great extent modelled after Low German examples, thanks to the lively contacts with the Hanseatic world.[6] However, Stockholm was not a Hanseatic town because it never was an official member of the Hanseatic League. Nor were the Germans the only culturally distinct group there. Swedes came into contact with visitors and immigrants from a wide range of places. Thus, foreign legal cultures other than solely Low German ones may have influenced the local legal practices in Stockholm, but that has been virtually ignored by the research so far, the only actual exception being Sofia Gustafsson's comparison between possible German, Danish, Dutch and English patterns within the medieval Swedish town administration, Stockholm included.[7] However, not even her study discusses whether and how different legal traditions met and clashed with each other, or if elements that were regarded as foreign were tolerated or rejected.

Elsa Trolle Önnersfors points out in her dissertation how influences from Roman Law began to be tolerated and actively applied in Sweden during the seventeenth century, albeit not without resistance from domestic legal experts who feared excessive cultural differences and their consequences. During the seventeenth century, the number of professional lawyers acquainted with Roman Law started to grow within the Swedish realm; likewise the number of conflicts dealing with property and economy. That is why new legal sources

---

series *Privilegier, resolutioner och förordningar för Sveriges städer*, vols. 1–7 (Stockholm, 1927–1985). Regarding Stockholm solely, ordinances have been also published in *Stockholms stads privilegiebref 1423–1700*.

5 *Stockholms stads tänkeböcker 1483–1492*, p. 162.

6 See, for example, the discussion in the introduction in *Magnus Erikssons stadslag as well as in* Karl Benckert, *Bidrag till inteckningsinstitutets historia* (Stockholm, 1920), p. 43–52, See also Schück 1926 and the chapter of Gustafsson 2006.

7 Cf. the previous note.

were needed,[8] but that development was still under way during the fifteenth, sixteenth and early seventeenth centuries.

Consequently, this chapter is meant to fill a gap in the existing research dealing with interaction and coexistence between Swedish and non-Swedish legal practices in Stockholm. This topic – tolerance or intolerance towards influences from foreign legislation – is highly relevant when we think of the development of the commercial law in the early modern Swedish context. Neither the Swedish central power nor any Swedish local community issued any separate coherent legislation for international commerce; instead, the commercial activities were regulated by means of national legislation like the Town Law as well as numerous ordinances issued by kings, regents and local courts. Moreover, like the dispute regarding the closing times of taverns in Stockholm in 1486, also local legal traditions stipulated how trades should be practiced.

The main question in this chapter deals with if and how external legal patterns were accepted by the local justice system in Stockholm, especially the town council (*stadens råd*), which consisted mainly of local merchants and which formed the Town Court (*rådstugurätten*). During the period studied, there were also two other permanent courts that functioned in Stockholm as well. One of them was the poorly known "market court" or "little court" (*torgrätten, lilla rätten*) subordinated to the Town Court. In the sixteenth century, it seems to have evolved into a lesser court called *kämnärsrätten*.[9] During the early seventeenth century, the Swedish state started to strengthen its grip on local communities and this was done, in part, by founding completely new high courts, the so-called courts of appeal (*hovrätter*) that supervised the judiciary system in the realm. The first of them was the Svea Court of Appeal (*Svea hovrätt*), founded in Stockholm in 1614.[10]

The tolerance or intolerance towards foreign influences cannot be analysed merely by focusing on foreigners and their interactions with the Town Court. Pre-modern culture has often been labelled as xenophobic, not only against people coming from other countries but against other local communities, that is from other parts of the same realm, as well. Even a person living in a neighbouring village was seen as a stranger, at least on certain occasions.[11] On the other hand, pre-modern towns were dependent on continuous immigration due to high mortality rates. In towns, virtually the entire population were

8 Trolle Önnerfors 1690, p. 76–79.

9 Karonen 1994, p. 44–47; Lamberg 2001, p. 192–194.

10 See the entire book Korpiola (ed.) 2014.

11 See, for example, Tak 1990, p. 90–100; Snell 2003, p. 1–30; Mäkinen 2007; Lamberg 2007, p. 211–220.

immigrants or descendants of immigrants.[12] Especially in greater harbour towns, it was possible to come into everyday interaction with people from several parts of the realm as well as with foreigners. But the concept of "foreigner" is very complex, as there were those who had moved directly from abroad as well as those who were descendants of earlier immigrants, those who had dwelt in some other community in Sweden before moving further, and those who had come from areas that had been brought into the Swedish realm due to changes in its borders. Not all foreigners were regarded as aliens, at least not in a similar way. Likewise, there were also Finns and occasionally also Sámi living in Stockholm: they were not formally foreigners as they had become subjects of the Swedish Crown centuries ago, but nevertheless they spoke their own languages and had a partly different cultural background – thus, they were, at least occasionally, regarded as strangers, different from the Swedes.[13] Considering the cultural mosaic that the local community of Stockholm consisted of, a study on possible foreign influences on jurisdictional practices also has to be contrasted with domestic external influences.

Although the scope of this chapter is holistic, its analysis excludes one important judicial factor, the Church and its law and jurisdiction. Originally, the Church was an external, transnational agent in Swedish society, but even in the Middle Ages, it had already become more national in its character and during the Reformation it was connected more intimately to the national administrative and judicial system subordinated to the King.[14] But because the Town Law and the ordinances issued for Stockholm mostly omitted religious and ecclesiastical matters, cases that dealt with religion, sexual behaviour or marital life were also regularly referred to the representatives and courts of the Church.[15] Thus, the Town Court shared its jurisdictional authority with the ecclesiastical authorities and their practices, which stemmed from transnational traditions or, especially after the Reformation, from the aspirations of the Crown. Many members of the local clergy were the offspring of local burgher families, which must have accelerated cooperation and diminished the possibility of severe antagonism.[16] The question of the role of canon law and other ecclesiastical

12 Calley 1995, p. 448–469.

13 Still in the seventeenth century, Sámi, i.e. members of the Nordic aboriginal population, lived in more southern areas in Finland and in Scandinavia and not just in the north, in Lapland. At least occasionally, some Sámi lived in Stockholm, too, or at least visited it temporarily. Nordin 2017, p. 45–71; Lamberg 2007 "Ethnic imagery".

14 Montgomery 1995, p. 144–178.

15 See entire book Murray 1949; Trolle Önnerfors 2010, p. 67–69.

16 Lamberg 2001, p. 112–114.

influences is important, but on this occasion, the analysis concentrates on secular activities and practices, mainly in the context of interregional and international commerce. The Reformation, however, did mean that the role of the Bible in the jurisdiction was strengthened as courts started to apply it, especially the Old Testament, in issuing sentences for different crimes.[17]

This analysis is mainly based on the protocols from the Town Court of Stockholm between 1474 and 1635. The protocols were called *tänkeböcker,* which literally means "notebooks." The term had been adapted from Middle Low German, which speaks of the German influence on local administrative practices. Not all the protocols have been preserved: besides the earlier books, which have been completely lost, there are some gaps in the preserved volumes, the biggest one concerning the years 1530–1543. The preserved records are kept at the Town Archives of Stockholm, but they are also accessible as printed source editions.[18] The contents of the protocols changed a lot during the period studied, the main trend being that the medieval records are usually shorter but more varied, occasionally mentioning other things than crime affairs or administrative matters, whereas especially seventeenth-century notices are more focused but simultaneously longer and more detailed. The foundation of courts of appeal, starting from the Svea Court of Appeal, which functioned in Stockholm from 1614 onwards, created greater demands on the contents of the protocols as they had to be sent regularly to the court of appeal to be checked.[19]

The foundation of the Svea Court of Appeal was a part of early modern Swedish state formation, which forms a framework for this study: the kingdom of Sweden was slowly evolving into a centralised nation-state in which the role of literary communication expanded and the central power attempted to tighten its control of local communities, even in the peripheries. This process is usually linked to the Vasa dynasty (1523–1654), but its roots can also be traced to late medieval development trends, especially in Stockholm during the later fifteenth century.[20]

---

17 Trolle Önnerfors 2010, p. 67–69.

18 *Stockholms stads tänkeböcker 1474–1520, Stockholms stads tänkebok under Vasatiden: 1524–1529*, (Stockholm, 1915) [This volume has also been published as *Stockholms stads tänkebok 1524–29 m.m. av M:r Olauus Petri Phase,* Skrifter utgivna av Vetenskapssocieteten i Lund, vol. 11 (Lund, 1940).]; *Stockholms stads tänkeböcker 1544–1591, Stockholms stads tänkeböcker 1592–1635.*

19 Wrede 1912, p. 270–271.

20 Kouri 2016, p. 44–59. Regarding Stockholm in particular during the later Middle Ages, see Sjöden 1950.

Regarding the main sources of the study, it must be remembered that they were not entirely objective reflections of the existing reality. Firstly, *tänkeböcker,* like all other court protocols, follow conventional patterns in their contents, and they omit a lot of what happened or what was actually said. Such events as changes between town scribes have also influenced the contents of the records: especially during the fifteenth and sixteenth centuries, the role of the individual scribe is very visible. Moreover, some scribes' interest in making notices seem to have diminished the longer they had been serving the town – such human development trends can also be traced in the protocols.[21] These changes, as well as the gaps, make it difficult to trace actual changes and continuities in practices: a new feature in the records does not necessarily indicate a novel practice, and if some patterns vanish, they may still have continued to exist in reality. Nevertheless, with the above-mentioned reservations, it is possible to trace several features and discuss the motivations and mentalities behind them.

This chapter is structured in the following fashion: the first chapter presents a concise synthesis of migration movements to Stockholm and discusses the relationships between different ethnic groups. Because the Germans continued to be an important group amidst the growing multiculturalism in Stockholm, the second chapter focuses on Germans living in or visiting the town. The third chapter treats a special category of foreigners in the urban community, namely guests or merchants on a shorter or a longer stay. The fourth chapter deals with the Swedish legislation and its flexible character. The fifth chapter discusses the opposition to the Swedish legal traditions. The sixth and final chapter before the conclusion analyses the cooperation between the Town Court of Stockholm and courts in other places and other countries – attention is paid to how and to what extent external influences were tolerated. Finally, the results of the study are summarised and re-evaluated in the conclusion.

2 Aliens in the City

In the Middle Ages, most foreigners visiting or residing in Stockholm were German merchants, sailors and craftsmen. There were Finns, too, but they had been subjects of the Swedish Crown since the twelfth and thirteenth centuries, so officially they were not foreigners. Occasionally, court protocols or other sources also mention sporadic visits by other Scandinavians, Estonians,

21 Lamberg 2001, p. 198, 203.

Russians as well as Italians and Frenchmen – but of course these ethnic concepts did not have exactly the same connotations as they have today.

The number of people who spoke German dialects in medieval Stockholm is unknown, and the same holds true for the size of the total urban population. On the basis of preserved taxation lists from the 1460s, it has been estimated that the number of the town dwellers was probably c. 4,500–5,500.[22] Of course, the number must have varied a lot due to occasional epidemics, fires and periods of societal unrest. Approximately one-third of the persons in these taxation lists have names that can be regarded as German. But since in principle only the heads of the households were registered and not all single members of the households, the actual proportion of the German population was most likely smaller. The servants in the households seem mostly to have been either Swedes or Finns, seldom Germans.[23] Thus it is plausible to assume that the share of the German speaking element was clearly smaller than one-third at the end of the Middle Ages and most likely even smaller later, when the town population grew and became even more ethnically heterogeneous, containing also Dutchmen, Englishmen and Scotsmen, among other nationalities. In the 1630s, the total number of all town dwellers grew rapidly, from approximately 15,000 to at least 30,000.[24]

The influence of the Germans, especially German-speaking merchants, varied a lot over the course of history. Due to its greater economic resources and cultural lead, the German-speaking population held great influence on Swedish society in the Middle Ages: norms and forms of urban life were in many respects modelled after German examples and even the Swedish language changed rapidly due to the lively interaction with German-speakers.[25] However, the Swedish central power tried, in an early phase, to limit the Germans' societal and political influence: the treaties with important Hanseatic towns Lübeck and Hamburg (made in the early 1250s and in 1261 respectively) stated that all Germans who settled down in Sweden should follow the Swedish legislation and be called Swedes.[26] The concept of Swede (*svensk*) in this context was most likely not an ethnic one; instead, as the use of "Swede" in several other contexts suggests, it was applied to all subjects of the Swedish Crown regardless of their linguistic, geographic or cultural background. This is also evident in late medieval laws issued for the towns and the countryside respectively: the

---

22 Lilja 1995, p. 307–309.

23 Ahnlund 1929, p. 7; Dahlbäck 1987; Lamberg 2001, p. 58–59; Sidén 2008.

24 Lilja 1995, p. 315.

25 Schück 1926, p. 308–314, 346–347; Bergman 1968, p. 60–64, 79–83.

26 *Sveriges traktater med främmande magter jemte andra dit hörande handlingar,* vol. 1, (Stockholm, 1877), p. 197–198, 216–218; Schück 1926, p. 266–267, 271; Kumlien 1953, p. 217.

FIGURE 2 For more than four centuries, St. Gertrude's Church has reminded on the German presence in Stockholm.

concept of Swede seems to have covered also Finnish co-subjects and other ethnic minorities residing in the realm.[27]

However, the concept of Swede is used in the Swedish Town Law in a way that seems to imply that it also had ethnic connotations, referring to geographical background or language or both: firstly, the town councils were supposed to be divided into two halves, one of which should be filled with Swedes and the other with Germans. There is written evidence showing that this principle was also practiced elsewhere and even before the Town Law was composed and issued. According to Nils Ahnlund, the principle may have originated from the

27 Kumlien 1953, p. 218; Lamberg 2000, p. 506–510; Lamberg 2006, p. 127; Gustafsson 2002, p. 91–113.

contracts mentioned above.[28] Secondly, the Town Law stated that if there were not enough German burghers in the town, it was allowed to fill the empty posts in the German half of the council with Swedes, but the opposite procedure was prohibited – once again we see an attempt to regulate German societal influence. We also see how the terms signifying Swede and German had, on these occasions, clearly ethnic connotations. This interpretation is strengthened in the paragraph that stipulated that a man who had a German father should be regarded as a German, regardless of whether his mother was a Swede or a German. Such a definition left possibilities for interpretation since it was not said exactly on what grounds one's father should be regarded as a German.[29] Most likely, the language spoken by the individual as well as his possible background as an immigrant or as a descendant of an immigrant played an important role in the interpretations made by the community.[30] In 1599, Nils Eriksson, apparently a Swede and a candidate for a burgomaster's post, made a speech in which he finished by saying that he "regarded all foreigners who had sworn their burgher oaths and who had a righteous Swedish heart as Swedes." In other words, he shared – at least in his public relations – the view that had been maintained by the Swedish authorities since the Middle Ages.[31]

Regarding the self-perceptions and identities among the German-speaking population in late medieval Stockholm, Justyna Wubs-Mrozewicz concludes that medieval individuals did not necessarily possess fixed, stable identities, any more than modern men and women. Thus, one and the same person appears in the sources sometimes as a German, at other times as a Swede.[32] Ethnic boundaries were in several cases blurred by intermarriages between German-speakers and Northerners. Hans Lambertsson, a burgher and councillor in Stockholm in the late fifteenth century, is an example of an individual who had German roots but who had adapted himself to Scandinavian cultural patterns to such an extent that he did not have a heritable family name any more, as most German-speakers had, but instead he had a patronymic, which was the most common feature among Swedish-speakers.[33]

But considerable differences existed precisely in the family patterns of the German-speaking burghers living in Stockholm: some families were more

28 Ahnlund 1929, p. 5.

29 *Magnus Erikssons stadslag*, p. 3–4 (Konungsbalken, paragraph 11); Lamberg 2000, p. 509.

30 Moberg 1989, p. 28; Lamberg 2001, p. 63–64.

31 *Stockholms stads tänkeböcker 1596–1599*, p. 272 ("*...at the främmande som sin borgere eed suoredh och et rätsijnnigt swenst hiertha vthi sigh haffua, hölle hann alle för suenske...*").

32 Wubs-Mrozewicz 2004, p. 53–67.

33 Lamberg 2001, p. 333 note 15.

open to intermarriage with Swedes and other language groups, whereas other stuck solely to other Germans and resisted assimilation.[34] There is also some evidence that at least certain German-speakers considered themselves a group of their own – a group whose societal interests differed from those of the Swedish-speakers and other groups. In some cases, one can even detect a hostile attitude towards Swedish societal supremacy.[35]

However, such findings are rare and cannot be overgeneralised. They merely tell of individual modes of thinking, not the mentality of the completely German-speaking population. It has to be stressed that there were no large-scale aggressions between different ethnic groups in Stockholm. In Bergen in Norway, the German merchants were so numerous and powerful that they could act quite independently till the middle of the sixteenth century and they were occasionally even responsible for serious violent acts which sometimes claimed numerous lives.[36] But nothing similar happened in Stockholm, although a late medieval tradition claimed that Germans killed several Swedish burghers in 1389 or 1392, according to one source as many as 75 men, by burning them alive, as a counteraction when King Albrecht of Mecklenburg, who was of German origin, had been forced into exile. But many details in this tradition are unclear and there is no definitive evidence from the local community of Stockholm to support the claim that this alleged massacre really took place.[37] In the fifteenth century, the aristocratic Swedish literature presented the Germans as an alien group that opposed the interests of the lesser social groups and the nobles fighting German and Danish kings, but such descriptions seem to reflect patriotic, proto-nationalistic propaganda. Consequently, only the supporters of the Swedish regents and kings were spoken of as Swedes in this tradition.[38]

Regarding the position of the town scribe – the official employed by the council and responsible for official record keeping – the Town Law stated that he should be a Swede and never a foreigner: apparently, this was an attempt to ensure that the court records and other important documents within the urban administration would be written in Swedish.[39] Correspondingly, another paragraph in the Town Law stipulated that transactions with landed property had to be confirmed in official documents written in Swedish or that they should at least be noted in official record books kept by the town council. In

34 Ahnlund 1929, p. 7; Sjödén 1950, p. 218-314; Lamberg 2001, p. 94–95.
35 Lamberg 2001, p. 94–95; Lamberg 2004, p. 13–14.
36 Helle 1982, p. 475–485, 700–701, 766-773; Lamberg 2001, p. 236–237, 291.
37 Heyde 1989, p. 9–27; Lamberg 2001, p. 64–66, 171, 176, 234, 237, 243, 289.
38 Lamberg 2001, p. 62–63.
39 *Magnus Erikssons stadslag*, p. 4 (Konungsbalken, paragraph VI).

Stockholm, both customs were usually applied and this ensured that the local textual culture remained mainly Swedish.[40] Thus, it would have been more difficult for German burghers to turn Stockholm into a Hanseatic town – if any of them ever had such aspirations.

3 Shifting Tides for Germans

The German influence diminished from the later fifteenth century onwards, partly because of growing proto-nationalistic tensions intertwined in power struggles between societal elites. In 1471, due to a political conflict that also involved Stockholm, the Town Law was changed so that no foreigner was allowed to act as a burgomaster or town councillor, or take up any other post within the urban administration and jurisdiction.[41] The reform affected every town of the kingdom of Sweden, and it was carried out in Stockholm even before its formal ratification. The German burgomasters and councillors lost their positions, but some of them, like the above-mentioned Hans Lambertsson, were permitted to continue nevertheless – a practical example on how blurred ethnic boundaries sometimes were.[42] Likewise, we occasionally meet men with German names among those who were elected to communal offices and positions of trust after the legal reform of 1471. Among them was Helmik van Nörden who acted as a town scribe in Stockholm in 1487–1511 and who was apparently bilingual.[43] It is evident that certain foreign traits, like German background, continued to be tolerated – after all, Swedish culture had borrowed a considerable number of words and concepts from German speakers, among them the word *stad,* which replaced the earlier Scandinavian word *by* in the sense of "town."[44] Moreover, the town council tolerated German being spoken occasionally in court; certain notices and sometimes even whole documents composed in Low German dialects were copied or written down in the court records.[45]

When the Vasa dynasty cut Sweden's ties to Denmark in the 1520s and put an end to the political supremacy of the most notable Hanseatic town, Lübeck, in the 1530s, the remains of the German influence diminished drastically, and the

40 *Magnus Erikssons stadslag*, p. 73 (Jordabalken, paragraph VI).

41 *Magnus Erikssons stadslag*, p. 21 (Konungsbalken, (new) paragraph II).

42 Moberg 1989, p. 28; Lamberg 2001, p. 63–64.

43 Moberg 1989, p. 31–34.

44 Bergman 1968, p. 62.

45 For example, *Stockholms stads tänkeböcker 1568–1575*, p. 435–437.

number of Germans in the population of Stockholm fell as well.[46] Foreigners continued to live in Stockholm nevertheless, not only Germans but also increasingly numerous groups consisting of Dutchmen and Scotsmen in particular. Several other "nationalities" were sporadically present. Moreover, the direct contacts of the Swedish burghers widened considerably. On the basis of notices in court records, Stockholm in the middle of the sixteenth century was far more international than it had been in the late Middle Ages and its range of international cooperation stretched to the Pyrenees and Italy.[47] Nevertheless, even in the late sixteenth century, the formulations in royal ordinances as well as in decisions made by the town council reflected an understanding that the burgher community of Stockholm consisted of Swedes and Germans.[48]

The number and role of the Germans started to grow again before the end of the sixteenth century, and the Germans received certain favours from the king, especially regarding the localities for their own congregation – the Reformation had split the earlier joint congregation of Stockholm into Swedish, Finnish and German congregations; in the seventeenth century, as the town grew, there were several Swedish congregations, and a French-English congregation was founded. But the Germans never regained their former societal or cultural position. The fact that King John (Johan) III allowed the German congregation to share its church building – a former guildhouse founded by medieval German merchants – with the Finnish congregation, which consisted mostly of the poorest Stockholmers, can also be interpreted as a token of the new social hierarchies. However, after three decades, the church was given solely to the Germans.[49]

According to the privileges granted to Stockholm by King Gustav Vasa in 1529, a German merchant seeking burgher rights in Stockholm should present written confirmation from the local authorities in a community where he had possessions. That is how the town council of Stockholm was expected to be able to acquire reliable information on the newcomer and whether he had fled any responsibilities.[50]

---

46 Peterzén 1945, p. 37.

47 For example, *Stockholms stads tänkeböcker 1549–1553*, p. 242–243; *Stockholms stads tänkeböcker 1584–1588*, p. 74, 127–129.

48 For example, *Stockholms stads privilegiebref*, p. 59, 73; *Stockholms stads tänkeböcker 1592–1595*, p. 133; *Stockholms stads tänkeböcker 1596–1599*, p. 272; *Stockholms stads tänkeböcker 1616–1617*, p. 287.

49 Murray 1954, p. 12–28.

50 *Stockholms stads privilegiebref*, p. 46; *Stockholms stads tänkeböcker 1603–1604*, p. 140.

King Eric (Erik) XIV felt it necessary to explicitly prohibit dual citizenship in Stockholm and in foreign, especially German, towns, when he issued privileges for Stockholm in 1563. A general prohibition against being a burgher in several towns simultaneously had already been mentioned in the privileges for Stockholm of 1436. King Eric also wanted to abolish the apparently existing state of matters that had allowed even foreigners to acquire de facto burgher rights even if they had not sworn loyalty to the Crown.[51] His brother and successor, King John III, maintained the control policy in the privileges and ordinances he issued in 1570. However, his ordinances also stated that disputes between domestic and foreign merchants should be handled by groups consisted half of domestic men and half of foreigners so that the matter could be clarified smoothly and so that the foreigners would not complain that injustice was done to them.[52] While acting as a Regent before becoming King himself, the youngest brother Carl (Karl),[53] made it clear in 1603 to the inhabitants of Stockholm that he wanted to guarantee the judicial rights of all people living in the realm, regardless of whether they were foreigners or locals.[54] These principles had medieval roots: the Town Law stipulated that a member of the Council of the realm (*riksrådet*), together with a member of the archbishop's council, should visit the town twice a year, first on Whitsunday and then on Saint Jacob's day (that is, on 25 July), to ensure that justice was done to everyone, guests as well as local burghers.[55] But King John apparently stressed – or perhaps it was the wish of the town council of Stockholm – that the burghers themselves should bear responsibility for impartial examinations and fair sentences.

Although the principle of impartial examinations mentioned by King John did not automatically mean that foreign legal practices were to be applied in Stockholm, it underlined the role of negotiation when disputes were to be solved. The ultimate goal was to achieve an outcome that foreigners were also able to accept and regard as lawful. However, the court records do not actually state that the principle was followed in practice. In 1584, a committee was formed for reconciliation between two French merchants on one part and an apparently German ship owner on the other. The committee consisted of town councillors and burghers as well as one "foreign" ship owner from Amsterdam. Apparently, the last-mentioned examiner was regarded as a warrant of

51 *Stockholms stads privilegiebref*, p. 6, 61–62.

52 *Stockholms stads privilegiebref*, p. 70, 76.

53 Also Karl.

54 *Stockholms stads tänkeböcker 1603–1604*, p. 90.

55 *Magnus Erikssons stadslag*, p. 127 (Köpmålabalken, paragraph XXX).

impartiality towards foreigners.[56] But neither in this case nor at other times was it stated that the Town Court actually appointed foreign examiners for each dispute which involved foreigners.

Most often, the notices refer merely to "good men" as examiners.[57] So the actual significance of the principle of impartiality in the privileges issued by King John remains obscure. Of course, the silence in written sources does not necessarily mean that the custom did not exist – on the contrary: it may have been so commonplace that it was not considered worth mentioning. Neither do we know if the medieval rule regarding the visits of the king's and archbishop's representatives was ever followed. The protocols of the town court from the late fifteenth century and the early sixteenth century do occasionally mention the presence of one or more lay members of the Council of the realm, sometimes even the Regent himself, but such notices do not concentrate on Whitsuntide or Saint Jacob's day.[58] Apparently, they merely reflect the travels of the high nobility: it was natural for the leaders of the realm to participate in the local administrative and judicial activities during their stay.

In the seventeenth century, language seemed to have become an issue: the Town Court usually required that German-speakers had their written statements and other written evidence translated into Swedish – only then the court was able to handle them. Apparently, German was felt to be, or at least was presented as, more foreign in the seventeenth century than before. Such a policy was quite new in Stockholm – for example, as late as in 1573, the sentence given by the Town Court was read aloud in German, as one party was apparently of German origin. Even royal sentences were occasionally written in German.[59] The new requirement posed problems for some guests – not all were able to find someone who would translate the necessary documents into Swedish.[60]

One of the earliest cases in which the court demanded that documents written in German be translated into Swedish can be found among the notices dealing with the year 1601.[61] Besides proto-nationalistic tendencies, a very practical reason may explain the need for translations: High German was

56 *Stockholms stads tänkeböcker 1584–1588*, p. 171–172.

57 See, for example, *Stockholm stads tänkeböcker 1601–1602*, p. 118–119.

58 See, for example, *Stockholms stads tänkeböcker 1483–1492*, p. 563; *Stockholms stads tänkeböcker 1504–1514*, p. 132.

59 *Stockholms stads tänkeböcker 1568–1575*, p. 440–441.

60 *Stockholms stads tänkeböcker 1616–1617*, p. 264.

61 *Stockholms stads tänkeböcker 1601–1602*, p. 137.

replacing Low German as a written code in the Hanseatic sphere as well, and this version of German was more remote from Swedish and other Scandinavian languages than Low German had been.[62] Documents written in Dutch also had to be translated into Swedish before the Town Court was able or willing to accept them, although the Dutch language bore great resemblance to Low German.[63] However, several documents written in German as well as in Latin were later copied in the court records, apparently without any problems. In 1616, a warrant written in German was read aloud before the court of Norrmalm; this medieval northern suburb of Stockholm was administered as an independent town in 1602–1635 until it was again merged with Stockholm as one of the districts in the capital. The contents of the letter were most likely understood, at least for the most parts.[64] Oaths were allowed to be sworn in French as well, although most likely only a few domestic burghers spoke or understood it.[65]

In 1630, a widow of a local merchant, who may have been at least partly of German origin on the basis of his name (Hendrich Löök), complained that a merchant from Lübeck had caused his husband's death by having put him in jail for no legal reason. Löök had died shortly afterwards. She described the accused as a "stranger" or a "foreign man" (*dänne främmande mannenn*) who had had her husband jailed "against all law and justice, yes [against] the burghers" privileges and the court's sentence' so that her husband had not been able to "enjoy that justice which our merciful authorities and the law have mercifully allowed and permitted." Indeed, the ordinances given by the King should have prevented a burgher of Stockholm being imprisoned in a case concerning an alleged debt, but naturally that principle was not necessarily applied abroad, where the husband had been jailed. The angered widow claimed that their opponent was more ruthless than "a Turk or a heathen." On the basis of her name, Elin, she was of Swedish origin.[66]

62 Hartweg and Wegera 2005, p. 34. I thank fellow historian Ilkka Leskelä for pointing out this language historical fact.

63 *Stockholms stads tänkeböcker 1605–1608*, p. 68.

64 *Stockholms stads tänkeböcker 1568–1575*, p. 435–437; *Stockholms stads tänkeböcker 1616–1617*, p. 400. Regarding Norrmalm's short period as a town of its own, see Wolke 2001, p. 40–47.

65 *Stockholms stads tänkeböcker 1616–1617*, p. 159.

66 *Stockholms stads tänkeböcker 1630*, p. 15–16, 59–60: ("*...emott all laag och rättwijsa, iaa emoot borgerlige priuilegier och rättenns doom...,*" "*...intet niutandes dänn rätt som wår nådige öffuerheet och laagenn sine vndersåter nådigest undt och efterlåthet hafuer...,*" "*iagh icke troor, att hoos enn turck eller hedninng eenn sådan obarmhertigheet finnas skulle...*"). Cf. *Stockholms stads privilegiebref*, p. 122–123 (the paragraph was repeated in certain other charters as well).

Such rhetoric underlined the alien character of the German guests, at least regarding the opponent in question. But while Elin Löök attacked one single foreign merchant, the vicar of the Finnish congregation hinted that even more permanent residents and holders of burgher rights should be seen as aliens. In 1627, Vicar Thomas Georgii, of Finnish origin, considered the Germans residing in Stockholm as a separate nation of their own (*then Tydska nation*), unjustifiably favoured by the Crown, whereas the Finns were "compatriots" to Sweden (*Sweriges egne Patrioter*) and should therefore receive better locales for their congregational life. He, of course, was frustrated by the fact that the Crown had given the Germans the church that they had earlier had to share with the Finns.[67]

But despite occasional tensions and certain mistrust against foreigners and immigrants from abroad, it was in the interests of the local community to maintain a well-functioning relationship with foreigners. That is why the Town Court also controlled the behaviour of the town dwellers and the local officials towards visitors. Even in the fifteenth century, communal rules had stressed the importance of speaking respectfully to noblemen and noblewomen, and that was still important approximately one hundred years later, when King Sigismund arrived in Stockholm together with his companions. It was stressed that the foreign visitors should not be given a negative image of rude and uncivilised Swedes. Nevertheless, the Town Court paid also attention to the interests of common visitors: occasionally it had to remind inn-keepers on the necessity of marking inns and taverns with clear signs so that strangers were also able to find them. In addition, in one respect many members of the local community sometimes preferred certain foreign elements to domestic ones: in times of economic uncertainty, especially during the internal wars in the 1590s, many Swedes distanced themselves from the official currency and preferred to receive all payments in the form of foreign coins.[68]

4 Temporary and Semi-permanent Visitors

A grey zone between the burghers and foreigners was formed by those visitors – foreigners as well as Swedish subjects from other places – who stayed in the town, sometimes for a short time, sometimes longer or sometimes coming back repeatedly during subsequent sailing seasons. Then there were also those who supported themselves by commerce or by some artisan's trade

67 Lamberg 2007 "Expressions", p. 115–116.
68 *Stockholms stads tänkeböcker 1592–1595*, p. 42, 134, 168, 216–218, 331.

without officially being burghers or members of the crafts guilds. At least occasionally, there were also several burghers who had not sworn any oath of loyalty towards the town, although the oath was prescribed in the Town Law, which otherwise gave detailed instructions and norms regarding how one could obtain burgher rights in a Swedish town.[69]

It was also possible to participate in trade without being a burgher, as a visitor, provided that one followed the legal norms regarding that status. The Town Law had adopted the term "guest" (Sw. *gäst*) from Low German (cf. Ge. *Gast*) when it spoke of merchants visiting from other towns, foreign or domestic. Of course, the rights of guests were more limited than the rights of burghers and merchants in the town in question. Guests were prohibited from making business trips into the countryside – it was easier to control and tax import and export in towns and in licit market places. Moreover, the only form of trade allowed for guests was the wholesale trade. If the guests needed something for their stay, they were supposed to buy it from local burghers. Thus, the law clearly protected the local merchants' interests. But the law also prohibited local merchants from helping guests to bypass this rule, so there must have been domestic merchants who were willing to cooperate with foreigners in spite of competition. Because guests posed a potential societal threat to the town, especially when their number grew as usually happened during the sailing season, the Town Law prohibited foreigners from bearing weapons in the town.[70] Burghers, on the contrary, were allowed to bear weapons if they owned an estate in the town or a considerable amount of other property – domestic guests were also allowed to keep their weapons when they visited other towns.[71]

Those foreign merchants who stayed in a Swedish town the whole winter were called "winter lodgers" or "winter stayers" (*vinterliggare*). The Town Law prescribed that guests who stayed the time period between Christmas and Easter were obliged to pay the same taxes as the local burghers. However, the law did not mention any special fees for the stay. Nevertheless, even those foreigners who had sailed away but left some of their goods in the town were supposed to pay tax to the town.[72] In principle, a stay over the winter was allowed only in the case that guests had been surprised by rapidly deteriorating weather

69 For example, *Stockholms stads tänkeböcker 1592–1595*; p. 311–312; *Stockholms stads tänkeböcker* 1614–1615, p. 58, 60–62. Cf. *Magnus Erikssons stadslag*, p. 8–10 (Konungsbalken, paragraph XV).

70 *Magnus Erikssons stadslag*, p. 126–131, 183 (Köpmålabalken, paragraphs XXX–XXXIV, Rådstugubalken, paragraph XXXIV).

71 *Magnus Erikssons stadslag*, p. 183 (Rådstugubalken, paragraph XXXIV).

72 *Magnus Erikssons stadslag*, p. 12 (Konungsbalken, paragraph XIX).

conditions which prevented them from sailing back home. This idea is expressed in some versions of the Swedish Town Law, although not in the law book used in Stockholm.[73]

The fact that the Town Law was to be read aloud to the public once a year, a day after Saint John's day[74] i.e. in midsummer, during the best sailing season, was most likely meant to make Swedish legal customs known to short-time visitors from abroad as well. However, it remains unknown if the whole law book was really read aloud or merely excerpts from it, and at what time of the year this actually happened. One notice in the records of the town council shows that the law book was read, at least in 1482, in early August.[75]

Nevertheless, it was customary to read aloud each year at least the local communal rules and regulations, issued by the town council and called *burspråk* (this term and this practice were also borrowed from Hanseatic traditions), which completed the Town Law. This reading seems to have happened completely outside the sailing season, during either the Christmas week, or during the early phase of the sailing season, that is around Whitsuntide.[76] That is how those rules reached, at least in principle, some visitors as well as all the foreign merchants who stayed in the town over the winter. Of course, most likely not all foreigners were able to understand the contents entirely, because the reading took place in Swedish.

The Vasa rulers (from 1523 onwards) sought to control local communities and foreign elements in their realm. They sought, among other things, to see that guests would not stay longer in Sweden than was prescribed.[77] Their policy is also reflected in several royal ordinances as well as in notices in court records, in the form of recurring rules and regulations that were read aloud to the town dwellers and that contained an obligation to report the presence of any stranger or foreigner to the local authorities.[78] But this surveillance had in fact

73 Yrwing 1976, p. 144. *Magnus Erikssons stadslag*, p. 148 note 182; *Codex iuris urbici Magnæanus. Konung Magnus Erikssons stadslag*; p. 209 note 10, p. 212 note 35.

74 *Magnus Erikssons stadslag*, p. 15 (Konungsbalken, paragraph XXIII).

75 *Magnus Erikssons stadslag*, p. 37 note 149; *Stockholms stads tänkeböcker 1474–1483 samt burspråk*, p. 366.

76 Published in *Stockholms stads tänkeböcker 1474–1483*; cf. previous note.

77 Sandström 1990, p. 60.

78 For example, *Stockholms stads privilegiebref*, p. 79; *Stockholms stads tänkeböcker 1553–1567*, p. 227–228, 260; *Stockholms stads tänkeböcker 1568–1575*, 349; *Stockholms stads tänkeböcker 1575–1578*, p. 285; *Stockholms stads tänkeböcker 1578–1583*, p. 253; *Stockholms stads tänkeböcker 1592–1595*, p. 80; *Stockholm stads tänkeböcker 1603–1604*, p. 18.

begun even earlier, in the 1480s at the latest: the preserved municipal ordinances (*burspråk*) from the 1450s–1470s stressed that each burgher should be careful whom he lodged because he was responsible for his guest's actions, but in the 1480s this paragraph received an addition that required burghers to report their guests to the royal bailiff and the burgomasters.[79] Already in the 1450s and possibly even earlier, the guests themselves had been obliged to report to the town council before they left the town.[80]

Moreover, the town council occasionally appointed burghers to collect information on the inhabitants of each house.[81] This had already been customary in the Middle Ages, when the town council had appointed burghers to act as "quarter masters" (*kvartersmästare*) or "district scribes" (*mantalskrivare*) for different parts of the town.[82] Of course, such examinations and supervision activities were enacted not only to control visiting merchants but the whole population in general.

In one case in 1616, the Town Court had a letter written in Scottish translated into Swedish. After that, a burgher from Nyköping, of Scottish origin, testified that its contents were trustworthy. He did this by putting one hand on the law book, as "our law requires" (*som wår lagh kräfuer*).[83] Thus it can be concluded that a background outside the town and even from abroad did not necessarily diminish the legal credibility of a person. After all, many if not most town dwellers were migrants or children of migrants, although the majority originated from areas where the population spoke Swedish.

The prohibition against acting as a burgher in several towns caused a curious outcome at least once. In 1617, a burgher living in Lübeck was denied any claim towards a house in Stockholm, with the reason that it was against the law to have a house and be a burgher simultaneously in Stockholm and in Lübeck. When the man asked, via a representative, if his children were allowed the right of inheritance towards the same house, it was replied that "the children do not go before the father – if the father cannot come [to the inheritance], the

79 *Stockholms stads tänkeböcker 1474–1483*, p. 487.
80 *Stockholms stads tänkeböcker 1474–1483*, p. 492.
81 For example, *Stockholms stads tänkeböcker 1592–1595*, p. 137.
82 These appointees have been occasionally listed in the court records (*tänkeböcker*), but more consequently in the office holder lists. The first preserved "book of offices" (*ämbetsbok*) begins with the year 1419; it has also been published as a source edition whereas the later lists are available at the Town Archives of Stockholm; see *Stockholms stads ämbetsbok 1419–1544*.
83 *Stockholms stads tänkeböcker 1616–1617*, p. 86–87.

FIGURE 3 Parts of Stockholm in the late seventeenth century seen from the east, where the mainpart of the visitors and migrants came from.

children come neither."[84] The Town Law did not allow people living abroad to own real estate in Swedish towns, but it gave such an heir one year to sell the estate he had inherited. Thus, being a burgher in a foreign town should not automatically have been an obstacle to receiving an inheritance.[85] For some reason, the Town Court of Stockholm wanted to prevent a foreign burgher from getting his share of the inheritance in question. But since foreigners occasionally won their cases, even against local burghers of Swedish origin, it cannot be said that the Town Court was systematically suppressing the rights of the foreigners.

5 Flexible Jurisdiction

As has already appeared above, in several cases, the Town Court justified its rulings by reference to the Swedish Law and "our law" (*wår lag*). Of course, this concept usually meant the Town Law and, on certain occasions, the ordinances and rules completing it. For example, in 1612, the Town Court of Stockholm

84 *"barnen gå icke för en, kan fadren icke der till komma icke kommer barnen der till": Stockholms stads tänkeböcker 1616–1617*, p. 264.

85 *Magnus Erikssons stadslag*, p. 9 (Konungsbalken, paragraph XV).

justified one verdict by referring to Swedish law and the orders of the King.[86] The Town Court was also able to make jurisdictional additions by means of municipal ordinances, *burspråk*, as mentioned above.

However, it must be remembered that as a law text, the Swedish Town Law, although formally codified and maintained by the king, was not an entirely homogeneous entity. In practice, it contained considerable local variation. Firstly, until 1618, all the existing versions of the Town Law were hand-written books. As was the case with any other manuscript, the copying processes occasionally led to involuntary errors and thus there were small differences between different versions. Secondly, the written law book was also intertwined with local traditions, which were never written down but nevertheless had an influence on how societal practices were structured within the local community. This is sometimes implied in the court records in Stockholm: In 1575, it was stated that it was "since ages customary here in the town" (*så är och af ålder här i staden brukligit*) that children who had renounced their right of inheritance were not held responsible for the debts of the deceased parent.[87] Moreover, regarding house and land transactions made in the suburbs of Normalm and Södermalm, Stockholmers seem to have applied legal practices that differed slightly from what was expressed in the Town Law. This becomes evident in a dispute which took place in 1594 and where the involved parties are, on the basis of their names, Germans or possibly Dutchmen. The Town Court explained to the quarrelling parties that transactions regarding estates in the suburbs were to happen in a different way from transactions regarding estates in the town. The Town Court stated that "for ages the custom had been" (*och haffuer aff ålder waret den sedwane*) that those who wanted to sell and those who wanted to buy property in Norrmalm or in Södermalm made an agreement in the presence of witnesses. When they had shaken hands, the sum in question had been paid and an official transaction document had been written in the presence of the officials of the suburb, the transaction was regarded as valid. Apparently, the semirural character of these suburbs explains why such a tradition had developed. However, one of the men involved in the dispute did not approve of the Town Council's solution. Instead, he made a petition to the Council of the realm.[88]

86 *Stockholms stads tänkeböcker 1608–1612*, p. 149.

87 *Stockholms stads tänkeböcker 1568–1575*, p. 626.

88 *Stockholms stads tänkeböcker 1592–1595*, p. 211–223. The custom described by the Town Court was probably a free adaptation of the paragraphs in the Town Law dealing with real estate transactions in the town and in the countryside: *Magnus Erikssons stadslag*, p. 73, 75 (Jordabalken, paragraphs VI, XI). See also *Magnus Erikssons landslag*, p. 75, 78

Indeed, it was already stated in the very first privileges for Stockholm, issued in 1436, that the Town Court had the right to fill all potential gaps in the written law according to their judgement and conscience.[89] However, the significance of unwritten traditions was diminishing in early modern Sweden: written law had already become the main source of justice by the early seventeenth century.[90] Regarding local traditions and interregional commerce, it is noteworthy that an important principle, that a case should be tried and examined where it had occurred and fines should be paid where the involved party lived, is missing from several versions of the Town Law. Thus it is obvious that it was not included in the original fourteenth-century version. But by the fifteenth century at the latest it had been borrowed from the Law of the Realm (*Landslagen*), which was applied in the countryside. This seems to have occurred for the first time in Stockholm because the paragraph in question is mentioned in law books that were based off the law book of Stockholm. Since the privileges issued for Stockholm in 1436 seem to refer to this principle, it is possible that the paragraph was added then or somewhat later.[91]

It is significant that it apparently was via Stockholm that the above-mentioned principle was imported into the urban legal tradition. Most likely, the Town Court of Stockholm was seeking ways to diminish the number of the cases it had to deal with. Disputes between foreign merchants and people coming from other towns could be very difficult because they often stemmed from events that had taken place outside the town and sometimes outside the realm entirely.

Occasionally, the Town Court did deal with cases that actually had taken place outside Stockholm. This is explained by the fact that the Town Court of Stockholm acted as a regional superior court before the foundation of the Svea Court of Appeal, which took place in 1614.[92] But since most burgomasters and councillors continued to receive their incomes from their trades, they were not eager to widen their clientele in judicial matters nor were they anxious to

(Jordabalken, paragraphs XII, XXIII–XXIV). Regarding local customs and traditions within jurisdiction, see Trolle Önnerfors 2010, p. 65, 86–87.

89 *Stockholms stads privilegiebref*, p. 6.

90 Pihlajamäki 2013, p. 168–188.

91 *Magnus Erikssons stadslag*, p. 175 (Rådstugubalken, paragraph XII), p. 198 note 85; *Stockholms stads privilegiebref*, p. 6; *Magnus Erikssons landslag*, p. 165 (Rättegångsbalken, paragraph XVIII).

92 For example, *Stockholms stads tänkeböcker 1474–1483*, p. 17–19, 28; *Stockholms stads tänkeböcker 1589–1591*, p. 31. Likewise, the consistory consisting of the local priesthood in Stockholm and founded most likely in the 1570s, examined cases that had taken place in the countryside; see Murray 1949, p. 126–130.

expand their own workload in the Town Hall.[93] This view is evident in the late 1610s and 1620s, after the Svea Court of Appeal had been founded: in spite of certain tensions and differing views on certain cases between the two courts, the Town Court usually happily submitted difficult cases to superior judges.[94]

Occasionally, the Town Court of Stockholm justified its sentences by reference to the Law of the Realm, as was the case in 1635 when it condemned a young maidservant to death because she had stolen an ox – the sentence was justified by both the Town Law and the Law of the Realm.[95] Most likely, the stolen ox had been taken to the countryside and that is why the court felt that a reference to the Law of the Realm was also needed. The Law of the Realm was applied as a subsidiary law in other Swedish towns as well.[96]

In 1617, in dealing with another theft case, the Town Court applied the Law of the Realm (originally from the middle of the fourteenth century, renewed in 1442) and the Law of the Province of Östergötland. The accused party in the case was a Dutch shipper who had been imprisoned but then released, thanks to a burgher who had guaranteed that he would appear at the hearing. However, the man had fled. His wife, called "the Dutchwoman" (*hollenderskan, Hållenskan*), wanted to have a favourable sentence regarding her role in the case. According to the law paragraphs in question, she should have sworn a purifying oath with twelve men, because she was "unknown and a stranger" (*okendh och fremmende*); the court accepted that it was enough that she only swore the required oath, without anyone else confirming it.[97]

In other words, the court took into consideration the fact that a person from another place did not necessarily have many contacts within the local community. Perhaps it also wanted to show some leniency towards the abandoned wife, who seems to have been stranded in Stockholm at least for a while. The curious fact that the Law of the Realm as well as the even older Law of the Province of Östergötland was applied in this case does not necessarily imply that the theft had taken place somewhere in that province and in the countryside. A more plausible explanation is the fact that both these laws contained more detailed norms than the Town Law regarding cases in which the wife had

93 Lamberg 2001, p. 206–211.

94 Lamberg 2014, p. 123–127.

95 *Stockholms stads tänkeböcker 1635*, p. 61.

96 Sommar 1942, p. 421.

97 *Stockholms stads tänkeböcker 1616–1617*, p. 323 (see also *Stockholms stads tänkeböcker 1616–1617*, p. 314; *Stockholms stads tänkeböcker 1618*, p. 272, 277); *Magnus Erikssons stadslag*, p. 280 (Tjuvabalken, paragraph x).

been unaware of the theft committed by her husband.[98] Such a procedure reflects the idea of a holistic national legislation, although it still took more than a century before Sweden received its first general law to be applied in towns and in the countryside alike. Provincial laws were still valid in principle, at least as supplements to the Town Law and the Law of the Realm.[99] However, it was very rare that the Town Court justified its sentences by means of reference to the Law of the Realm and it was even rarer that it looked in provincial laws for guidance. Most likely it did not even have copies of all provincial law books available. Perhaps some councillor had migrated from Östergötland and possessed a copy of the law of that province and that is how the Town Court was able to use it as a base for its sentence.

In another case, the Town Court felt that the contents of the Town Law were not enough to deal with the relationship between a husband and a wife. Adultery cases and marital problems had traditionally belonged to the jurisdiction of the Church as well, but once the Town Court had to discuss the role of "natural law," a concept that is otherwise missing from the court records. In that case a husband was accused of adultery and his wife wanted to swear him free. Finally, the court decided that the wife should be allowed to defend her husband.[100]

Thus, there existed a considerable amount of jurisdictional variation even within domestic judicial legislation and its adaptations. This variation and the fact that virtually all Stockholmers were immigrants or at least descendants of immigrants from other places and countries may have made the city tolerant to influences coming abroad as well, at least to a certain degree. Problems arose only when individuals felt that their interests and lawful rights had been violated or when the Town Court felt that the Swedish Law (meaning the whole complex of legal texts and practices applied in Stockholm) was violated.

---

98 *Magnus Erikssons stadslag*, 278, p. 280 (Tjuvabalken, paragraphs I–II, X); *Codex iuris Ostrogotici. Östgöta-lagen*; p. 89–90 (Vådamålsbalken, paragraph XXXIII); *Codex iuris communis Sueciae Christophorianus. Konung Christoffers landslag*; p. 372–373 (Tjuvabalen, paragraph IV).

99 Trolle Önnerfors 2010, p. 64–65.

100 *Stockholms stads tänkeböcker 1596*, p. 70. The Natural Law was mentioned more often by the Court of Appeal, but its contents were vaguely defined if at all: the concept had already existed in medieval legal and philosophical thinking and it was utilised as a reference to a human core essence that was even more important and significant than the laws created by humans; see Trolle Önnerfors 2010, p. 72–75.

6 Foreign Aspirations

One sentence, issued in 1601, reveals that the Town Court regarded it normal that the price that a merchant had to pay or that he had to sell his goods for in another town varied and was sometimes higher and sometimes lower than had been expected. If a shipper had promised his associates a higher price, they had to accept that their goods were sold at lower prices. Market prices outside one's own local community were apparently and unsurprisingly acknowledged as something that remained outside the control of local authorities and courts.[101] However, the Town Court of Stockholm became involved in a case, in which some brimstone (sulphur) had been sold in Danzig by the pounds that were used in Sweden, although the merchants in Danzig should have been bound to that pound that was used in Cologne and which was approximately 50 grams heavier. The buyer had met the wife of the seller in Stockholm and raised a case before the Town Court, which examined the case and allowed the buyer to receive the money that the wife of the seller had deposited in the court.[102]

Actually, in only one case did the Town Court of Stockholm approve of foreign legal customs being applied directly in Stockholm. In 1592, the Town Court had to examine a contract that had been made between a burgher and his father-in-law. The agreement was found to be contradictory to the Swedish legislation on the widow's and her children's rights to inheritance. The burgher in question, a Wolter Laurentz, had been married at least once before he entered his second marriage. He had children from his first marriage and apparently he had believed that he would not have any during his second marriage because he had made a deal with the father of his fiancée, Adam Distelerer. According to that pact, his second wife would inherit only her clothes, her best bed, her wedding ring and presents given by godparents to her potential children. Because the couple had five children in all, his widow sought to annul the contract. The other party most likely held a copy of the agreement. According to the Swedish Town Law, if a widow had had children with her deceased husband, she had no right to any dowry. Instead, she had the right to the best bed (although it is debatable how many beds there in fact were in medieval households), her best church clothes, albeit without any smith work, and half of the estate; the rest would go to the children of the couple. The Town Court regarded

101 *Stockholms stads tänkeböcker 1601–1602*, p. 120–124.

102 *Stockholms stads tänkeböcker 1549–1551*, p. 150. Jansson 1971, p. 64–65.

the contract as contradictory to Swedish legislation, but it was held to be valid because her father had approved it and because he had been her rightful guardian at the time of its making. Moreover, the late husband had not altered the contract before his death. The Town Court also decided "that hereafter such unlawful contracts and foreign subtlety are not to be approved, but it [= each division of inheritance] shall go according to the Swedish Town Law."[103] So the Town Court gave its reluctant acceptance, but it is unclear why it did not annul the contract – it would have been completely possible to do so and actually the court should have followed traditional Swedish norms in this case. Apparently, the Town Court valued the patriarchal societal order more than the legislation. In another case, dealt with in 1615, the Town Court forced a German-speaking family to follow the Swedish norms when it divided its inheritance, but in that case it was protecting the interests of the male heir.[104] Most likely, there were several immigrant families that followed the norms of their original home places, but the Town Court of Stockholm did not become involved in most such cases. Attempts to deviate from the law can also be traced among some Finnish immigrants when they made decisions regarding the inheritance they were about to leave, but such solutions or attempts can be explained by the great geographic distance between the immigrant living in Stockholm and the main part of his living relatives, dwelling far away in Finland – it was understandable that an elderly immigrant would wish to favour relatives who were nearby and who had helped him.[105]

In the 1630s, when Sweden was fighting ardently against Catholicism, divisions of inheritances became problematic if one or more of the heirs were Catholic or lived in Catholic parts of Europe. The judgements issued by the Town Court of Stockholm show that individuals who served the enemies of the kingdom or who were Jesuits had no right to inherit anything from Sweden. But if a person merely lived in a Catholic area, he had a right to his share.[106]

The court records from Stockholm mention recurring disputes and problems that arose when several foreigners tried to break the norms of the local community, not only regarding how inheritance should be divided. Most often, such offenses were connected to commercial interests. Several foreign merchants wanted to have greater freedom in their trade than allowed them by

103 *Stockholms stads tänkeböcker 1592–1595*, p. 34, 36–38 ("*…at her effter skole sådana olaglige contracter och främmende spitzfundigheet icke gilles, vthann thet skal ghå effter Suerigis stadzlagh*"). Cf. *Magnus Erikssons stadslag*, p. 42–43 (Giftermålsbalken, paragraph IX).

104 *Stockholms stads tänkeböcker 1614–1615*, p. 122.

105 *Stockholms stads tänkeböcker 1596–1599*, p. 14.

106 *Stockholms stads tänkeböcker 1634*, p. 18; *Stockholms stads tänkeböcker 1635*, p. 19.

their roles as guests. Consequently, individual foreigners were repeatedly fined for such offences. Such cases could create tensions among burghers: in 1635, a local merchant of German origin turned in a young merchant's aide (*köpsven*), on the basis of his name most likely a German too, because the aide had gone against the "privileges of the town" (actually against the Town Law as well as the royal ordinances regarding merchant's trade) by travelling to the villages in the Swedish copper mine areas as well as to several inland towns and conducting commercial activities during his voyage. Such illicit business trips were in fact quite common and a constant source of minor conflicts between the burghers and the guests. In this case, another burgher, also with a German name, was summoned to witness against the aide, but he was unwilling to do so until he was reminded that his burgher oath obliged him to do so: that is, he was supposed to prioritise the interests of his fellow burghers and not those of his compatriots.[107]

But what apparently was the most difficult thing for many guests staying over the winter to accept was the responsibility of paying taxes to the local community, as the Town Law prescribed. In late May 1551, all the German merchant's aides were called to the Town House of Stockholm. They were accused of not having paid their taxes although they had spent the whole winter in the town. Nevertheless, the aides explained that they had been exempted from the taxes earlier and asked to keep those "liberties which they had had a long time" (*frijheter, som the en tiid lång haft haffue*). The town council replied that they should have thanked the King for that liberty but they had neglected to do so – even when he had visited the town. That is why the council declared that they were each obliged to pay a fine of 40 marks according to the Swedish Law and besides that pay their taxes as the law prescribed.[108]

On the basis of the aides' answer, it is possible that the winter stayers had been exempted from local taxes at some stage but this burden was re-introduced later, apparently under the reign of King Gustav. The obligation to pay tax after a stay of more than six weeks is mentioned in the ordinances given by King Gustav, but not earlier than six years after the above-mentioned case, that is in 1557. The ordinances make it known that foreign merchants and their aides had always paid tax to the town earlier, but such a formulation may merely have been a propagandistic attempt to hide the dissonance that had arisen.[109] It may indeed have been King Gustav who in the 1550s wanted to

---

107 *Stockholms stads tänkeböcker 1635*, p. 28–30.
108 *Stockholms stads tänkeböcker 1549–1551*, p. 127.
109 *Stockholms stads privilegiebref*, p. 51.

exploit more fully the economic potential of the German merchants and their aides.

The exemptions of winter stayers from taxes must have been focused merely on foreigners – it must be remembered that there were also domestic merchants or their aides among the guests and winter stayers. In April 1546, that is five years before the case regarding the obligations of the German guests, a dissatisfied merchant's aide claimed, apparently in an outraged state, that he would not pay any taxes to Stockholm thereafter. Instead, he announced that he would pay his taxes to Lübeck because there was, at least according to him, an annual maximum limit of 24 *penningar*, which he felt was more reasonable. Moreover, he stated that he would become a German aide and act in Stockholm like any other German visitor, so that he would not be obliged to serve the kingdom of Sweden anymore. The outraged aide had a Scandinavian name, Oluf Larsson, so he was most likely a Swede, although a Finnish origin cannot be excluded. The same holds true for the burgher supervising the taxation, Erik Svensson. He reprimanded Oluf by pointing out that "You owe more to Sweden, where you have been born, than to Lübeck." The quarrel soon escalated into a violent battle, but luckily, no one lost his or her life because of it.[110]

The case shows no doubt how two contradicting ideas clashed: the modern idea of becoming a "tax refugee" and the patriotic idea of one's native country as something one owed responsibilities in spite of how onerous they might be. But if Oluf Larsson's (alleged) strategy appears modern in our eyes, neither was Erik Svensson's standpoint outdated in the 1540s. On the contrary, his point of view can be regarded as a positive reception of the leading elites' patriotic propaganda, which had been disseminated in different ways into lesser layers of Swedish society, firstly during the last decades of the fifteenth century when Swedish regents had combated Danish kings, and even more intensively during the reign of King Gustav Vasa (1523–1560). That propaganda aimed to make the subjects of the Swedish Crown aware that they were first and foremost Swedes, both as loyal subjects and taxpayers and as a nation.[111]

The obligations of longer-staying guests were delineated in later ordinances.[112] The town council reminded guests of their obligations: in 1576, it was stated that all "strangers" who stayed in the town more than six weeks would be obliged to pay taxes to the town and subordinate other responsibilities

110 *Stockholms stads tänkeböcker 1544–1548*, p. 177 ("*Dhu wore mere plictug Swerige, ther thu jnfödder är, än Lubke.*").

111 Nordquist 2015, p. 126–127.

112 *Stockholms stads privilegiebref*, p. 57, 67.

towards the town as well. This was repeated in 1577. Then it was decided that visiting merchants would be allowed to stay seven weeks at most.[113]

It had happened in several Danish towns that Hanseatic merchants had been unwilling to subordinate themselves to local legislation and regulations. Conflicts arose when Germans occasionally refused to pay for the right to stay in the town during the winter. Paradoxically, the Danish practices had been modelled after German examples, but as guests abroad themselves, Germans were seeking wider rights.[114] At least occasionally, guests were able to bypass the tax-paying obligations because they either did not report their presence or their hosts and business partners did not do so. This why it was possible, like in May 1601, that the council became aware that, in all, eighteen foreign merchants from different countries had stayed in Stockholm longer than was allowed in the law.[115]

In spite of all regulations regarding guests' rights and obligations, at least one local burgher, Hans Fougtt, who on the basis of his name was of foreign origin, felt that the foreigners had greater rights in Stockholm than the domestic persons. His viewpoint was written down in the protocols of the Town Court in 1599.[116] It is revealing how an individual of non-Nordic origin apparently felt no solidarity with merchants from areas where he had his genealogical roots; instead he regarded himself as a part of the local community or perhaps foremost a member of the local burgher community. Therefore, he felt that the rights of the locals should have been defended better than was the case.

In some cases, the Town Court acted harshly towards foreigners. In 1601, the Town Court decided to treat Elias Bylow, a burgher from Lübeck, with hard hands because he had not handed over to the court a certain sum of money (73 dalers), contrary to the decision of the court. Elias Bylow was willing to pay the required sum of money so that the court would read the actual law paragraphs aloud for him in return. The court kept the money but did not allow him to enjoy the Swedish law. It did not help that Elias Bylow and the burgher who was lodging him offered to gather eight guarantors for him. Elias was put in prison and he was not even allowed to visit the church on the following morning. He was told that he would be imprisoned as long as he did not follow the sentence issued by the court. Three days later Elias Bylow appeared before the court. He now asked for his sentence to be read to him and this happened after

113 *Stockholms stads tänkeböcker 1576–1578*, p. 32, 252, 281–282, 302.

114 Enemark 1960, p. 689, 691.

115 *Stockholms stads tänkeböcker 1601–1602*, p. 33–35.

116 *Stockholms stads tänkeböcker 1596–1599*, p. 372.

he had paid 5 *öre* more. Regarding the 73 dalers he should submit to the court, he asked if he could present a guarantee for them. But his counterpart referred to a case in the court of Norrköping where he had been obliged to pay immediately, so he asked that the same would be applied this time, too. Finally, in spring 1604, Elias Bylow was obliged to leave Stockholm together with his family within two weeks after Easter or when the sea was free from ice.[117]

In 1593, an Italian called Nicolaus Stangniole, dwelling in Norrmalm, accused six young men of being thieves and asked that they be imprisoned. He asked also for the men to be tortured so that they would confess, but the court did not approve it because the Swedish law did not allow for such practices. Apparently, Stangniole was used to more drastic judicial practices. When Stangniole found the real thief himself, the man was hanged as Swedish law stipulated, but the six wrongly imprisoned young men demanded compensation. The court read aloud a "harsh text" (*enn hård täxt*) from the law book for "the Italian" (*italianen*) – the formulation reveals that his ethnic background was regarded as an alienating and aggravating factor in this context. Thus Stangniole became informed on the penalty for ungrounded accusations and actions, but the court was apparently not willing to punish him – instead, it recommended that he should reconcile with the young men in question, which seems also to have happened although not all the details have been written down.[118]

In 1593, when the chamois leather tanners' (*sämskmakare*) guild asked the council for a confirmation letter for a certain Hans Andress who had served his year as an apprentice and wanted to be his own master in another Swedish town, the council denied the petition. Instead, the tanners were reminded of the fact that they should train as many Swedish apprentices as German apprentices – apparently, Hans Andress was regarded as a foreigner. The same seems to have held true for the tanner masters as well, because they claimed that they had sworn abroad that they would not have Swedes or any other "nations" (*ingen svensk eller annan nation*) as their apprentices but only their compatriots, Schlesians. "With that they were turned away without any confirmation letter" (*der medh blefue the affwijste, vthan laere breff*).[119] Apparently, the Town Court of Stockholm disapproved of such patriotic and anti-Swedish sentiments.

117 *Stockholms stads tänkeböcker 1601–1602*, p. 130; *Stockholms stads tänkeböcker 1603–1604*, p. 182.

118 *Stockholms stads tänkeböcker 1592–1595*, p. 117.

119 *Stockholms stads tänkeböcker 1592–1595*, p. 133.

7 Courts in Co-operation

By the middle of the sixteenth century, the range of the Stockholmer merchants' activities had reached the Iberian Peninsula. A burgher called Brynolf Skräddare ("Tailor") was imprisoned while visiting Lisbon, accused of having had intercourse with a young Jewess. At last, he was freed because local honourable wives examined the young woman and concluded that nothing had happened. However, during his imprisonment Brynolf had been obliged to borrow money from another merchant, called Lyder Timme, apparently in order to buy himself food and other necessities. On the basis of his name he was most likely of German origin, whereas Brynolf was probably of Scandinavian origin. Far from the Baltic area, these two men had somehow come into contact with each other, or perhaps they already had known each other. In a notice from 1556, Lyder Timme has the epithet "from [actually to] Lisbon" (*Lyder Tymme tiill Lijsbonn*) which signifies that he dwelled there more or less permanently.[120]

Soon there arose a dispute between these two men, because they had differing opinions regarding how much Brynolf had borrowed and who actually was in debt to whom and by how much. In 1555, Lyder brought a case against Brynolf before the Town Court of Stockholm. The court decided to handle the case but in return Lyder was obliged to accept that the matter was to be solved in Sweden and especially in Stockholm and not elsewhere. He had to present a local burgher, namely Antonius Hagennow – another German based on his name – as a guarantor of that commitment. The necessity of having a guarantor in a case like this shows that the council was not able to trust that its verdict would be shared by other judicial courts in other places.

In the following year, the dispute between Brynolf and Lyder was heard twice at the Town Court of Stockholm. Lyder had acquired written statements from Germany – apparently from one or more German town courts – as well as from Lisbon. The Town Court of Stockholm examined the statement written by the public notary in Lisbon and concluded that it must be regarded as reliable.

Brynolf's case was in many respects unique, but even every-day business transactions and deals often involved merchants and other parties in several towns and other places. Moreover, several burghers living in different towns and countries sometimes owned a ship used for commercial trips. Besides

---

120 *Stockholms stads tänkeböcker 1549–1553*, p. 242–243; *Stockholms stads tänkeböcker 1553–1567*, p. 112–115, 157–158.

these patterns, genealogical bonds often connected individuals living even far away from each other.

Thus, the capital and resources utilised within commerce often had a transnational character. Consequently, interregional and even international interaction was traditionally a part of virtually all town courts' activities. Usually, that interaction was based on written communication, but the contacts between different courts could be direct, meaning that the courts corresponded directly with each other, or indirect, meaning that the courts issued certificates and confirmation letters that were transmitted to other courts and authorities via the individuals who had received them.[121] Regarding problems with international commerce, the communication between the Town Court of Stockholm and its peers took almost entirely indirectly, via burghers or guests who brought written statements from other courts or who were obliged to acquire such documents. Likewise, the Town Court occasionally produced confirmation letters and other documents for burghers and guests who were contacting authorities and courts in other places.[122]

It was in fact quite usual for the Town Court to require justice seekers to acquire some kind of written evidence from other courts in foreign cities in order to be able to hear the case. In the 1620s and the 1630s, the Town Court sometimes appears stricter than the Court of Appeal in its policy of requiring written confirmed documents as evidence. In 1621, when hearing a dispute between a German guest from Copenhagen and a burgher living in Stockholm, the Town Court wanted to see the original agreement or at least an attested copy of it. But when the claimant raised his case in the Court of Appeal, it regarded the evidence as entirely sufficient and returned the case back to the Town Court. However, the Town Court still insisted on more evidence from the claimant. This gave the claimant reason to express his astonishment regarding the Swedish judicial system: he said that he was unable to understand what proof could be presented against a debt agreement and he claimed that in Denmark the debt would have been collected even on the basis of the "*Gastrecht.*" However, the accused party was able to free himself from the claims through the help of two men who testified that he had already paid the debt. The claimant's aide did not appear in the court any more – apparently because he understood that the case had been lost.[123]

121 Kallioinen 2017, p. 1–22.

122 *Stockholms stads tänkeböcker 1578–1583*, p. 113–114.

123 *Stockholms stads tänkeböcker 1620–1621*, p. 174; *Stockholms stads tänkeböcker 1622–1623*, p. 24–25, 38.

Sometimes the Town Court received contradictory evidence from different courts and then it applied Swedish criteria for the written statements in order to conclude which confirmation should be regarded as the most reliable. Thus, even written statements from other courts were occasionally denied judicial cogency in Stockholm if they were not oath-sworn or if they were not regarded as detailed enough. The evaluation was done by comparing the documents to the Swedish laws.[124] The Town Court was also able to make modifications to statements presented to it. For example, when a German burgher was appointed by the council of Lübeck to collect debts in Sweden on behalf of a deceased merchant's widow, the Town Court of Stockholm confirmed his warrant but required that everything the deceased one owed to others in the kingdom of Sweden should be paid off first.[125]

Because the Town Court still consisted mostly of merchants at the beginning of the seventeenth century, it showed understanding for their affairs, for example in the case of a German merchant who had not been able to fulfil his promise and appear before the court since he had been involved in Regent Carl's actions and travels. Because the case involved the most prominent person in the whole realm, at least indirectly, the court gave the defendant more time to order evidence from Danzig and Rostock.[126] In several cases, however, the Town Court of Stockholm did not actually seek to resolve the case; instead it obliged one or both parties to appear in court at some other place, for example in Lübeck or in Riga or in Kopparberget, that is the copper mine district in Sweden. Usually, the Town Court then also set a time limit for the involved parties.[127]

If a case had already been raised or tried in another court in some other place, in Sweden or abroad, the Town Court of Stockholm seems to have been happy merely to refer the quarrelling parties to it. This happened especially in cases in which both parties were non-Stockholmers.[128] In one case, noted in 1604, one might suspect that the town councillors were not willing to get involved in a case that concerned one of their peers in another Swedish town: when the Town Court was informed that Jöns Staffensson, who was burgomaster in Bogesund in the province of Västergötland, had insulted the royal coinage and called it mischievous money (*skälmskt mynt*), the councillors washed

124 For example, *Stockholms stads tänkeböcker 1584–1588*, p. 267–270, 332–333.

125 *Stockholms stads tänkeböcker 1596–1599*, p. 42.

126 *Stockholms stads tänkeböcker 1601–1602*, p. 84–85.

127 For example, *Stockholms stads tänkeböcker 1592–1595*, p. 249; *Stockholms stads tänkeböcker 1596–1599*, p. 302–303.

128 For example, *Stockholms stads tänkeböcker 1576–1578*, p. 120–121, 296–297; *Stockholms stads tänkeböcker 1592–1595*, p. 132.

their hands of it by referring the case to "down there" (*dit neder*), that is to Bogesund, because the alleged blasphemy had happened there and all the witnesses lived there.[129]

But on several occasions, the Town Court did deal with a case that was already being heard or had been heard in another town in Sweden or abroad. For example, in one case, heard in 1619, the disputed goods had been seized in Lübeck, but the Town Court of Stockholm heard the case and applied Swedish Town Law. The Town Court justified its actions by referring to the following facts: the debt in question had been made in Sweden, both parties traded in Stockholm, and the claimant had promised to pay the debt in Stockholm.[130] In another case, also heard in 1619, one party did not live in Stockholm but instead elsewhere in Sweden, in the duchy belonging to the younger son of late King Carl IX, but because the house under dispute was situated in Stockholm, the Town Court accepted the suit, which was quite understandable.[131]

However, on several occasions the Town Court of Stockholm refused to hear further such cases and justified this by referring to the verdicts or ongoing processes in other places. In 1619, one case was referred to England, without précising to which actual court, although it appears that the property in question was situated in London. The justification was that the guardians were living in England, the account books were there, both the family and the house were in London and all parties involved were subjects of the King of England.[132]

Nevertheless, there were numerous cases that the Town Court accepted in spite of the fact that the case had already been tried elsewhere. This held true, among other things, for a dispute regarding a certain debt in 1624: the case had already been heard in Holland but the Town Court of Stockholm was willing to accept it when a merchant, apparently of Dutch origin, contacted it. However, the Town Court wanted to know how the Dutch court had resolved the case.[133]

In the very same year, the Town Court of Stockholm dealt with a debt dispute between two Germans living in Copenhagen and Söderköping and concluded, on the basis of the written documents, that the debt had to be paid – although the transaction had taken place in Copenhagen.[134] This and similar cases were actually contradictory to the traditional policy of the Town Court

129 *Stockholms stads tänkeböcker 1603–1604*, p. 285–288.
130 *Stockholms stads tänkeböcker 1619*, p. 28–29.
131 *Stockholms stads tänkeböcker 1619*, p. 29.
132 *Stockholms stads tänkeböcker 1619*, p. 38.
133 *Stockholms stads tänkeböcker 1624–1625*, p. 169, 192.
134 *Stockholms stads tänkeböcker 1624–1625*, p. 143.

and its legal basis, the Town Law, which claimed that a case had to be tried where it had originated. A year later, the Town Court dealt with a calamity that had happened abroad and that had been caused by stormy weather condition. The Town Court confirmed the verdict of the court in Rostock where the disaster had occurred.[135] By dealing with cases that actually belonged elsewhere, the Town Court of Stockholm occasionally gave itself a status as a kind of a higher court or a court with a higher authority – a court that had the power to confirm or not to confirm sentences issued by other, even foreign courts.

These exceptions from the main policy sometimes also dealt with criminal affairs. For example, in 1612, the mother of a student killed in Uppsala, the Swedish university town, raised the case against the manslayer, a Frenchman, and although the last mentioned was not present and even though the Town Court of Uppsala had already heard the case. But the Town Court of Stockholm examined the case and heard a Frenchman who was a companion of the alleged killer. He stated that he had already given a statement at the Town Hall of Uppsala and was not able to add anything more. There is no indication that the Town Court of Stockholm consulted their peers in Uppsala. Nevertheless, the Town Court of Stockholm concluded that the alleged killer should be condemned to death.[136]

In certain cases the Town Court of Stockholm let the foreign court resolve the case, but because it, too, had been contacted, it decided that the disputed sum of money should be kept at the Town Hall in Stockholm until the process had come into an end. The idea was, of course, that the winning party should get the money.[137] But in at least one case, the Town Court did not follow the sentence given by a foreign court: in a dispute regarding an unpaid debt between a German from Hamburg and another who had moved to Stockholm in 1620, the Town Court decided that it was unable to deal with the case because it already had been resolved by the council of Stralsund as well as by the Court of Appeal of Wolgast.[138] It is unclear, though, why the Town Court did not require the merchant who had moved to Stockholm to pay the debt, according to the sentence given in Stralsund, although in several other cases it acknowledged the validity of verdicts issued abroad. Most likely, the Town Court was for some reason protecting a member of the local burgher community, although he was of foreign origin.

135 *Stockholms stads tänkeböcker 1624–1625*, p. 337.

136 *Stockholms stads tänkeböcker 1608–1612*, p. 185.

137 For example, *Stockholms stads tänkeböcker 1584–1588*, p. 5.

138 *Stockholms stads tänkeböcker 1620–1621*, p. 84.

There were also cases that were brought before the Town Court by non-residents merely because one or both of the disputing parties happened to be in Stockholm, as happened, among other things, in the above-mentioned case dealing with brimstone trade that had taken place in Danzig. Similar patterns can be found in several other cases as well. For example, in 1620, regarding a dispute between a merchant's widow from another Swedish town and a Scottish merchant's aide, both visiting Stockholm at the time, the Town Court obliged the male party to appear before any court or send a representative if the case should be continued in another place.[139] In a case examined in 1594, the disputing parties originated from the town of Turku (Åbo in Swedish) and the village of Åketorp in the province of Västergötland: a farmer from the last-mentioned village was allowed to present his evidence before the Town Court of Stockholm with the justification that the parties involved lived so far away from each other.[140]

Sometimes it is difficult to understand why certain information dealing with foreign merchants was written down in court records. For example, in 1586, a merchant called Dirik Bökman had a total of five letters from the council of the town of Kolding written down in the record book. The letters had been written between 1579 and 1584 and they dealt with the exemption of Kolding from certain internal Danish tariffs, its medieval privileges and Dirik Bökman's intention to quit his position as a burgher and move to some other place. In particular, the last mentioned letter functioned simultaneously as testimony to Dirik's societal reputation, but it is difficult to understand why the Town Court of Stockholm should have been interested in details regarding internal Danish regulations.[141]

Of course, foreign and even domestic merchants could escape the verdict and judicial processes. They could simply disappear or not return even though the process was incomplete. This was in fact easier in the sixteenth century than during earlier times, as the increasing role of written documents and judicial representatives made it unnecessary for both claimants and defendants to appear personally before the courts.

The Town Court was able to require certain measures from such individuals, but if they stayed away, no one was able to require them to follow the decisions. A foreign defendant could also refuse to answer to the claims in Sweden if they wanted to do so in some other country, by claiming that the dispute was already undergoing judicial treatment there. Naturally, the Town Court of Stockholm

139 *Stockholms stads tänkeböcker 1620–1621*, p. 52–53.
140 *Stockholms stads tänkeböcker 1592–1595*, p. 239–240.
141 *Stockholms stads tänkeböcker 1584–1588*, p. 183–186.

was not bound to any defendant's wishes, but in one such case the court consulted noble authorities before making any decision.[142] In certain cases, when a condemned party had fled a verdict given by a court abroad, the Town Court of Stockholm was able to assist the other court by allowing the case to be reopened or continued in Stockholm – of course, provided that the party who had fled had come to Stockholm.[143]

8 Conclusions

This chapter has proved that Swedish legislation was continuously prioritised and even emphasised in the jurisdictional activities of the Town Court of Stockholm. The Swedish legislation was regarded as the sole base for all sentences and decisions, but since in practice it consisted of numerous judicial texts and not solely one law book containing the Swedish Town Law, that foundation made it possible for the judges to select and apply different norms and rules. Together with the fact that most town dwellers, even the domestic ones, had some kind of immigrant background, this must have made mentalities open to negotiation and external influence. Thus, the early modern roots of the commercial law in Sweden did not grow in an entirely domestic ground. However, the Town Court was apparently neither willing nor able to let people staying or dwelling on Swedish soil to follow foreign legal practices exclusively. The official goal seems to have been that all were subject to Swedish legislation, regardless ethnic or cultural background. This was also the policy of the ruling domestic dynasty, which sought to control happenings and circumstances in local communities more intensively than its predecessors had been able to do. The central power gave courts less and less freedom in their actions. However, at least on the idealistic level, the Town Court of Stockholm sought to make even the foreigners accept the verdicts and not just subordinate themselves to them. With certain exceptions, the Town Court sought to appear impartial in front of foreigners as well. This policy also coincided with the aspirations of the kings and regents, and it had already been expressed in the medieval Town Law.

Interregional and international commerce in particular launched cases in which the Town Court of Stockholm had to interact with other courts in other places and even outside the realm. Communication with other courts – either

142 *Stockholms stads tänkeböcker 1616–1617*, p. 89–90.

143 *Stockholms stads tänkeböcker 1627*, p. 86.

directly in the form of correspondence or indirectly via individuals seeking justice and asking for confirmation letters or other documents – forms the channel that constantly maintained external influences within the judiciary system in Stockholm. In several cases, the Town Court willingly let other, even foreign, courts resolve cases that individuals tried to bring before it. Many cases required cooperation between at least two different courts before they could be resolved. But especially in this area the Town Court was not quite consistent and sometimes it did hear cases that had undergone a judiciary process in some other place or that were currently undergoing such a process.

The notices in the court records changed greatly over the course of time, so it is difficult to make comparisons between different eras and detect what might have changed. The overall image emphasises continuities, which is a plausible interpretation because the central power had more and more tools to ensure that the ideas and norms expressed in laws and ordinances actually became lived practices. However, as several examples presented above have proved, the Town Court of Stockholm nevertheless also possessed a certain freedom of choice that in some occasions resulted in solutions that actually contradicted the written law.

Source Editions

Codex iuris communis Sueciae Christophorianus. Konung Christoffers landslag, (eds.) H.S. Collin and C.J. Schlyter, Corpus iuris sueo-gotorum antiqui. Samling af Sveriges gamla lagar, vol. 12, (Lund: Berlingska boktryckeriet, 1869).

Codex iuris Ostrogotici. Östgöta-lagen, (eds.) H.S. Collin and C.J. Schlyter, Corpus iuris sueo-gotorum antiqui. Samling af Sveriges gamla lagar, vol. 2 (Stockholm: P.A. Norstedt & Söner, 1830).

Codex iuris urbici Magnæanus. Konung Magnus Erikssons stadslag, (ed.) C.J. Schlyter, Corpus iuris sueo-gotorum antiqui. Samling af Sveriges gamla lagar, vol. 11 (Lund: Berlingska boktryckeriet, 1865).

Magnus Erikssons stadslag i nusvensk tolkning, (eds.) Å. Holmbäck and E. Wessén (Stockholm: Nordiska bokhandeln, 1966).

Privilegier, resolutioner och förordningar för Sveriges städer, vols. 1–7, (eds.) N. Herlitz et al. (Stockholm: Stadshistoriska institutet, 1927–1985).

Stockholms stads privilegiebref 1423–1700, (eds.) K. Hildebrand and A Bratt (Stockholm: Wahlström & Widstrand, 1900–13).

Stockholms stads tänkeböcker 1474–1520 (5 vols), (eds.) H. Hildebrand et al. (Stockholm: Kungl. Samfundet för utgivande av handskrifter rörande Skandinaviens historia and Samfundet S:t Erik, 1917–1944).

Stockholms stads tänkebok under Vasatiden: 1524–1529, (ed.) N. Sjöberg (Stockholm: Samfundet S:t Erik, 1915).

Stockholms stads tänkebok 1524–29 m.m. av M:r Olauus Petri Phase, (ed.) L. Larsson (Lund: Vetenskapssocieteten i Lund, 1940).

Stockholms stads tänkeböcker 1544–1591 (8 vols), (eds.) J.A. Almquist et al. (Stockholm: Kungl. Samfundet för utgivande av handskrifter rörande Skandinaviens historia and Samfundet S:t Erik, 1936–1948).

Stockholms stads tänkeböcker 1592–1635 (24 vols), (eds.) D. Almqvist et al. (Stockholm: Stockholms stadsarkiv, 1939–2009).

Sveriges traktater med främmande magter jemte andra dit hörande handlingar, vol. 1, (ed.) O.S. Rydberg (Stockholm: Norstedt, 1877).

Literature

Ahnlund, Nils. 1929. "Svenskt och tyskt i Stockholms äldre historia" in *Historisk Tidskrift* 49, 1–34.

Bergman, Göstä. 1968. *Kortfattad svensk språkhistoria* (Stockholm: Prisma).

Calley, Chris. 1995. "A Model of Early Modern Urban Demography" in *Economic History Review* 48, 448–169.

Dahlbäck, Göran. 1987. *I medeltidens Stockholm* (Stockholm: Stockholmia).

Enemark, Poul. 1960. "Gæster" in *Kulturhistoriskt lexikon för nordisk medeltid*, vol. 5 (Malmö: Allhem).

Gustafsson, Harald. 2002. "The Eight Argument. Identity, Ethnicity and Political Culture in Sixteenth-Century Scandinavia" in *Scandinavian Journal of History* 27, 91–113.

Gustafsson, Sofia. 2006. "Svenska städer i medeltidens Europa. En komparativ studie av stadsorganisation och politisk kultur" in *Stockholm Studies in History* vol. 86, 109–129.

Hartweg, Frédéric, and Wegera, Klaus-Peter. 2005. *Frühneuhochdeutsch. Eine Einführung in die deutsche Sprache des Spätmittelalters und der frühen Neuzeit* (Tübingen: Niemeyer).

Helle, Knut. 1982. *Kongssete og kjøpstad. Fra opphavet til 1536* (Bergen: The Town of Bergen).

Heyde, Astrid. 1989. "Käpplingemorden år 1389 – ett 600-årsminne?" *Sankt Eriks årsbok* 87, 9–28.

Jansson, S.O. 1971. "Skålpund" in *Kulturhistoriskt Lexikon för nordisk medeltid* vol. 16.

Kallioinen, Mika. 2017. "Inter-Communal Institutions in Medieval Trade" *The Economic History Review* vol. 70, 1–22.

Karonen, Petri. 1994. *Kämnerinoikeudet Suomen kaupungeissa suurvalta-ajan alkupuolella (noin 1620–1660)* (Jyväskylä: University of Jyväskylä).

Koppe, Wilhelm. 1933. *Lübeck-Stockholmer Handelsgeschichte im 14. Jahrhundert* (Neumünster: Wachholtz).

Korpiola, Mia (ed.). 2014. *The Svea Court of Appeal in the Early Modern Period. Historical Reinterpretations and New Perspectives* (Stockholm: Institutet för rättshistorisk forskning).

Kouri, Erkki. 2016. "The Reformation in Sweden and Finland" in Kouri, Erkki and Olesen, Jens E. (eds.), *The Cambridge history of Scandinavia* (Cambridge: Cambridge University Press, 2016).

Kumlien, Kjell. 1953. *Sverige och hanseaterna. Studier i svensk politik och utrikeshandel* (Stockholm: Wahlström & Widstrand).

Lamberg, Marko. 2001. *Dannemännen i stadens råd. Rådmanskretsen i nordiska köpstäder under senmedeltiden* (Stockholm: Stockholmia).

Lamberg, Marko. 2017. "Ethnic Imagery and Social Boundaries in Early Modern Urban Communities. The Case of the Finnish Immigrants in Swedish Towns, c. 1450–1650" in Lamberg, M. (ed.), *Shaping Ethnic Identities. Ethnic Minorities in Northern and East Central European States and Communities, c. 1450–2000* (Helsinki: East West Books Helsinki).

Lamberg, Marko. 2007. "Expressions on Ethnic Self Concepts among Low-Status Finnish Immigrants in Early Modern Swedish Towns" in S. Prühlen, L. Kuhse and J. Sarnowsky (eds), *Der Blick auf sich und die anderen. Selbstbild und Fremdbild von Frauen und Männern im Mittelalter und früh er Neuzeit* (Göttingen: University of Göttingen Press) 113–133.

Lamberg, Marko. 2000. "Finnar, svenskar eller främlingar? Inblickar i den finska befolkningsdelens status i det svenska riket under senmedeltiden" in *Historisk Tidskrift* vol. 120, 506–510.

Lamberg, Marko. 2006. "Finns as Aliens and Compatriots in the Late Medieval Kingdom of Sweden" in O. Merisalo and P. Pahta (eds.) *Frontiers in the Middle Ages. Proceedings of the Third European Congress of Medieval Studies (Jyväskylä 10–14 June 2003)* (Louvain-la-Neuve: Brepols), 121–132.

Lamberg, Marko. 2004. "Perceptions of Finns and Ethnic Boundaries in Sweden during the Middle Ages and the Early Modern Era" in *Nordeuropaforum* 14 (N.F. 7), 3–23.

Lamberg, Marko. 2014. "The Tale of Two Courts in One Town. The Relationship between the Stockholm Town Court and the Svea Court of Appeal 1614–1624" in M. Korpiola (ed.) *The Svea Court of Appeal in the Early Modern Period. Historical Reinterpretations and New Perspectives* (Stockholm: Institutet för rättshistorisk forskning).

Lilja, Sven. 1995. "Stockholms befolkningsutveckling före 1800. Metoder och förklaringar," in *Historisk Tidskrift* vol. 115, 304–337.

Mäkinen, Kirsti. 1989. *Lollot ja kollot. Suomalaista naapurihuumoria* (Helsinki: Otava).

Moberg, Lena. 1989. *Lågtyskt och svenskt i Stockholms medeltida tänkeböcker* (Uppsala: Kungliga Gustav Adolfs akademien).

Montgomery, Ingun. 1995. "The Institutionalization of Lutheranism in Sweden and Finland" in O.P. Grell (ed.) *The Scandinavian Reformation* (Cambridge: Cambridge University Press), 144–178.

Murray, Robert. 1954. *Finska församlingen i Stockholm. Intill tiden för Finlands skiljande från Sverige* (Stockholm: Svenska kyrkans diakonistyrelses bokförlag).

Murray, Robert. 1954. *Stockholms kyrkostyrelse intill 1630-talets mitt* (Lund: Svenska kyrkans diakonistyrelse).

Nordin, Jonas. M. 2017. "Samer i imperiets mitt. Samiskt liv i det tidigmoderna Stockholm – en glömd historia" in Götling, A. and Lamberg, Marko (eds.) *Tillfälliga stockholmare. Människor och möten under 600 år* (Stockholm: Stockholmia).

Nordquist, Margareta. 2015. *A Struggle for the Realm. Late-Medieval Swedish Rhyme Chronicles as Ideological Expressions* (Stockholm: University of Stockholm).

Peterzén, Ingvar. 1945. *Studier rörande Stockholms historia under Gustav Vasa*, (Stockholm: Kommittén för Stockholmsforskning).

Pihlajamäki, Heikki. 2013. "Legalism before the Legality Principle? Royal Statutes and Early Modern Swedish Criminal Law" in Martyn. G., Musson. A. Pihlajamäki. H. (eds.), *From the Judge's Arbitrium to the Legality Principle. Legislation as a Source of Law in Criminal Trials* (Berlin: Duncker & Humblot).

Regner, Elisabet. 2013. *Det medeltida Stockholm. En arkeologisk guidebok* (Lund: Historiska Media).

Sandström, Åke. 1990. *Mellan Torneå och Amsterdam. En undersökning av Stockholms roll som förmedlare av varor i regional- och utrikeshandel 1600–1650* (Stockholm: Stockholmia).

Schück, Adolf. 1926. *Studier rörande det svenska stadsväsendets uppkomst och äldsta utveckling* (Uppsala).

Sidén, Per, Gunnar, "*Hur tyska var de svenska städerna under högmedeltiden?*" paper presented at the Svenska Historikermötet Conference 2008, https://www.historia.su.se/polopoly_fs/1.27755.1320939842!/SidenTyskaSvenskaStader.pdf.

Sjödén, C.C. 1950. *Stockholms borgerskap under Sturetiden med särskild hänsyn till dess politiska ställning* (Stockholm: Kommittén för Stockholmsforskning).

Snell, K.D.M. 2003. "The Culture of Local Xenophobia" in *Social History* vol. 37, 1–30.

Sommar, C.O. 1942. "Till Kristoffers landslags 500-årsjubileum" *Svensk Juristtidning* vol. 27.

Svanberg Ingvar and Tyden, Mattias. 1990. "Invandringen genom tiderna" in G. Lindberg (ed.) *"Sicken turk" Om invandrarnas svenska historia* (Stockholm: Riksförbundet för hembygdsvård).

Tak, Herman. 1990. "Longing for Local Identity. Intervillage Relations in an Italian Mountain Area" in *Anthropological Quarterly* vol. 63, 90–100.

Trolle Önnerfors, Elsa. 2010. *Justitia et Prudentia. Rättsbildning genom rättstillämpning – Svea hovrätt och testamentsmålen 1640–1690* (Lund: University of Lund).

Wolke, Lars Ericson. 2010. *Stockholms historia under 750 år* (Lund: Historiska Media).

Wrede, Rabbe Axel. 1912. "Bidrag till kännedom om processen under 1600-talet. Utdrag ur Åbo stads dombok 1623–1638" in *Tidskrift utgifven af Juridiska föreningen i Finland* vol. 48, 263–299.

Wubs-Mrozewicz, Justyna. 2004. "Interplay of Identities. *German* Settlers in Late Medieval Stockholm" in *Scandinavian Journal of History* vol. 29, 53–67.

Yrwing, H. 1976. "Vinterliggare: Sverige" in *Kulturhistoriskt lexikon för nordisk medeltid*, vol. 20 (Malmö: Allhem), 142–144.

CHAPTER 3

Chartered Companies in Sweden, the Dutch Republic and England (*c.*1600–*c.*1630): Experiments in Corporate Governance

Dave De ruysscher

1 Introduction[1]

This chapter analyses the organisational structures of chartered companies in North-West Europe in relation to economic, cultural and political variables. The focus is on developments during the first three decades of the seventeenth century, in Sweden, the Netherlands and England.

First, the chapter argues that in this period rules of governance for chartered companies were national, but also that the crafting of these norms was a dynamic and interactive process. The drafters of charters devised rules with elements that were drawn from foreign company statutes and practices. In this era, the Dutch *Verenigde Oost-Indische Compagnie* (1602, henceforth VOC), and the English East India Company (1600, henceforth EIC), as well as the Dutch *West-Indische Compagnie* (1621, henceforth WIC), were regarded as paragons of commerce. It is true that contemporaries – and in particular governments of other states – considered their charters as examples. This was due to the success of these companies. Policies of establishing chartered companies also related to the coming into being of a "mercantilist" political-administrative culture all over Europe. However, the aura of the mentioned companies should not be inflated to the point of considering them predecessors of present-day "corporations." A "genealogical" approach to the history of chartered companies is highly problematic.[2] The first regulations of the Dutch and English chartered companies lacked many features of present-day corporations. Moreover, in the

1 This chapter was made possible with the support of the Academy of Finland and the European Research Council. I would like to thank Katja Tikka (University of Helsinki) and Jussi Sallila (University of Helsinki), for sending me copies of company statutes and for guiding me through the Swedish archives.

2 On hindsight bias in analysing the history of chartered companies, see Cordes and Jahntz 2007, p. 5–19 (nos. 4–6), Arguing that early chartered companies did not develop in linear ways from medieval examples, and because of their combined political and economic features. See more Steensgaard 1981, p. 245–251.

 | DOI:10.1163/9789004436046_004

eyes of contemporaries, the chartered companies were not considered to have a fixed corporate governance regime. Indeed, the organisational characteristics of these companies were subject to swift, often fundamental changes.[3] Moreover, not all changes were implemented by way of new charters; sometimes decisions about structuring were taken by the companies' boards that were not communicated widely.[4] As a result, in the early seventeenth century, the successive charters and decisions, even practices, that adjusted the structures of the Dutch and English licensed companies precluded a perception of their charters as "models" for organisations of overseas trade. Legal borrowing was concerned with parts of charters, with practices and views, not with the transplanting of charters as such, or as a whole. Furthermore, the developing rules of organisation could serve as inspiration but they were not simply replicated. Instead, all over Europe rules and charters for companies reflected new ideas on such issues as limited liability of investors, legal personality and directors' liability. But, again, such new ideas could be borrowed from elsewhere.

In this regard, plans for setting up chartered companies in the Scandinavian and Baltic regions, and in Sweden in particular, are highly illustrative. Drafts and charters of company statutes, which were often written by or in close cooperation with merchants, contain elements selected from Dutch and English texts and practices. This demonstrates legal borrowing, but also, the Swedish plans and charters built on novel interpretations of problems of corporate governance. The Dutch and English companies have received ample attention, and they have often been compared.[5] By contrast, chartered companies in Sweden have been analysed less, and they have not yet been linked to recent literature that delves into the developing corporate regulations in the Dutch Republic[6] and England.[7] Moreover, the relative wealth of source materials

---

3 With regard to the VOC, this point was raised in Steensgaard 1982, p. 238–239; Gelderblom 2013, p. 1050–1076. Both publications argue that permanence of capital was not envisaged from the start. The second publication contends that several new organisational features (limited liability of directors, permanence of capital, pooling of debt) were developed in response to shortages that were due to unforeseen events. Steensgaard considers the changes of structure to be the side effects of practical decisions, and of differences in approach between the company's offices in the Netherlands and in Batavia.

4 Kirti 1965, p. 33. (1615, different minimum admissions for merchants, shopkeepers and members of the gentry); Gelderblom, Jong and Jonker 2013, p. 1061. (1617, pooling of debt).

5 Heckscher 1994, p. 223–254.

6 Jongh 2016, p. 61; Jongh 2014, p. 60–102, 133–164; Gelderblom, Jong and Jonker 2011, p. 26–62; Gelderblom, Jong and Jonker 2013, p. 1050–1076.

7 See the entire book by Gialdroni 2011. See also the older, rich monograph by William Robert Scott, which is often overlooked: Scott 1912.

for Sweden, as compared to the Dutch Republic and England, allows us to reconsider the coming into being of corporate governance norms in North-West Europe.

A second point of this chapter is that the variables that determined which foreign characteristics of organisation were chosen could be, and often were, cultural and political, rather than economic. The penholders of statutes did not select such features on the basis of economic conditions, but rather from within convictions on the properties of successful companies. The auras of the Dutch and English chartered companies hindered assessments of the regional and national situations, and on how to adapt companies' structures accordingly. Early seventeenth-century Sweden is a case in point. The mercantile settings in Sweden in the first years of the seventeenth century were modest overall. Swedish chartered companies were devised mainly to attract or channel flows of Scandinavian and Baltic trade to harbours of the Swedish heartland, in order to stimulate commerce at home and to generate revenue for the Crown. These licensed companies did not often perpetuate existing mercantile ventures, even though they were proposed by or written in cooperation with (foreign) merchants. Plans were drawn up and adjusted according to the political-economic views of the Swedish government. They were not just private business ventures that were rubber-stamped by the Swedish kings. Reasons for why constraints were political and cultural rather than economic include that it was unclear which institutional characteristics of monopolistic, chartered companies were the most efficient. Throughout North-West Europe, ideas regarding core problems were diverse, and the motives underlying comparable changes in the charters could differ. Moreover, the impact and success of chartered companies depended not only on their institutional frameworks, but also on other factors such as policy continuity, territorial acquisitions, and the availability of capital and knowhow. In Sweden, lack of capital and unwieldy politics of trade were crucial factors.

2 Sweden's Trade Policy and Foreign Mercantile Relations in the Early Seventeenth Century

Dutch merchants have traded in Scandinavia and the Baltic regions since the later Middle Ages. Particularly from the beginning of the sixteenth century onwards, many merchants from the Low Countries set up trading associations venturing to those areas, and traders, or their servants or apprentices, commonly settled for some time in ports in the Scandinavian, Baltic and Russian territories.[8] From around 1590, within these provinces Sweden and Denmark became more integrated in North-Western European trading networks than before. This arose from a mix of mercantile demand, territorial expansion and state intervention. In the later years of the sixteenth century, Swedish exports of iron, copper, tar and pitch increased. In particular, the export of copper from Sweden and tar from Finland rose quickly.[9] In addition, mining proved lucrative in the Norwegian territories, which depended from Denmark.

Early on, Dutchmen had stakes in these trades. In October 1605, the Swedish King Carl IX (1604–1611) started negotiating with Dutch merchants on trade from the newly established city of Gothenburg, on the island of Hisingen.[10] These and other contacts amounted to the further integration of the markets of Sweden and the Dutch Republic. In the 1610s, many copper mills in Dutch cities were processing shipments that had come from Sweden.[11] In Sweden, Dutch merchants started investing in mining infrastructures, and this also happened in the larger Scandinavian area.[12] In matters of trade, the Swedish state drew on the expertise of foreigners. Because of the intertwining of commerce and government affairs, shortly after 1605 many Dutchmen – merchants but also diplomats and jurists – had already been awarded high positions in the Swedish administration.[13] These Dutchmen came not only from the County of Holland, or from its capital Amsterdam, but also from other constituencies of the Low Countries, in particular from French-speaking regions.[14]

The Baltic and Russian trades were at least as important as the Swedish export trade. Local products from the Baltic and Russian mainland were exchanged. But the Baltic and Russia commerce also penetrated into the

8 Grell 2016, p. 229–245; Jeannin 1996, p. 221–262; Müller 2005, p. 60; Wijnroks 2003. One can also refer to Dutch whaling expeditions, which were directed to the coasts of Norway and surrounding territories.

9 Klein 1978, p. 459; Klein 199, p. 245–247.

10 Thomson 2005, p. 336.

11 Israel 2002, p. 96, 116.

12 Van Bochove 2008, p. 63, 103. Examples include the de Marselis family, which invested in Norwegian mining, and the de Geer family, which had stakes in Swedish mines.

13 Wrangel 1901, p. 22–23. (on Abraham Cabelliau, who – besides major of Gothenburg and governor of the Gothenburg Company – was also the chairman of the royal mint), and p. 23–25 (concerning dr Jacob van Dijck, councilor at the royal court in 1609). See the biographies of Abraham Cabelliau and Jacob van Dijck, respectively G. Jacobson, on Svenskt biografiskt lexikon. For the intense Dutch-Swedish relations of lawyers and law professors in the 1630s and thereafter, see Modéer 2014, p. 69–77.

14 Businessmen Louis de Geer and Peter Minuit were Walloons, as were many workers in the Swedish mining and iron industry. See Jespersen 2016, p. 374.

heartland of Central Asia. Via Narva and Archangelsk, Moscow was reached, where merchandise as raw silk, leather and rugs were sold that had been imported from Persian cities through Astrakhan. The infiltration of Sweden in the Baltic and Russian trades rose in concordance with its territorial ambitions. From the middle of the sixteenth century onwards, important Baltic and Russian ports were conquered. They included Reval (1561), Narva (1581), Ivangorod (1612), Ingria (1617), and Riga (1621). During the reign of Gustav II Adolphus (1611–1632) a "derivation" policy was pursued, which entailed the maximisation of taxation opportunities on freights going to and from the captured harbours. However, at the same time, attempts to stimulate commerce through Swedish cities and to create a Swedish bourgeoisie were at odds with this "eastern" programme. Ships did pass through Stockholm or Gothenburg, but the attractiveness of these harbours was limited; acknowledging the prominence of the Baltic and Russian ports meant that Swedish ports remained underdeveloped.[15]

The ambitions of the Swedish and Danish kings to increase trade to and from their nations, and at the same time raise income for the Crown drew merchants from the Dutch Republic, carrying with them plans for chartered companies. Before the seventeenth century, companies with many silent partners uninvolved in the trade had generally not been set up in Scandinavian and Baltic regions.[16] After 1605, this changed, mostly because of Dutch influence. In Sweden, the reinvigoration of Gothenburg and negotiations on trade privileges were accompanied by the grant of a royal charter for a trading company in 1607. This company was planned as a venture for all trade over Narva, to Russia and also Persia, but it did not last.

When Gustav II Adolphus became king in 1611, a new era of intense Dutch-Swedish relations began. In 1614, Sweden and the Republic signed a peace treaty for fifteen years.[17] At the beginning of 1615, Dutch merchants approached the Swedish King with a scheme for a ten-year "Swedish Company in Stockholm."[18] The Swedish government drafted over the Dutch-language

15 Kotilaine 2005, p. 142–178.

16 Arrangements involving limited liability of investors (*wedderlegginghe*, *sendeve*) had been known in the late medieval Hanseatic trade. The investing partner was shielded in these arrangements, albeit more practically than legally. However, in contrast to many chartered companies, the *wedderlegginghe* and *sendeve* were cooperative ventures, which were established by way of an agreement between the partners. See Cordes 1998, p. 121–154.

17 Lindblad 2014, p. 23–25; Wetterberg 2014, p. 40–54.

18 Riksarkivet Stockholm (henceforth RAS), *Ämnessamlingar, Handel och sjöfart*, no. 46. This project draft is written in Dutch and is labelled "*Voorslach ofte concept van een compagnie*"

proposal and changed some of the characteristics of the proposed Stockholm company. The final charter of the Stockholm company reflects a change in Swedish trade policy, which had become markedly more investor-oriented. The Stockholm company was destined for trade of any merchandise, as was the 1607 Gothenburg company, and it was of long projected duration (ten years). The charter took into account the rights of investors, even though control over the venture remained in the King's hands.[19] In spite of all this, the Stockholm company was not launched. In 1619 another company was set up, the charter of which was renewed several times.[20] This "Swedish Trading Company" was of more limited duration (three years), and in 1620 was combined with a monopoly in copper at the mine of Stora Kopparberg.[21] The company had similar structural characteristics as the 1615 company.

Even though the 1607, 1615 and 1619 companies were very different, their charters all reflect Dutch influence, as will be detailed further. But Dutchmen were also active in Denmark. In March 1616, the Danish King Christian IV established an East India Company, after he had been courted by two Dutch merchants, Herman Rosenkrantz and Jan de Willem, with plans for such a company.[22] In tandem with the success of their business ventures, Dutch merchants

("Proposal or concept of a company"). It contains 32 sections, followed by an "Instruction" of 19 sections. The text does not bear a date or the names of its authors. *Terminus ad quem* is 1 February 1616, when the first subscriptions were accepted. The document is described in the books by Wittrock 1919, p. 12–15; Thomson 2005, p. 336–337.

19 *Samling utaf kongl. Bref, stadgar och forordningarr angaende Sweriges Rikes commerce, politie och oeconomie ...*, vol. 1, p. 660–667 (the Väsby-charter, 1 March 1615), p. 668–671 (instruction), p. 671–678 (the Stockholm-charter, 24 April 1615) (all hereafter 1615 StoC). The first charter is discussed in Wittrock 1919, p. 16–19, the second one is not. See on the 1615 Stockholm company, also Johnson 1911, p. 45; Thomson 2005, p. 336–337.

20 For the first charter, see von Stiernman, *Samling*, 1, p. 708–710 (24 July 1619) (henceforth SwTC 1619). In December 1619, December 1620, December 1622, January 1625, January 1626 and June 1626 new statutes for this "general" company were issued. See von Stiernman, *Samling*, 1, p. 718–731 (21 Dec. 1619) (henceforth SwTC 1619/2), and p. 761–774 (21 Dec. 1620) (henceforth SwTC 1620); RAS, *Ämnessamlingar, Handel och sjöfart*, no. 50 (22 Dec. 1622) (henceforth SwTC 1622); von Stiernman, *Samling*, 1, p. 923–926 (10 Jan. 1625) (henceforth SwTC 1625); RAS, *Ämnessamlingar, Handel och sjöfart*, no. 46 (1 Jan. 1626) (henceforth SwTC 1626); RAS, *Ämnessamlingar, Handel och sjöfart*, no. 46 (June 1626) (henceforth SwTC 1626/2). The labels that have been given to this company differ. Ligtenberg and others refer to a "copper company." See Lightenberg 1914, p. 90. Even though the focus was on copper trade, for which in 1620 a monopoly was granted, all kinds of merchandise could be traded. See in this regard Johnson 1911, p. 45; Roberts 2013, p. 118.

21 Styrker 2014, p. 136.

22 Diller 1999, p. 24–25; Rindom 2000, p. 100; Sørensen 2005, p. 109; Willerslev 1944, p. 608.

infiltrated Swedish and Danish high society, to the extent that they granted loans to the monarchs.[23]

The Swedish Trading Company of 1619 had potential, but it struggled early on and was eventually wound up in 1628, largely because of King Gustav's incessant borrowing from the firm.[24] Yet the idea of a "general" Swedish trading company persisted, and this resulted in the founding of a new company, the Swedish South Company (1626), which was oriented towards the West Indies. This was done in close cooperation with Dutchman Willem Usselinckx. He had come to Sweden in October 1624,[25] and under his instigation new initiatives on chartered companies were taken. Usselinckx, born in Antwerp, had migrated to the United Provinces in the early 1590s after many years abroad. Ever since the later years of the sixteenth century, he had advocated for a Dutch West India company. At first, the plans were not implemented because of the Dutch-Spanish conflict. When the project was revisited during the Truce with Spain (1609), Usselinckx' ideas were seriously challenged by the Dutch state authorities. Drafts of statutes circulated in political bodies of the Netherlands, and Usselinckx drew up another project charter in 1619. However, when in 1621 it was ultimately decided to launch a West India Company, most of Usselinckx' proposals were ignored. Usselinckx had envisaged the WIC as a purely commercial organisation that would trade with permanent Dutch settlements in South America. A Council would control these colonies, which would be a political body. By contrast, in matters of commerce, only traders would decide: the investors and not institutional bodies of cities and regions were to elect the directors, as was the case in the VOC. In this regard, the Estates-General, which wielded the highest political authority in the Dutch Republic, were not to interfere with the directors. The proposed separation of commerce and foreign policy was not accepted: the Estates-General opted for a company that was devised as a military structure, with broad powers for the central government and little control by shareholders.[26]

In December 1624, the Swedish King Gustav granted Usselinckx a license to establish a general trading company in Sweden, which would become the South Company.[27] Even before that time, in November 1624, Usselinckx had

23 The Trip family lent to the Swedish king. See Müller 2005, p. 68. The de Marselis family extended loans to the Danish King Christian IV. See Van Bochove 2008, p. 248.

24 Roberts 1958, p. 2, 92–99; Stryker 2014, p. 135.

25 Jameson 1887, p. 93; Lightenberg 1914, p. 97.

26 Jameson 1887, p. 61–63.

27 Samling utaf kongl. Bref..., p. 910–911. (21 Dec. 1624).

FIGURE 4
Portrait of Willem Usselincx (1567–1647).

written a draft of statutes.[28] In June 1626, King Gustav issued a charter, thereby founding the South Company for a period of twelve years (1627–1639).[29] Usselinckx was appointed director-general of the company, and boasted of his achievements among his former compatriots by translating the charter into Dutch and having it printed in The Hague in 1627.[30] Usselinckx' views on corporate structuring had been novel around 1605, when they were first formulated, but they had become somewhat out-dated by 1626, considering the

28 RAS, *Ämnessamlingar, Handel och sjöfart*, no. 48. This document is in Dutch. Jameson refers to two (Dutch-language) copies of the November 1624 draft. Only one of them could be located. See Jameson 1887, p. 214 (no. 18) and p. 215 (no. 19).

29 See for the Swedish version Samling utaf kongl..., p. 1, 932–947 (14 June 1626) (henceforth: SC 1626). A Dutch version (which in fact was nearly the same as the 1624 draft) is W. Usselinckx, *Octroy ofte Privilegie, soo by den alderdoorluchtigsten grootmachtigen vorst ende heer heer Gustaeff Adolph van Sweden ... aen de nieuw opgerichte Zuyder Compagnie in't koningrijck Sweden, onlangs genadigst gegeven ende verleend is, ...* (The Hague: Aert Mueris, 1627), no fol. The charter was also translated in High German: *Argonautica Gustaviana; das ist nothwendige Nachricht von der Newen Seefahrt und Kauffhandlung ...* (Frankfurt am Main: Caspar Rodteln, 1633), no. fol. The *Argonautica Gustaviana* was inserted into Johann Marquardt, *De iure mercatorum et commercium* (Frankfurt: Matthias Gotzius, 1662), p. 373–540. There also exists a "contract," probably from 1625, which lists 12 sections (complementing the 37 sections of the 1626 charter) resuming the basic features of the company. See Samling utaf kongl..., p. 1, 911–922 (1625).

30 Usselinckx, *Octroy ofte Privilegie*.

changes that had been implemented in the Dutch Republic in the intervening years. In other respects, the ideas of Usselinckx were closely attached to Dutch examples, which were not always fit for the Swedish context.

The changing contents of Swedish statutes of chartered companies, and their interactive features vis-à-vis Dutch and English plans and charters of such companies, are evident from a comparison of Swedish, Dutch and English source materials. In total, for the analysis of developments in the Netherlands and Sweden, ten drafts and seventeen issued charters were used. They were written and/or issued in the period 1601–1630. Of the drafts, three concern the Dutch East India Company (dating 1601 and 1602),[31] four projects relate to the Dutch West India Company (three dating 1606, and one 1619),[32] and three proposals regard Swedish companies (dating from 1615, 1624, and 1627–28).[33] The Dutch-issued charters of the VOC (1602,[34] 1622,[35] 1623[36]) and the WIC (1621[37] and two of 1623[38]) were consulted as well. The Swedish charters include those of the Gothenburg Company (1607), the Stockholm company (1615), the Swedish Trading Company (1619, 1619/2, 1620, 1622, 1625, 1626, 1626/2), and the South Company (June 1626, as well as the 1625 "Contract"). In addition to the ten

31 *De opkomst van het Nederlandsch gezag in Oost-Indië (1595–1610). Verzameling van onuitgegeven stukken uit het oud-koloniaal archief*, vol. 1, p. 257–261 (petition, 1600–1601), p. 262–271 (Dec. 1601 – Febr. 1602), and p. 271–278 (Jan. 1602).

32 The first ones were published in A.C. Meijer, ""Liefhebbers des vaderlandts ende beminders van de commercie." De plannen tot oprichting van een generale Westindische compagnie gedurende de jaren 1606–1609," *Mededelingen van het Koninklijk Zeeuwsch Genootschap der Wetenschappen* 1984, p. 21–70, here p. 50–59 (integrated version of the "*Project*" (middle of 1606), "*Rapport*" (Aug. – Sept. 1606), and "*Concept-Octrooi*" (Oct. 1606)). The 1619 draft by Willem Usselinckx was published in Otto van Rees, *Geschiedenis der staathuishoudkunde in Nederland tot het einde der achttiende eeuw*, vol. 2 (Utrecht: Kemink, 1868), p. 384–408.

33 See footnotes 18 and 27. The 1627–1628 draft is preserved in RAS, *Ämnessamlingar, Handel och sjöfart*, no. 49. It is a French document, containing 103 sections, and detailing the features of a new "*compagnie du sud*," for a duration of 18 years. The name of the author is not mentioned, but Willem Usselinckx is the most likely candidate. Jameson does not mention this document in the bibliography added to his monograph.

34 The 1602 VOC charter was published and translated in English in Gepken-Jager 2005, p. 1–38. Henceforth it will be referred to the (numbered) version published in Van der Chys 1865, p. 98–115.

35 *Groot-Placcaet-Boek vervattende de placaten, ordonnantien ende edicten van de doorluchtige, hoogh mog. heeren Staten Generael der Vereenighde Nederlanden*, vol. 1 (c. 539–544 (22 Dec. 1622) (henceforth VOC 1622).

36 *Groot-Placcaet-Boek*, 1, c. 543–546 (13 March 1623).

37 *Groot-Placcaet-Boek*, 1, c. 566–578 (3 June 1621).

38 *Groot-Placcaet-Boek*, 1, c. 584–586 (13 Febr. 1623); *Groot-Placcaet-Boek*, 1, c. 585–590 (21 June 1623).

drafts and seventeen issued charters listed above, comparisons can be drawn not only with the English EIC (charter of 1600[39]), but also with the first French Company for East India trade (1604),[40] the Danish East India Company (1616) and the Danish Icelandic Company (1619).[41] The French and Danish companies have been linked to proposals that were written by Dutchmen as well.[42]

3 The Gothenburg Company (1607): a State Venture without Shareholders' Rights

In its initial phase, until around 1615, corporate governance was not considered important in Sweden. The Gothenburg company was established in September 1607. King Carl IX granted a charter that was written in Low German, and even though it nominally addressed both Swedes and non-Swedes, it clearly targeted foreign merchants. The newly located Gothenburg, on the island of Hisingen, was proposed as their place of business. The venture would focus on trade with Russia and Persia. The company's charter is peculiar in terms of trade policy. This is evident in the fact that no formal monopoly was awarded, even though low taxes for imported merchandise were promised. Around 1607, elsewhere in Europe, trading companies without monopolies were being set up, but it had become very rare by then to launch a chartered company without a monopoly.[43] It is probable that the Swedish King was hesitant on how to impose a monopoly considering that the trade within the scope of the company moved mostly through the Swedish Baltic ports of Narva and Reval. Gothenburg was not given a right of staple. In this regard, the "eastern" approach was clearly interfering with plans to launch commerce through Swedish towns. Another indication of this indecision might be that

39 See the published charter in Gialdroni 2011, p. 299–319.

40 In 1600, a *compagnie des mers orientales* was established. Royal *lettres patentes* for an East India Company were accorded in 1604, 1611 and 1615. The 1604 and 1615 lettres were published in Francheville 1746, p. 161–162 (1 June 1604), and p. 161–166 (2 Sept. 1615).

41 Their statutes were published in Feldbæk 1986, p. 25–33 (17 March 1616), p. 489–494 (16 Dec. 1619), and p. 494–504 (29 Jan. 1620). The 1616 charter, together with a German translation, can also be found in Lehmann 1895, p. 91–105. For a description of these statutes, also with a focus on corporate governance issues, see Diller 1999, *Die Dänen in Indien, Südostasien und China*, 17 *seq.*; Rindom 2000, "Ostindisk Kompagni"; Willerslev 1944, "Danmarks første aktieselskab."

42 Diller 1999, p. 17; Willerslev 1944, p. 608. 17; Willerslev, "Danmarks," 608, and p. 614–620. For Dutchmen negotiating on chartered companies in France, see Van Dillen 1958, p. 41 (Pieter Lijntgens 1604); Van Dillen 1930, p. 5–10 (Isaac Le Maire 1605–1610).

43 Gelderblom 2009, p. 226–232.

investments in the Gothenburg company could be made not only at Gothenburg and Stockholm, but also at Reval.

At the same time, many efforts were made to attract as many investors as possible. Investments could be made in kind. There were no requirements on minimum investments. Admittedly, the latter was not unusual in this period. Minimal nominal contributions had not been imposed in the original VOC and EIC charter either. But other parts of the charter also reflect a policy of lowering the bar for participants. Investors in the Gothenburg company were promised very high returns. Investments were possible during the course of the first two years, and a 12 per cent interest on injected capital during those years was guaranteed. In the Dutch VOC of 1602, instalments could be made within five months (s. 11) and a minimum 7.5 per cent interest was granted after a period of ten years (s. 9).

In spite of its attractive characteristics, accountability towards investors in the Gothenburg company was weak.[44] A closing account of the company was to be made only after twelve years. It was vaguely promised that – "no doubt" – investors would receive their share of profits regularly, but implicitly it was meant that the company's directors, and practically the King (see hereafter), would decide on this. The mentioned 12 per cent interest only concerned the first two years. Withdrawal of investments and a guarantee of a share in the profits – if any – were only provided for after twelve years. It was prohibited to cancel investments before that time. The statutes of the Gothenburg company stipulated that at the end of the twelve-year lifetime of the company investors could sell, assign or pledge their invested capital and accrued profits. This reflects, to some extent, contemporary commercial practice in Amsterdam and London, but it was markedly stricter. As early as 1602, the subscription ledgers of several chambers, i.e. regional units, of the Dutch VOC had provided that transfers of debentures of investments could be made, even when expeditions had not been rounded up. This ultimately resulted in a vibrant secondary market in shares.[45] Also, shares of the EIC were sold as early as 1601, before the closing of accounts.[46] However, in contrast to Dutch and English mercantile practice, the shares of the Gothenburg company could not be sold before its date of expiry.

Minimal exit options were not counterbalanced with voting rights. The charter did not detail the relationship between investors and directors. The underlying idea was clearly that the King would appoint the managers and that investors would not participate in the policy of the company. In fact, the

44 See also Hagströmer 1872, p. 83.

45 Heijer 2005, p. 95, 107; Gelderblom and Jonker 2004, p. 653–663.

46 Chaudhuri 1965, p. 215.

Amsterdam merchant Abraham Cabelliau was granted the position of governor by royal decree, which conflated with his post of mayor of Gothenburg.[47] Moreover, provisions regarding a right of audit and the responsibility of directors vis-à-vis investors were lacking. This conforms to the contents of the charter of the Dutch VOC around that time. Investors did not control or have a part in the nomination of directors, which were proposed by the chambers. The chambers were units organised by cities or provinces, and their administrators chose directors from among the main investors (s. 26), who were closely linked to the political class.[48] By contrast, in the English EIC, the council of directors, i.e. the Court of Committees, responded to investors before the closing of the accounts of each expedition. Each decision on policy was submitted to the General Court, a gathering of all investors, and this general assembly also appointed directors annually.[49]

For Sweden, all the above points to unwieldy trade policies and a minimal knowhow in devising structures of companies, in combination with an aim of close supervision by the Swedish sovereign. In terms of corporate governance, the charter of the Gothenburg company followed the charter of the VOC closely in some respects, and was not influenced by the English examples very much. As was the case for the Dutch company, it was thought that investors' capital was to be locked in and that the participants had to rely on the board and the royal government.

4 The Stockholm Company (1615) and the Swedish Trading Company (1619): Corporate Governance as Invitation

The charter and instructions of the 1615 Swedish "Stockholm company" differed fundamentally from the statutes of the – by then collapsed – Gothenburg Company. The Stockholm company was more commercially orientated. The charter granted a monopoly, and it also listed detailed tax cuts (s. 20). Moreover, the exit options for investors were more generous. Participants were granted the right to sell or pledge their shares at any time, even during the ten-year duration of the venture, provided that the directors agreed and no harm would accrue to the company (s. 5). In terms of administration, distinctions were made between general policy and day-to-day business. It was provided

47 Johnson 1911, p. 45; Wittrock 1919, p. 16. On the synchronicity of the mayorship with the post of governor, see Cronholm 1871, p. 32.

48 Heijer 2005, p. 110–115.

49 Chaudhuri 1965, p. 31–33; Gialdroni 2011, p. 274, 281.

that a governor, a number of directors appointed from among Stockholm investors and a secretary would constitute the executive committee of the company, called the *Collegium*. This committee would meet on a daily basis in Stockholm (s. 3 *instruction*). The board of the new company, which was called the General Council ("*General-Collegium*"), consisted of the directors of Stockholm and other directors who represented other cities of Sweden. The board decided issues of importance, such as the buying of new products, and whether to demand the renewal of the charter (s. 5 *instruction*). The General Council chose a governor from among the directors and the investors; the *collegium* chose and appointed all directors, even those outside Stockholm. The governor swore an oath to the King, and the directors pledged allegiance to the governor. In spite of the level of detail of the charter, it was not clearly stated how many directors would be appointed (either as members of the General Council or as members of the executive committee), and who was eligible to be given the post of director. Since the governor depended directly from the sovereign, and presided over the *collegium*, it is a fair assumption that this was left to the discretion of the royal government.

4.1 *Dutch Influences Concerning Investors' Rights*

The charter and instruction of the 1615 Stockholm company resembled the abovementioned Dutch proposal that had been written some time before. For example, both were for ventures of ten years that started on the same date, 1 March 1616. The 1615 charter clearly incorporated ideas taken from the 1615 Dutch draft, which were of Dutch origin. For the first time in a Swedish charter, the act of investing was called "*participere*" (s. 1) and an investor was described as "*participant*" (s. 5), which was the common term for investors in contemporary Dutch company statutes. The debenture that the "*participant*" received upon making an investment was called "*action*" (s. 5), from the Dutch "*actie.*" The latter notion had become common in the Dutch Republic since 1602.[50] Furthermore, the compound organisational structure of the Stockholm company was comparable to the one in the 1615 draft, which had proposed an executive committee as well as a board. However, both the draft and the 1615 charter largely followed the organisational scheme of the VOC as well. The VOC's board of Seventeen Directors (*Heeren XVII*) consisted of selected

50 The date of 1606 or 1607 has been proposed in older literature, but does not hold in view of more recent findings. See Heijer 2005, p. 95, footnote 103. For the older view, see Colenbrander 1901, p. 383–387; Van Dillen 1958, p. 32. Critical on the idea that the "*actie*" only covered the dividend, not the share of capital, which was uttered by Lehmann and Colenbrander, is Van Brakel 1908, p. 155–156.

directors, and this body decided on the policy of trade and important affairs (s. 2–3), as the General Council of the Stockholm company did. In the VOC, cities and provinces selected directors ("*bewindhebbers*") for their chambers from the main investors and these in turn delegated directors to the board (s. 26). The dominant presence of Stockholm directors in the *collegium* is reminiscent of the prominence of Amsterdam *bewindhebbers* in the VOC board. Moreover, the idea of an executive committee had been known in the Netherlands as well.[51]

In some regards, the Stockholm company implemented ideas from Dutch commercial practice that had not always been written into company charters. For example, a distinction was made between active and non-active directors. This was not mentioned in the VOC charter or in the drafts for the WIC, for example, but it was common in Dutch commercial practice.[52] Other rules, both in the Dutch draft and in the charter of the Stockholm company, had merely been proposed and discussed, but had not received approval in the Dutch Republic. This was clearest with regard to the right of audit of large investors. According to the 1615 draft, accounts were closed every year and the results were presented to the executive committee. To this end, the executive committee was supplemented with a number of investors (s. 17 draft charter, s. 7 draft *instruction*). According to the charter of 1615, six selected "*partipanter*" were to assist the board in the annual closing of accounts (s. 7 *instruction*). Ideas on a right of audit and participatory powers for main investors in important decisions had been elaborated on in drafts for the Dutch WIC since 1606, even before the protests of shareholders in the VOC,[53] but it took another seven years

51 The *collegium* resembled the gatherings of all directors of each chamber of the VOC. On the emergence of the executive committee of directors acting as one, see Gelderblom 2013, p. 42.

52 In the so-called Dutch "Nordic" company ("*Noordsche compagnie*"), which had been granted a monopoly on whaling in 1614, the body of active directors of each chamber was called the "*Magistraet*" (magistracy). The 1617 charter of this company provided that candidate-directors were proposed by the directors, as was the case in the VOC, and then selected by the "*Magistraet*," which suggests a distinction between executive committee members and other directors. See 1874, p. 425 (s. 10) (24 Jan. 1617). One of the drafts of the 1602 VOC charter also mentions "*gemene bewindhebbers*" of chambers, most probably as opposed to directors who were not members of the steering committee of a chamber. See De opkomst van…, p. 270 (s. 30).

53 Meijer 1984, p. 55–56 (s. 21). This section provided that directors would appoint some of the main investors ("*hoofdparticipanten*"), who would delegate one or some of them to assist at the annual closing of accounts. The delegate main investors could check partial accounts intermittently as well. They sat with the directors when they discussed "important affairs." These rules had not been proposed during the negotiations leading up to the 1602 VOC charter. See also Gelderblom, Jong and Jonker 2011, p. 48–49. The right of assisting at

after 1615 before they were imposed in the Netherlands. In the English EIC, the dissent of shareholders denouncing the secrecy of the Court of Committees dates from 1619. They called for auditors to be chosen among the investors, but they did not succeed.[54] Overall, dynamics in the Dutch VOC and English EIC were different. In the latter, merchants were at the steering wheel, and they shielded the business of the company from non-merchants.[55] By contrast, in the Dutch VOC, the shareholders' grievances were mostly of merchants advocating access to the closed circles of *regenten*, to which the directors belonged.

With regard to investor-director relationships, one must be cautious not to be anachronistic. The absence in the 1615 Swedish charter of the right of investors to select directors was not backward. In 1615, rights of shareholders to nominate directors were non-existent in the Dutch Republic as well. The Dutch draft of 1615 provided that directors and not the investors chose and appointed directors. In the 1602 VOC charter, it was said that new directors were proposed by existing directors and installed by the political body (provincial estates, city) that had a chamber (s. 25). Admittedly, in the Dutch Republic, before the implementation of the mentioned VOC charter and again in 1606 in negotiations on the new WIC to come, it was proposed that the major shareholders would elect the directors.[56] But this was a view that was not widely shared and it met with resistance from above, resulting in its late implementation, well after 1615. For example, in the first WIC charter of 1621 the provisions of the VOC statutes on the issue were reproduced.[57] Only in 1622 and 1623 was the election of (some) directors by large shareholders accepted, for both the VOC and the new WIC (see hereafter, under 4.), but only following long and severe contention amongst the investors.[58] In the Danish East India Company of 1616, new

the annual closing of accounts did not entail a right to decide on dividends. According to the 1606 proposal, the delegate main investors only controlled their chamber, not the Board of Seventeen Directors.

54 Chauduri 1965, p. 58–60.

55 Chauduri 1965, p. 33–38.

56 Meijer 1984, p. 55 (s. 19); Gelderblom, Jong and Jonker 2011, p. 48–49. In 1601, it had been proposed that both directors and "main and qualified" investors would elect and appoint the directors. See De opkomst van…, 1862, p. 259–260.

57 Jongh 2014, p. 107–108. Another example is the 1617 charter of the Nordic company, which stated that directors proposed candidates, from among main investors, and that the nomination was done by the magistracy of the chamber. See footnote 52.

58 About the changes in the charters of 22 December 1622 (VOC), 13 February 1623 (WIC), 13 March 1623 (VOC) and 21 June 1623 (WIC), see Jongh 2014, "Shareholder Activists *Avant la Lettre*," p. 74–80; Jongh 2014, p. 83–84; Frentrop 2002, p. 88–105.

directors were proposed by the board of directors, and the ultimate choice was in the hands of the Danish King (s. 6).

In this regard, the 1619 Swedish Trading Company changed the rights of investors slightly. Participants with high stakes formed a council. This council was consulted not only on the annual rendering of accounts, as in the 1615 company, but on also when a director's position had to be filled. When a director had to be replaced, the council of investors, together with the directors and the governor, proposed two candidates, one of which would be selected by the King. The directors presented accounts to the governor and to eight selected investors. The latter were also involved when the board deliberated on "important" issues. Every year, the governor and directors had to summon all investors to Stockholm. They proposed sixteen investors, of whom the King chose eight.[59]

In the charters of the Swedish Trading Company of 1619, it was also more clearly provided that dividends were to be paid annually.[60] This was a remarkable innovation, which had much to do with the projected durations of expeditions of one year.[61] Even so, it was very new. It would take several decades after 1619 before annual dividends became part of corporate practice throughout Europe.[62] In this regard, the Swedish government had altered the Dutch proposal.[63] According to the Dutch draft, at the checking of accounts, a decision was to be taken, by the executive committee and the chosen investors together, on the payment of dividends (s. 17 draft charter). But this provision was absent in the 1615 Swedish charter.

4.2 *The Liability of Directors: Sweden ahead of the Dutch*

In another respect, the 1615 Stockholm Company was a testing ground for ideas that were imposed in the Netherlands only later. In the VOC, the liability of directors was related to a complex system of checking and turning over of company-related debts. The company was considered an overarching structure, and the practical implementation of trade decisions was to be done by the chambers. As a result, each chamber had personnel, ships and a shipyard;

59 SwTC 1619, 709; SwTC 1619/2, 720, and 730–731; SwTC 1620, s. 5 and s. 40; SwTC 1622, s. 3, s. 5, s. 38. See also Lehmann 1895, p. 59.

60 SwTC 1619, 709–710.

61 SwTC 1619/2, 719.

62 Lehmann 1895, p. 70–73.

63 See, on the correcting notes made by councillor Axel Oxenstierna in the margins of the Dutch proposal: Wittrock 1919, p. 14–15.

merchandise imported from overseas was sold by the chambers.[64] In terms of capability to engage in contracts, the chambers of the VOC and WIC did not have legal personhood. Chambers were not considered as *corpora* that were liable for debts, and neither were the chartered companies as such. Instead, liability for debts was centred on the directors. In the VOC and WIC, the *bewindhebbers* of the different chambers were held to execute the contracts that they had signed, even if these contracts were nominally linked to their chamber.[65] The first contacts when enforcing company-related debt were the directors, or their cashiers. Directors of a chamber were liable, jointly and severally, for debts signed by their colleagues if they concerned company-related matters.[66] As a result, even personal effects could respond for these debts. After the debts had been paid by one of the directors, they were checked and if considered legitimate taken over by the chamber. The same happened in the relation between the chamber and the company.[67] The final control was annual, even though accounts of equipment made by each chamber had to be sent over to other chambers before that, i.e. three months after the departure of ships (s. 14). The Board of Seventeen Directors issued directives on the equipment of ships and other matters, which were further detailed in the meeting of directors within each chamber. As a result, the practical relevance of the system of turnover of debt depended on the level of detail of these instructions. If the orders were precise, and precisely executed, then there was no question that the debts were inscribed in the final accounts of the company.

In the first years of the VOC, the Board usually made broad directives.[68] This provided considerable leeway for chambers and their directors, but with it went the danger of debts being bounced afterwards, partially or entirely.

64 Heijer 2005, *De geoctroieerde compagnie*, p. 129–139; Van Brakel 1908, *De Hollandsche handelscompagnieën*, p. 76; Van der Heijden 1908, p. 56.

65 Sometimes the debts of the "*comptoir*" of the chamber were mentioned (s. 16), but from other sections of the VOC charter it is clear that directors were debtors for the debts that had been made on behalf of the chamber (s. 30–33).

66 In seventeenth-century Dutch doctrine, a distinction was drawn between the co-ownership of ships, for which limited liability for investors applied, and mercantile companies, including the chartered ones, in which directors were jointly and severally liable. Associates were sometimes put on the same level as co-owners of ships, and then their liability was occasionally defined as *pro parte*. However, this seems not to have been done with regard to the "*bewindhebbers*" in the VOC, who were shareholders as well. See Asser 1983; Punt 2010, p. 108–110; Van der Heijden 1908, p. 50–56.

67 This view is only partially acknowledged in literature. According to Van Brakel, the chambers were administrative units. Any debt made by the directors was the chamber's (Van Brakel contends that directors were not liable for company-related debts), and all debts of the chambers were the company's. See Van Brakel 1908, p. 76–77.

68 Heijer 2005, p. 76.

Moreover, since until 1612 the VOC's capital was not permanent, and the closing of accounts was not regular, the relative freedom of directors in engaging in debt was particularly tricky. Stock and gains could be floated from one expedition to the next, but sometimes pressure from investors mounted and dividends had to be distributed, irrespective of the financial situation of the company at a given moment.[69]

The director's liability instead of the liability of chambers or of the company was a strange construct. It related to a haphazard floating of capital. Investments were made through a chamber. They were nonetheless considered investments in the company, and the Board of Seventeen Directors decided the amount of dividends granted and they were the same for all chambers.[70] Dividends were determined by the Board, following the drawing-up of an integrated account of contributed capital, costs and profit of all chambers.[71] However, the chambers administered the capital that was formed by the investments that they had received. Again, this administration rested on the liability of the chamber's directors. The 1602 VOC charter provided that when a director came to a "state" that prevented the due payment of debts, or which caused damages, this was to be compensated with the capital of his chamber, not by the company (s. 32). It was added that the investment made by the director, which was a minimum of 1,000 *livres* Fl. (s. 28), was by priority used for this purpose. Directors were responsible for the cashiers that they hired (s. 33). These sections most probably indicate that any default on a contract signed by a director, for whatever reason (e.g. negligence, absence, maybe also bankruptcy), was considered the director's responsibility. Therefore, the capital of each director, and even his personal assets, was collateral for his debts, and the capital of the director's chamber constituted a supplementary collateral for the debts that were made through that chamber, that is by its directors.

However, this liability of directors was restricted from the start. In the business ventures ("*voorcompagnieën*") that preceded the VOC, it had sometimes been provided that directors could not be addressed for dividends or reimbursements of capital during the venture, but that this had to be done before

69 Gelderblom, Jong and Jonker 2013, p. 1059–1064.

70 Van Brakel 1908, p. 71. This was the policy in 1610. However, the 1602 charter mentions a dividend of 7.5 per cent "or more, for as much as what was promised" (s. 9). This may reflect remnants of an earlier – never applied – view that dividends were to be decided by the chambers, even though they could not ignore the imposed minimum dividend.

71 Gepken-Jager 2005, p. 75; Van Brakel 1908, p. 76–79. It was common that the chamber of Amsterdam advanced payments and recovered them from the chambers for which they had been made, at this rendering of accounts. See De Heer 1929, p. 58–59.

the board of the company at the end of the expedition.[72] This rule was closely related to a general prohibition of withdrawal for the duration of the company, but it also purported to ensure continuity of the business: the assets of the venture were shielded from attachment. In the later years of the sixteenth century, another provision emerged that restricted the procedural means of creditors addressing directors for debts. This rule was of larger scope: it did not only entail the rendering of account by investors, but also related to debts such as loans and wages. In one of the proposals made for the VOC charter, it was said that persons and merchandise on board ships could not be apprehended or attached for debts (of wages or other), but that payment was only done on arrival and by the directors, potentially following proceedings of arrest or attachment.[73]

According to the ultimate 1602 VOC charter and the 1621 WIC charter, directors could not be arrested or attached on their belongings for holding them accountable for their administration or for the payment of wages. Instead, creditors had to start ordinary proceedings in court (s. 42). This section has often been misinterpreted, in the sense of it providing that directors should not be personally liable towards creditors for company-related debts. Many authors have generally read this meaning into the text – implicitly following the example of nineteenth-century directors in corporations.[74] In fact, it seems

72 "De opkomst van…", 1862, p. 24; Gelderblom, Jong and Jonker 2011, p. 42; Van Dillen 1958, p. 22, footnote 3.

73 "De opkomst…", 1, 277 (s.12).

74 Gepken-Jager 2005, p. 65–66; Van Brakel 1908, p.123; Van Dillen 1958, p. 27: "Nieuwe gegevens" p. 352. See by contrast Heckscher 1994, p. 1, 368; Van der Heijden 1908, p. 56; Zeijlemaker 1945, p. 587. Van der Heijden suggests that proceedings were possible against directors in their role of director. It is not clear whether he considers that attachment of company-related assets found with the director was possible. The prohibition would then merely concern arrest and attachment of personal effects. This interpretation seems too far-fetched; arrest of company-related assets would have hampered the business of the chamber, and it seems that the protection of such assets was one of the motives of this provision. Moreover, it was stressed that ordinary proceedings – in contrast to arrest or attachment proceedings – had to be started. Zeijlemaker proffers – in my opinion – the right interpretation. Most of the authors mentioned have linked their views regarding s. 42 to a presumed liability of the company. This interpretation was *inter alia* based on an opinion by van Zurck in his *Codex Batavicus*. See Van Brakel 1908, p. 56, footnote 4, who however misinterprets Van Zurck's statement. Van Zurck stated that proceedings had to be started against the company, and not against the *bewindhebbers*. But this opinion dates only from 1727. See Eduard van Zurck, *Codex Batavus waer in het algemeen kerk-publyk en burgerlyk recht van Hollant, Zeelant, en het Ressort der Generaliteit kortelyk is begrepen …* p. 616–617. The statement is not present in earlier editions of this work.

that in the early seventeenth century, together with their share of capital, the personal assets of directors were considered a pledge for the debts they signed, or the damages that they incurred. It is likely that this was also the case when assets were found with the director that concerned the company, even to the extent that no distinction was made between personal and company-related effects.[75] The latter was not unusual for "office-holders": profits as well as debts made were personal, and personal and even office-related properties were not shielded in any way, even though they held an office for a political body. The aforementioned s. 42 of the VOC charter was copied into the WIC charter, and it had not been changed in the proposals that preceded this charter.[76]

By contrast, the 1615 Dutch proposal for the Stockholm company described the protection of directors in much broader terms. No directors could be apprehended, nor even addressed in an ordinary lawsuit, for company-related debts, which were defined in the broadest sense, and neither by investors nor others. Any suit on company-related debt had to be brought before the *collegium*, and in appeal before the Crown's court (s. 10). This provision was copied into the charters of the Stockholm and Swedish Trading Company. The innovative features of this rule are remarkable. For the first time, a strict distinction was being made between personal and company-related debts with regard to the liability of directors. The latter were reduced to the status of administrators, and any debt relating to the company was considered as a debt of the company. In the Netherlands, around the same time, in 1617, the Board of Seventeen Directors limited the leeway of chambers and their directors to engage in loans without their approval,[77] even though the complicated turnover system for debt remained. The partial, rather haphazard protection of directors was kept, and was never formulated in the same broad terms as in Sweden. In the Dutch Republic, directors remained jointly and severally liable for company-related debts, even with their own properties, even though neither their belongings nor the company's assets could be confiscated.

---

75 This was congruent with academic approaches on the joint and several liability of associates, which was commonly linked to the *actio institoria* or *exercitoria* of Roman law. See the example of a 1604 claim against all directors of the chamber of Zeeland (mentioned in de Jonghe, *Tussen* societas *en* universitas, 69), the examples of bonds signed by directors for company purposes but pledging their person and goods, and a 1611 threat to imprison the directors of the Zeeland chamber for company-related debts, in See the entire book Gelderblom, Jong and Jonker 2013; Gelderblom, Jong and Jonker 2011, p. 43.

76 Meijer 1984, p. 59 (s. 41); Rees 1868, p. 2, 394–395 (s. 25).

77 In 1617, the Seventeen Directors prohibited loans without prior consent. Gelderblom, Jong and Jonker 2013; Van Brakel 1908, p. 78 dates this decision 1607.

4.3 *A Combined English-Dutch Influence*

A non-Dutch element in the 1615 draft, in the 1615 Stockholm company charter and in the 1619 Swedish Trading Company, was the governor. This concept went back to the 1607 Gothenburg company, and had most probably been inspired by English examples.[78] The Swedish notion of "director," as well, is English rather than Dutch: Dutch charters typically mentioned "*bewindhebbers.*"[79] Dutch chartered and non-regulated companies did not generally have a CEO-like figure such as the governor in the 1615 Stockholm company, even though for the VOC a governor-general oversaw the administration of territories abroad.

This brings up the point of parallel English influence in Dutch and Swedish chartered companies. There are some examples of this, such as the 1615 Dutch draft providing for four directors to be responsible for mercantile transactions and two for the equipment of ships (s. 17–18 draft instruction). This reflects the English practice of specialising committees of directors. This had been in use in some of the Dutch *voorcompagnieën* that eventually merged into the VOC, and it was applied in the VOC chamber of Amsterdam as well.[80] Moreover, in the Dutch draft of 1615 (not in the official charter) the meetings of the executive committee were called "ordinary" and "extraordinary" assemblies (s. 8 draft charter). This terminology was rare in the Dutch Republic, whether in drafts, published statutes or in mercantile practice. These notions most probably hint at English influence. In the English EIC, meetings of directors were fixed; when they were unplanned and urgent, they were "extraordinary."[81] A similar point concerns the election of directors by investors, which was a feature of English chartered joint-stock companies, in particular the EIC. It is probable that the EIC also served as an example for proposals in this vein,

78 The notion of "Governor," as leading director, was already established in the fifteenth- and sixteenth-century companies of Merchant Adventurers. See Lingelbach 1902, xxiii–xxvi. It became common after 1600. See Scott 1912, p. 150–151.

79 It is noteworthy that the term "director" first appeared in an English charter in 1618. However, it was used in practice before that time. See Scott 1912, p. 151.

80 The Amsterdam "*Oude Compagnie*" (1597) had four committees, which were for the recruitment of personnel, for equipment, for the buying of victuals and for the buying of merchandise. See Heijer 2005, *De geoctroieerde compagnie*, p. 28; Van Brakel 1908, *De Hollandsche handelscompagnieën*, p. 100. On the 24 committees in the EIC, each of which was led by one director, see Gialdroni 2011, p. 279–283. It seems that in the EIC, committees acted more on delegation than in the "*Oude Compagnie*," in which each committee was said to have "full powers." See Heijer 2005, *De geoctroieerde compagnie*, p. 28. For the committees depending from the chamber of Amsterdam, see Heijer 2005, *De geoctroieerde compagnie*, p. 130–131.

81 See some mentions of "extraordinary courts," in the years 1622–1624, in Scott 1912, p. 2, 274, 277, 285.

which had been made in the Netherlands since the early years of the seventeenth century.

As a result, all the mentioned examples provide a caveat: an exclusively Dutch "style," even in the contents of Dutch-language projects of Swedish companies, was not present. Dutch influence often brought with it English views that had trickled into the United Provinces some time before. Furthermore, Sweden imported Dutch ideas, but the Swedish administrations also filtered and recalibrated them.

5 Usselinckx's Contributions to Swedish Chartered Companies

Willem Usselinckx contributed variously to Swedish and Dutch charters of companies. His attempts to set up religiously inspired colonies and impose a separation of politics from trade within chartered companies in the Netherlands failed, but he brought these views to Sweden. However, there again they were only partially implemented. But some of Usselinckx' ideas gained more ground. Among them were the further generalisation of shareholders' voting rights and guaranteed director positions for large investors. However, in considering the previous developments in Sweden, the role played by Usselinckx in the "modernisation" of Swedish companies has been over-stated. Usselinckx mostly built on what had been done before.

In some respects, Usselinckx was somewhat out-dated. For example, he imported chambers into Swedish chartered companies. Even though the 1607, 1615 and 1619 Swedish charters had already envisaged participation by more than one city, in Dutch chartered companies the structure of chambers, which were attached to city or provincial governments, had become less relevant by the middle of the 1620s. In the VOC, and also in the WIC, a central board monitored a fixed capital, which was decentralised only with regard to practical issues. The chambers in these Dutch companies merely laid out the policy that had been decided in detail by the board. Yet Usselinckx did not abolish the structure of chambers.

The statutes for the new Dutch WIC of 1621 contained one of the few of Usselinckx's ideas that had been accepted, which was that each investor, or group of investors, who put in 100,000 guilders, was granted the right to establish a chamber (s. 11). In 1621, this was novel, since the forming of a chamber had never before been linked to the amount of investment, which for the VOC had been due to the merger of existing city-companies at its foundation. In the Swedish South Company, Usselinckx introduced a rule similar to the one that was applied in the WIC. Cities or regions with expertise in maritime trade that invested 300,000 *thaler* were granted a chamber of their own (s. 16). The board of the South Company was assembled accordingly. The board was to consist of twelve directors. Each chamber was to appoint directors according to their share in the company's capital (s. 23). There were as many directors per chamber as there were shares of 100,000 *thaler*. When an investor made an instalment of 100,000 *thaler* by himself, or when investments were bundled in order to reach this threshold, the investors were given two directors of their own (s. 5). This latter direct representation was absent in the 1621 WIC, even though Usselinckx had proposed it in the Netherlands in 1619.[82]

The fact that chambers were introduced in Swedish companies has been labelled as unpractical and alien to Swedish tradition,[83] but in fact, in so doing Usselinckx conformed his plans to the royal policy of stimulating trade through the cities in Sweden. What was more stubborn than the organisation in chambers was the fact that chambers were created according to the level of investment, which did not account for the expertise that was required for equipping ships. In addition, the amounts required were very high, and in practice no additional chambers were created.[84] Moreover, the integration of chambers' finances, which in the Netherlands had been accomplished by 1617, was ignored. Usselinckx continued to provide that damages caused by directors, who were responsible for signing contracts, were not to be borne by the company, but only by the director, and – in subsidiary order – by the chamber from which he depended (s. 13).

Usselinckx expanded shareholders' rights. As had been done in the Stockholm Company, chief investors could check the accounts of the company. This was expanded in the charter of the Swedish Trading Company. However, between 1619 and 1624, provisions in Swedish charters became more vague. A second statute of the Swedish Trading Company of 1619 provided that some "qualified" shareholders were given a right of audit at the annual closing of accounts.[85] The charter of 1622 stated that only two chief investors would assist at the annual rendering of accounts, but it did not specify how they were to be selected and appointed.[86] However, Usselinckx' project of November 1624 re-injected ideas regarding participatory governance into Sweden's trade policy. It provided that every year, each investor with a share of minimum 1,000 *thaler* was entitled to be informed as to profits and losses (s. 3). This went much

82 Rees 1868, p. 2, 390–391 (s. 10). This had not been proposed in 1606. See Meijer 1984, "Liefhebbers des vaderlands" p. 54–56.

83 Heckscher 1994, p. 1, 371.

84 Roberts 1958, p. 2, 126.

85 SwTC 1619/2, 720, and 730–731.

86 SwTC 1622, s. 5 and s. 38.

further than the Dutch charters, which stuck to auditing by selected chief investors. Following protests, in 1622 it had been imposed in a new VOC charter that nine representatives of the majority shareholders would exert control over the board of Seventeen Directors and over individual directors of chambers as well. The nine auditors could sit at all meetings of the board and controlled the accounts on a yearly basis.[87] The 1616 Danish East-India Company also defined the (few) shareholders that could participate at the hearing of accounts, but this was an annual task.[88] A charter for the WIC, of June 1623, went further, by installing a committee of chief shareholders that could check books and other documents at any time.[89] The charter of the South Company of 1626 was even more generous to investors. It provided that all investors appointed as many delegates of (chief) investors as they thought fit, and that these auditors could check the accounts "every day" (s. 20). In 1619, Usselinckx had proposed this for the WIC as well.[90]

With regard to the right to appoint directors, Usselinckx clarified positions and strengthened the position of shareholders. Ever since 1615, not much attention had been paid to the selection and appointment of directors, because of the strong supervision of the king. In the South Company, the first directors were in principle appointed by all large shareholders (investing 1,000 *thaler* or more), who voted at a meeting (s. 6). They served six years, after which two-thirds were re-appointed by the chief investors. The other third was to consist of new directors, to be appointed by and from amongst the chief shareholders (s. 7). This clearly reflected Usselinckx' views, which had also inspired changes in the United Provinces. In new charters for the VOC (March 1623) and WIC (June 1623), new rules had been imposed. The result of these changes was that in the VOC all new directors were elected by both directors and chief investors, from amongst the chief investors. In the WIC some directors were chosen and appointed by and from amongst the chief shareholders. Since 1623, directors in both the VOC and WIC had occupied their positions for three years, and no longer for six years as had been the case before.[91] Usselinckx thus envisaged the right of representation for all (large) shareholders, and excluded (broad)[92] voting rights for directors in office. Yet, Usselinckx also struck compromises.

87 VOC 1622, s. 2.

88 s. 22. See also Rindom 2000, p. 102.

89 Heijer 2005, p. 82. This had been proposed in 1606 as well. See footnote 53.

90 Rees 1868, p. 2, 397–398 (s. 33–34).

91 Jongh 2014, p. 95, 101, 108–111; Heijer 2005, p. 82–84; Gepken-Jager 2005, p. 55–56.

92 Of course, directors were investors as well, and because of the requirements of minimum investments for directors they were all chief investors. However, their vote was capped: every shareholder had one vote.

One director was appointed by the King (s. 23), which reflected earlier tendencies of supervision by the monarch. In case of a tie vote, the King's director decided. In the VOC and WIC, the board could decide over all matters, independently from the States-General. The only exception was the waging of war. But even in the WIC of 1621, the States-General had a director of their own.[93]

Since shareholders' rights of control and exit were firmer than before, the duration of the South Company was longer than of previous Swedish chartered companies. In the period 1619–1622, three years had become common, and charters were often renewed every year. But now again – as had been the case in 1607 – a chartered company was set up for a longer period (twelve years). Usselinckx had always dreamt of a long-lasting merchant corporation.[94]

6 Conclusion

William Usselinckx introduced many of his views in Sweden, some of which had gained acceptance in the Netherlands after some strife. In 1627, 1633 and 1639, Usselinckx's combined ideas were re-inserted into Swedish company charters.[95] Usselinckx convinced the Swedish royal entourage to write high rewards for investors into the statutes. Reluctant investment had been an issue in the previous companies, and Usselinckx made the diagnosis that merchants and others had refrained from investing because of the agency problems implied within the older organisational schemes. If directors were appointed by the King, the shareholders not only had no say in this, they could also be confronted with directors who were not knowledgeable in trade. But the South Company failed in spite of the changes made. The company suffered from the same flaws as before. Local directors were not competent.[96] Moreover, the King continued to award monopolies to private companies and individual merchants, thus hollowing out the business of the government's chartered companies.[97]

93 Heijer 2005, p. 1, 123.

94 Rees 1868, p. 2, 387 (s. 2): this 1619 draft for the WIC, which was written by Usselinckx, reads "twenty-four years," but this was struck out and replaced with "twelve years." Eventually, the WIC was set up for twenty-four years.

95 RAS, *Ämnessamlingar, Handel och sjöfart*, no. 49, draft 1627–28 (see footnote 33), and no. 49, draft 21 March 1639 ("*Octroy et privilèges de la compagnie du sud*"). The "*ampliatie*" of the 1626 charter, dating 1633, was published in the *Argonautica Gustaviana*.

96 Roberts 1958, p. 2, 125.

97 Müller 2005, p. 67–68 (on the 1628 monopoly for Louis de Geer for iron gun casting); Van Dillen 1937, p. 213 (on the 1622 monopoly for Thomas Alsten Bloemaert, the brothers de Besche and Paulus Auleander for gun casting).

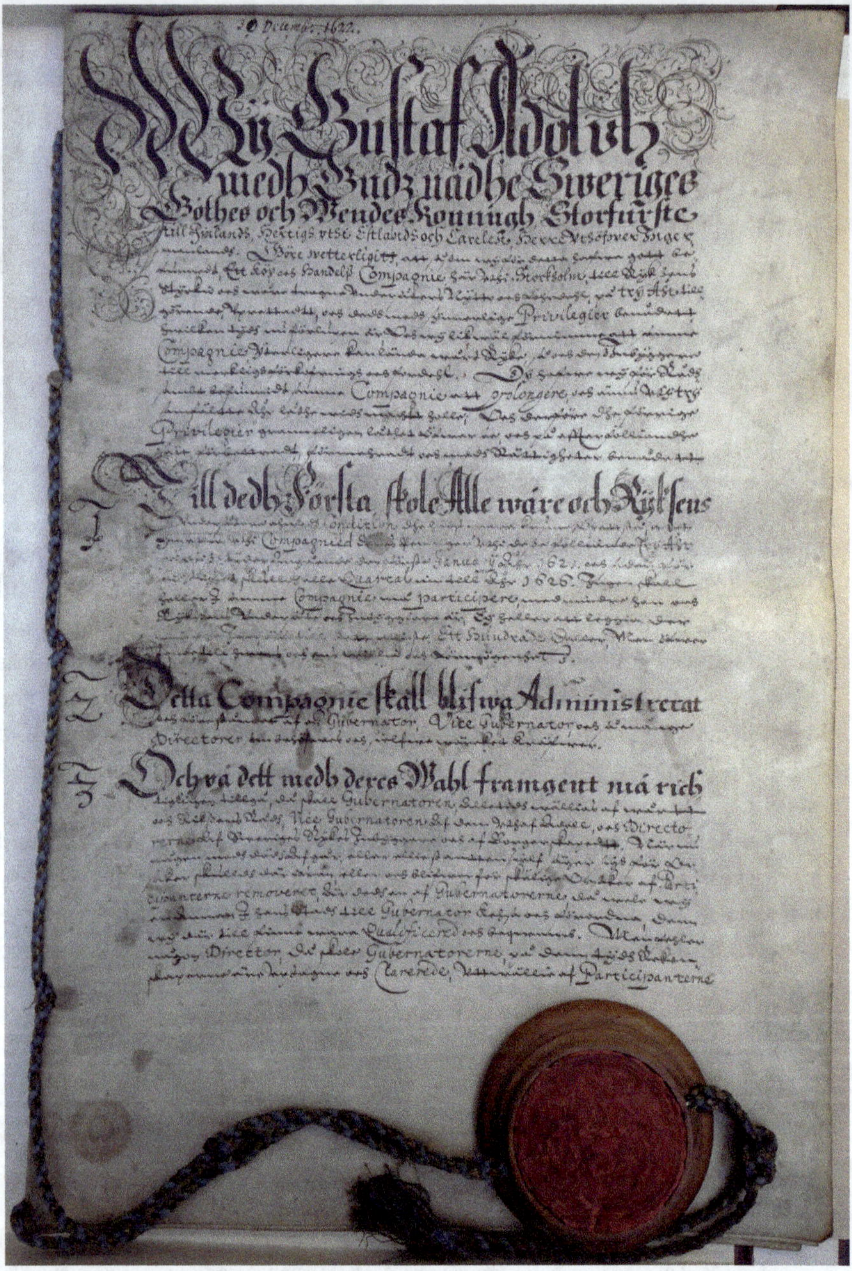

FIGURE 5 The Privilege of the South Company 1622.

Furthermore, in contrast with the Dutch VOC and also the Danish Icelandic company for example,[98] no pre-existing companies could be merged. The Swedish "general" companies had to be started up from nothing, and they did not draw in sufficient capital. The French East India Company of 1604, for example, suffered from comparable constraints.[99] It has been pointed out that the first Swedish companies could not flourish because of unfavourable preconditions, including lack of capital and entrepreneurial expertise.[100] It is evident that the high powers of chief shareholders in the Swedish companies, which were ultimately imposed, had to do with the fact that the ventures were top-down initiatives, an offer of public borrowing, whereas such chartered companies as the VOC could largely ignore shareholder rights because capital was widely available.[101] All this marks a caveat against considering the institutional characteristics of chartered companies as sufficient for generating trade.

Sweden provides an example of a nation that was largely inexperienced when it came to chartered companies. Notwithstanding these disadvantages, the country served as a testing ground for new concepts. It embraced the English idea that directors were to be chosen and appointed by the shareholders. Auditing rights were implemented in Sweden before they gained acceptance in the Netherlands. Swedish chartered companies went further in separating the company from chambers and directors than had been done in the Netherlands, even though the structure of chambers was out-dated when it was introduced in 1626.

The above demonstrates that the development of chartered companies was not a process of transplanting models of organisation, but rather that throughout North-West Europe there was an incessant exchange of ideas. In the understanding of the drafters of projects, it was clear that chartered companies could be successful, but the exact recipe for achieving high revenues remained unclear. The Swedish companies show that policy makers were hesitant, often shifting their approach, and that some formulas of organisation did not per se direct international trade to Swedish ports, even when they were features of successful companies elsewhere. An explanation for the contents of plans can therefore not be (exclusively) economic. Failures ultimately triggered adjustments to economic conditions (e.g. the widening of rights of large shareholders, because investments were limited). But, mostly, incentives were situated at

98 Willerslev 1944, p. 609–610. The Danish East-India Company seems to have been the exception to the rule; it was successful in a first phase and gathered large amounts of stock, mainly from Danish investors: Feldbaek 1981, p. 139–140; Feldbaek 1981, p. 105.

99 Haudrére 1991, p. 9–27. 12.

100 Klein 1981, p. 24–25.

101 Gelderblom, Jong and Jonker 2013, p. 1054.

a political level. An interventionist model of trade policy was emerging, and chartered companies were purported to generate profit. Their statutes were assembled while taking chunks of rules and practices from successful nations. A cultural influence lay in the example of prospering countries. The dominant presence of Dutch merchants was sufficient for the fact that mainly Dutch examples were used for inspiration. However, behind Dutch ideas there were often English views as well.

This prompts the question on the direction of organisational change in the early seventeenth century. The incremental extension of shareholders' rights, both in the Dutch Republic and Sweden, seems to point to convergence. Changes were made in England as well, which invites such a conclusion. By 1657, the EIC had a permanent capital and limited liability of investors,[102] which the Dutch chartered companies had achieved some decades before. Yet it is uncertain whether growing similarities really reflect convergence. This would suppose that the relationship between the organisational structure of companies and economic return was linear and fixed, across large areas. Such a conclusion would also take for granted a certain model of chartered company as ensuring success, and that this was perceived as such by seventeenth-century merchants and administrators. Also, an explanation of this kind would assume a final point in development, which would neglect the adaptability of law to – inevitably changing – economic circumstances. Furthermore, there are many indications that divergence lasted very long, and also with regard to core aspects of corporate organisation. For example, the shareholders' right to a yearly dividend was known in Sweden in 1615, but it took a long time to emerge elsewhere – in this regard, the Swedes were ahead of their times.

Online Sources

Hoek, D. and Hildebrand, Bengt, "Jacob Dijck, van" Svenskt biografiskt lexikon, https://sok.riksarkivet.se/sbl/artikel/17538 (consulted on 18 August 2017).

Jacobson, G., "Abraham Cabiljau" Svenskt biografiskt lexikon, https://sok.riksarkivet.se/sbl/artikel/16310 (consulted on 18 August 2017).

Unprinted Sources

Riksarkivet Stockholm (RAS), Ämnessamlingar, Handel och sjöfart, no. 46, no. 48, no. 49.

102 Gialdroni 2011, p. 286, 290.

Source Editions

De opkomst van het Nederlandsch gezag in Oost-Indië (1595–1610). Verzameling van onuitgegeven stukken uit het oud-koloniaal archief, vol. 1 Jonge, Johan K.J. de (ed.) (The Hague: Nijhoff, 1862).

Groot-Placcaet-Boek vervattende de placaten, ordonnantien ende edicten van de doorluchtige, hoogh mog. heeren Staten Generael der Vereenighde Nederlanden, vol. 1 (The Hague: Jacobsz van Wouw, 1658).

Samling utaf kongl. Bref, stadgar och förordningarr angaende Sweriges Rikes commerce, politie och oeconomie, vol. 1 Stiernman, And. Anton von (ed.) (Stockholm: Tryckeriet, 1747).

The Argonautica Gustaviana was inserted into Johann Marquardt, De iure mercatorum et commercium (Frankfurt: Matthias Gotzius, 1662).

Literature

Asser, Willem H.D. 1983. *In solidum of pro parte. Een onderzoek naar de ontwikkelingsgeschiedenis van de hoofdelijke en gedeelde aansprakelijkheid van vennoten tegenover derden* (Leiden: Brill).

Blussé, Leonard and Gaastra, Femme S. (eds.). 1981. *Companies and Trade. Essays on Overseas Trading Companies During the Ancien Régime* (Leiden: Leiden University Press).

van Bochove, Christian. 2008. *The Economic Consequences of the Dutch. Economic Integration Around the North Sea, 1500–1800* (Amsterdam: Aksant).

van Brakel, Simon. 1908. *De Hollandsche handelscompagnieën der zeventiende eeuw. Hun ontstaan, hunne inrichting* (The Hague: Nijhoff).

Chaudhuri, Kirti N. 1965. *The English East India Company. The Study of an Early Joint-Stock Company, 1600–1640* (London: Cass).

van der Chys, Jacobus A. 1856. *De stichting der vereenigde Oost-Indische compagnie en de maatregelen der Nederlandsche regering betreffende de vaart op Oost-Indië, welke haar voorafgingen,* Dissertation (Leiden University).

Colenbrander, Hermann T. 1901. "Über das erste Auftreten des Wortes Aktie in den Niederlanden", Zeitschrift für das gesamte Handelsrecht 50.

Cordes, Albrecht Cordes and Jahntz Katharina. 2007. "Aktiengesellschaften vor 1807?" in Walter Bayer and Mathias Habersack (eds.), *Aktienrecht im Wandel. I: Entwicklung des Aktienrechts* (Tübingen: Mohr).

Cordes, Albrecht. 1998. *Spätmittelalterlicher Gesellschaftshandel im Hanseraum* (Cologne: Böhlau).

Cronholm, Abraham. 1871. *Sveriges historia under Gustav II Adolphes regering. V/I* (Stockholm: Cronholm).

De Heer, Cornelis. 1929. *Bijdrage tot de financiëele geschiedenis der Oost-Indische Compagnie,* Dissertation (University of Rotterdam).

Diller, Stefan. 1999. *Die Dänen in Indien, Südostasien und China (1620–1845)* (Wiesbaden: Harrassowitz).

van Dillen, Johannes G. 1930. "Isaac Le Maire en de handel in actiën der Oost-Indische Compagnie" in *Economisch-Historisch Jaarboek* vol. 16, 1–165.

van Dillen, Johannes G. 1937. "Amsterdamsche notarieële acten betreffende den koperhandel en de uitoefening van mijnbouw en metaalindustrie in Zweden" in *Bijdragen en Mededelingen van het Historisch Genootschap* vol. 58, 211–301.

van Dillen, Johannes G. 1958. *Het oudste aandeelhoudersregister van de Kamer Amsterdam der Oost-Indische Compagnie* (The Hague: Nijhoff).

Feldbæk, Ole. 1986. *Danske Handelskompagnier 1616–1843. Oktrojer og interne ledelsesregler* (Copenhagen: Selskabet for udgivelse af kilder til dansk historie).

Feldbaek, Ole. 1981. "The Organization and Structure of the Danish East India, West India and Guinea Companies in the 17th and 18th Centuries" in Blussé et al. (eds.).

Francheville, Josephs du Fresne de. 1746. *Histoire de la compagnie des Indes avec les titres de ses concessions et privilèges …* (Paris: de Bure).

Frentrop, Paul. 2002. *Corporate governance 1602–2002* (Amsterdam: Prometheus).

Gelderblom, Oscar, Jong, Abe de and Jonker, Joost. 2011. "An Admiralty for Asia. Isaac le Maire and Conflicting Conceptions About the Corporate Governance of the VOC" in Jonathan G.S. Koppell (ed.), *The Origins of Shareholder Advocacy* (New York: Palgrave Macmillan).

Gelderblom, Oscar and Jonker, Joost. 2004. "Completing a Financial Revolution. The Finance of the Dutch East India Trade and the Rise of the Amsterdam Capital Market, 1595–1612", *The Journal of Economic History* vol. 64/3, 653–663.

Gelderblom, Oscar, de Jong, A. and Jonker, J. 2013. "The Formative Years of the Modern Corporation. The Dutch East India Company VOC, 1602–1623", *The Journal of Economic History* 73/4, 1050–1076.

Gelderblom, Oscar. 2009. "The Organization of Long-Distance Trade in England and the Dutch Republic" in Oscar Gelderblom (ed.), *The Political Economy of the Dutch Republic* (Surrey: Ashgate).

Gepken-Jager, Ella, Solinge, Gerard van and Timmerman, Levinus (eds.). 2005. *VOC 1602–2002. 400 Years of Company Law* (Deventer: Kluwer).

Gerner, K. (ed.) 2014. *The Swedes and the Dutch Were Made for Each Other. 400 years of Swedish-Dutch relations* (Lund: Historiska Media).

Gialdroni, Stefania. 2011. *East India Company. Una storia giuridica (1600–1708)* (Bologna: Il Mulino).

Grell, Ole Peter. 2016. "Dutch and English in the Baltic, North Sea and the Arctic" in Kouri, Erkki and Olesen, Jens (eds.), *The Cambridge History of Scandinavia.* vol. *II: 1520–1870* (Cambridge: CUP).

Hagströmer, Johan. *Om aktiebolag enligt svensk rätt*, Dissertation (University of Uppsala, 1872).

Haudrère, Philippe. 1991. "Jalons pour une histoire des Compagnies des Indes", *Revue française d'histoire d'outre-mer* vol. 78, 9–27.

Heckscher, Eli. 1994. Mercantilism (London: Routledge, first edition 1934).

van der Heijden, E.J.J. 1908. *De ontwikkeling van de naamloze vennootschap in Nederland voor de codificatie* (Amsterdam: Van der Vecht).

Heijer, Henk den. 2005. *De geoctroieerde compagnie. De VOC en de WIC als voorlopers van de naamloze vennootschap* (Deventer: Kluwer).

Israel, Jonathan I. 2002. *Dutch Primacy in World Trade, 1585–1740* (Oxford: Clarendon Press).

Jameson, Franklin J. 1887. *William Usselinx. Founder of the Dutch and Swedish West India Company* (New York: G.P. Putnam's sons).

Jeannin, Pierre. 1996. "Les relations économiques des villes de la Baltique avec Anvers au XVIe siècle" in Pierre, Jeannin (ed.) *Marchands du Nord. Espaces et traffics à l'époque moderne* (Paris: Presses de l'École normale supérieure).

Jespersen, Leon. 2016. "The Consolidation of the Nordic States: The Europeanisation of Scandinavia" in Kouri, Erkki and Olesen, Jens (eds.), *The Cambridge History of Scandinavia.* vol. II: 1520–1870 (Cambridge: CUP).

Johnson, Amandus. 1911. *The Swedish Settlements on the Delaware, 1638–1644*, vol. 1 (Philadelphia: Swedish Colonial Society).

Jongh, Johan Matthijs de. 2011. "The Dutch East India Company, 1622–1625" in Jonathan G.S. Koppel (ed.), *The Origins Of Shareholder Advocacy* (New York: Palgrave MacMillan.

Jongh, Johan Matthijs de. 2014. *Tussen* societas *en* universitas. *De beursvennootschap en haar aandeelhouders in historisch perspectief* (Deventer: Kluwer).

Klein, Peter W. 1978. "A 17th-Century Monopoly Game: the Swedish-Dutch Trade in Tar and Pitch" in Jürgen Schneider (ed.), *Wirtschaftskräfte und Wirtschaftswege. II: Wirtschaftskräfte in der europäischen Expansion* (Nuremberg: Zentralinstitut für Frankische Landeskunde und Allgemeine Regionalforschung).

Klein, Peter W. 1981. "The Origins of Trading Companies" in Blussé et al. (eds.).

Klein, Peter W. 1999. *De Trippen in de zeventiende eeuw. Een studie over het ondernemersgedrag op de Hollandse stapelmarkt* (London: Routledge).

Kotilaine, Jarmo T. 2005. *Russia's Foreign Trade and Economic Expansion in the Seventeenth Century. Windows on the World* (Leiden: Brill).

Lehmann, Karl. 1895. *Die geschichtliche Entwicklung des Aktienrechts bis zum Code de commerce* (Berlin: Heymann).

Ligtenberg, Catharina. 1914. *Willem Usselinx*, Dissertation (University of Utrecht).

Lindblad, J. Th. 2014. "Mirror Images of Progress" in Gerner (ed.).

Lingelbach, William E. 1902. *The Merchant Adventurers of England, their Laws and Ordinances* (Philadelphia: s.n.).

Meijer, A.C. 1984. "*"Liefhebbers des vaderlandts ende beminders van de commercie". De plannen tot oprichting van een generale Westindische compagnie gedurende de jaren 1606–1609*" (Mededelingen van het Koninklijk Zeeuwsch Genootschap der Wetenschappen)

Modéer, Kjell Å. 2014. "Law in Books and Law in Action. On Dutch Contributions to Swedish Legal Culture in Early Modern times" in Gerner (ed.).

Muller, Samuel. 1874. *Geschiedenis der Noordsche Compagnie* (Utrecht: Van der Post).

Müller, Leos. 2005. "The Dutch Entrepreneurial Networks and Sweden in the Age of Greatness" in Hanno Brand (ed.) *Trade, Diplomacy, and Cultural Exchange. Continuity and Change in the North Sea Area and the Baltic, c.1350–1750* (Hilversum: Verloren).

Punt, Martijn. 2010. *Het vennootschapsrecht van Holland. Het vennootschapsrecht van Holland, Zeeland en West-Friesland in de rechtspraak van de Hoge Raad van Holland, Zeeland en West-Friesland.* Dissertation (Leiden University, 2010).

Rindom, Jan. 2000. *Ostindisk Kompagni 1616–1650*, Handels- og Søfartsmuseets årbog 59.

Roberts, Michael. 1958. *Gustavus Adolphus. A History of Sweden*, vol. 2 (London: Longmans).

Roberts, Michael. 2013. *Profiles in Power. Gustavus Adolphus* (London: Routledge).

Rees, Otto van. 1868. *Geschiedenis der staathuishoudkunde in Nederland tot het einde der achttiende eeuw*, vol. 2 (Utrecht: Kemink).

Scott, William Robert. 1912. *The Constitution and Finance of English, Scottish and Irish Joint-Stock Companies to 1720*, 2 vol. (Cambridge: CUP).

Steensgaard, Niels. 1981. "The Companies as a Specific Institution in the History of European Expansion" in Blussé et al. (eds.).

Steensgaard, Niels. 1982. "The Dutch East India Company as an Institutional Innovation" in Maurice Aymard (ed.), *Dutch Capitalism and World Capitalism. Capitalisme hollandaise et capitalisme mondial* (Cambridge: CUP).

Stryker, Lawrence. 2014. ""Sharp Practice" among Merchants in Seventeenth-Century Amsterdam (1620–1632)" in *The Journal of European Economic History* 3, 131–164.

Sørensen, Karsten E. 2005. "The Danish East India Company" in Gepken-Jager et al. (eds.).

Thomson, Erik. 2005 "Swedish Variations on Dutch Commercial Institutions, 1605–1655" *Scandinavian Studies* 77/3, 331–346.

Wijnroks, Eric. 2003. *Handel tussen Rusland en de Nederlanden, 1560–1640: een netwerkanalyse van de Antwerpse en Amsterdamse kooplieden, handelend op Rusland* (Hilversum: Verloren).

Wetterberg, Gunnar. 2014. "Calming the Waves of the Baltic Sea. The Netherlands as the Midwife of Sweden During its Great Power Era" in Gerner (ed.).

Willerslev, Richard. 1944. "Danmarks første aktieselskab", in *Historisk Tidsskrift* vol. 10/6, 608–636.

Wittrock, Georg. 1919. *Svenska Handelskompaniet och kopparhandeln under Gustaf II Adolph* (Uppsala: Almqvist).

Wrangel, E.H.G. 1901. *De betrekkingen tusschen Zweden en de Nederlanden op het gebied van letteren en wetenschap, voornamelijk gedurende de zeventiende eeuw* (Leiden: Brill).

Zeijlemaker, Jacob. 1945–1946. "Verleden, heden en toekomst van de naamloze vennootschap", in *Rechtsgeleerd Magazijn Themis*, 581–665.

Zurck, Eduard van. 1727. *Codex Batavus waer in het algemeen kerk-publyk en burgerlyk recht van Hollant, Zeelant, en het Ressort der Generaliteit kortelyk is begrepen ...* (Delft: Adriaan Beman).

CHAPTER 4

The Swedish Tar Company – Balancing between Privileges, Commerce and Foreign Politics

Katja Tikka

1 Introduction

The peace treaties of Westphalia were finally signed between Sweden, France, Spain, the Netherlands and The Holy Roman Empire in 1648. Thereafter, Sweden gained a leading position in the Baltics and Scandinavia in terms of both politics and geography.[1] These novel circumstances expanded the commercial interests of Sweden, which meant a new era for commercial legislation. In the same year, the first Swedish tar company was founded in Stockholm. The Crown granted the company a privilege to export tar and pitch from the north of the country, which covered the whole of Finland and the greater Stockholm area. The right to export tar was in practice a monopoly; single merchants were afterwards barred from trading in tar.[2]

This chapter[3] studies the tar company as a corporation selling one specific article – tar – and its processed product, pitch: items desired by the trading powers of Europe. Meanwhile, Sweden had extensively begun to practise the government-based ideology of mercantilism as the guiding principle of the economy. Furthermore, the company was capturing the mind of the monarch.[4]

1 For more see Kirby 1990, p. 123, 171–180. In the year 1630, Sweden participated in the European war, which started as a religious war between the Catholic Church and North German protestant princes. King Gustav II Adolphus intervened in North-west Germany with the consent of the Elector of Brandenburg. After the victory of Sweden in 1626, the war shifted to Polish Russia. Stralsund became Sweden's first permanent base in Germany in 1628. After that, control over the Eastern Baltic ports was strengthened and Livonia was conquered. Peace negotiations continued for years before the parties finally managed to approve the complex parts of the agreements in 1648.

2 The original tar privilege "Privilegium för Tiäru Handels Compagniet" is printed in Anders Anton von Stiernman (1750), *Sweriges Rikes commerce. politie och oeconomie uti gemen uppå Hans Kongl.Maj:ts nodigsta belfallning*, p. 525–530; Hallberg 1959, p. 106.

3 The Chapter is partly based on Tikka's doctoral dissertation, *Shipping Legal Norms – Swedish Trading Companies in the Seventeenth century* (Helsinki: Unigrafia, 2020).

4 Israel 1989, p. 149. See also Dave De ruysscher's chapter p. 59.

 | DOI:10.1163/9789004436046_005

Nevertheless, the tar company failed to connect these two contradictory tendencies. The purpose of this chapter is to explain the management of the company, how it related to earlier Swedish companies, and whether any parts of the legislation regarding the company may be referred to as a legal transplant. The chapter discusses the rules, privileges and statutes that affected the company. Within the framework of the project[5] of Professor Heikki Pihlajamäki, some discussion has focused on company statutes. These often differ according to the branch of business. Moreover, the growing scale of businesses and the need for larger capital lent variety to the models. This chapter brings to the discourse a limited focus: only one sales article – tar – that brings a totally new aspect to this discourse.[6]

During the decades following establishment of the first Swedish tar company, several consecutive tar companies were founded, since the interests of the Swedish kings and merchants differed. The main intention of the Crown was to accrue financial capital by controlling prices and the amount of tar purchased from producers and sold to foreign traders. However, due to strict rules, the markets could not develop freely, and new legislation was introduced as the disadvantages came to light. This chapter surveys the background to the evolution of the tar companies' legal character in Sweden.

First and foremost, it is necessary to present a general overview of Swedish chartered companies before the tar companies. Swedish economic history has its own special character, influenced by both the country's northern location and the position of the estates, which differed from the Central European model. As a result, legal development also followed its own path. In addition, it should be noted that the structure of Swedish society had unique administrative characteristics during the seventeenth century.[7]

Before the tar company, a few nascent trading companies already existed in the 1610s. Dave De ruysscher's chapter in this book discusses the legal character of the first Swedish companies, which were influenced by the Dutch.[8] Hence, I will not discuss the details of the earliest companies here. Instead, this chapter explains the importance of the tar trade to Sweden and Europe, and answers the essential question as to who buyers, producers and traders were, and what kind of motives each side represents.

---

5 See a description of the project from the Introductory chapter, p. 1–3.

6 Hofstraeten 2017, p. 107–107; Amend-Traut 2017, p. 81–83; Gephen-Jager 2005, p. 75.

7 Lappalainen 2017, p. 131–132; Tikka 2020, see "Introduction."

8 Kirby 1990, p. 149; Wirta 2018, p. 30–32.

The main sources of this study consist of original documents in the *Riksarkivet* in Stockholm. The focus of earlier research has not been the operations of the company or its legal character or at least hardly at all. Therefore, fundamental research at a basic level is needed. Karl Oskar Fyhrvall's 1880 dissertation, *Bidrag till Swenska handelslagstiftingens historia* is the oldest known analysis of Swedish company law, and especially that relating to tar companies.[9] However, the primary approach in his research is narrative-based, without deeper analysis. For example, Fyhrvall claims that the development of tar companies had a negative effect on the national spirit of Sweden. The main reason for this lay in the company model, which easily led to illegalities. Moreover, Fyhrvall wrote his dissertation over 130 years ago, so his conclusions are partly outdated. The next – and broader – analysis of the tar company is Annagreta Hallberg's chapter *Tjärexport och tjärhandelskompanier under stormaktstiden.*[10] This research from 1959 represents aspects of the company's trading. Hallberg sees the tar companies as an example of a new business model in early modern Europe. Her focus is the tar trade and how it moulded Sweden's international relations with the Netherlands and England.

As existing research on this topic does not take a strong legal approach, the original archive materials need to be critically investigated. This material includes the company's privileges, orders from the monarch, proposals by the Commercial Collegium, complaints to the King from the burghers and peasantry, decisions by the lower courts, and parliamentary proceedings.[11] Most of these sources are in the Stockholm State Archive[12] in the "Miscellanea" section, and the collection in the "Commerce and Seafaring" section, where all the archive materials of Swedish commercial companies can be found.

One of the main methods used in this chapter is comparison between the early stages of privilege and the situation *vis-á-vis* the later companies. The change in regulation reflects the progress of the trading companies, which later became modern institutions. Surrounding elements, such as war, economic innovations, and the varying balance between the estates, created economic booms and recessions. These had a wide effect on the tar companies' future development.

9 Ernst Gustaf Palmén's study *Historisk framställning af den svensk-finska handelslagstiftningen från Gustaf Vasas regering till* 1766 was published in 1876, but its perspective is not as deep as Fyhrvall's.

10 The entire book Hallberg 1959.

11 Moreover, in printed versions you can find statutes, privileges and sessions of the Swedish Parliament.

12 In original called *Riksarkivet.*

The tar companies exerted a particularly strong influence on Finland.[13] For that reason, this chapter concentrates more on Finland than Sweden. Certainly legislation, regulations and administration concerning the companies were formulated in Stockholm, Sweden's capital. Nonetheless, the consequences of the foundation of the company were seen at grass-roots level mainly in Finland.

The following paragraphs first explain the characteristic features of Swedish society as a culture that allowed local mercantilism to form its own shape and expression. The next paragraphs deal with the tar trade and clarify the situation before the first tar monopoly. Without a detailed introduction, the essence of the tar company and the problems it faced would be impossible to understand fully. In subsequent paragraphs, the lifespans of the three individual tar companies are then described. Finally, the chapter concludes by describing the monopolised tar trade as a logical narrative of the pre-modern chartered company.

2 Mercantilism in Sweden

During the seventeenth century, the whole of Europe faced extensive change. War raged across the continent, and the need for financial capital, iron, weapons and food supplies grew rapidly at the same time. There was thus a broad interest in importing the conditions for commerce, as the country that managed to create the most effective trading system would also succeed on the battlefield. This new commercial system was the target of huge expectations, with tar and pitch seen as products over which Sweden could also have a monopoly in European markets.[14]

Mercantilism was the ruling economic tendency in Europe from the sixteenth century onwards. Its commercial ideology focused on profit-seeking at a national level. The roots of the ideology were in the European mineral industry and bullion trade, which was seen as a key element for countries to gain national capital. Mercantilism was considered the guiding principle for building an economically strong and independent country. Mercantilism strove to maintain a positive foreign trade balance, keeping export prices high and

---

13 Finland was ruled by the Swedish Crown for nearly 700 years: from the 12th century until 1809, when Finland became part of the Russian Empire.

14 Lindkvist and Sjöberg 2010, p. 306-312; Klein 1992, p. 39.

import prices low. Sweden adopted mercantilist ideas in the sixteenth century, when foreign trade was influenced by north German cities.[15]

In the first half of the seventeenth century, Sweden became a northern superpower. The period 1630–1720 is also known as the *age of greatness* in Nordic historiography. King Gustav II Adolphus led successful battles and conquered the most fertile territories around the Baltic Sea. The huge "granaries" of the Baltic States and Northern Germany fed the Swedish army and helped them to gain military victories. Finally, the King also had extensive administrative power over the country. The first Swedish commercial companies were founded during a time when mercantilism and monopolies were fundamental ideas in all commercial decisions. These economic notions dominated this age of greatness. At that time, financial ideologies were mostly adopted from France and Germany. In the theories of the historian Peter Englund, mercantilism took root in Sweden during the 1630s and the administration saw mercantilism as the only way to maintain a balance in trade. In contrast, the Netherlands followed its own trade policy based on free trade. Instead, in Sweden this kind of independence was not possible.[16]

These ideological tendencies had a strong effect on commercial legislation, causing its development to follow the trends prevailing in various periods. Legislation in the cities was based on city privileges, including permission to trade. In the 1350s, a common city law, known as the law of Magnus Eriksson, took effect. Even though the law mostly served Stockholm merchants, it was also used in other cities. The law defined how cities should be ruled. However, besides this, local rules – imposed by the mayor and the magistrate – existed in every city. In these cities, city bailiffs enforced the law. At the same time, immigrants and foreigners have traditionally had a great impact in Swedish cities by bringing with them new influences. Nevertheless, old customs were challenged with the founding of the first commercial companies.[17]

One of the main tools for fulfilling the idea of mercantilism was the legally complex notion of privileges. Rulers awarded privileges as advantages to certain people they wanted to control. Granting and receiving a privilege connected the parties to the contract, with both gaining benefits that were more or less unique.[18] Earlier, privileges were used as town privileges. However, when the first Swedish chartered companies were founded, privileges were adapted to a new field. The winner in this scenario was the nobility, as the lower estates

15 Klein 1953, p. 348.

16 Runefelt 2001, p. 15–17; Lappalainen 2006, p. 89–90.

17 Korpiola and Ojala 2019, p. 212–213; Björnsson and Magnusson 2011, p. 44–50; Gardberg 1981, p. 31–32.

18 Nováky 1990, p. 42–43.

could not even dream of receiving such privileges because of strict social hierarchy. In the ambitious theories of philosophers, privileges brought advantages to society as a whole. In reality, however, it was only the few that benefited. Having a privilege almost without exception included obligations.[19] For instance, in its first years the tar company attempted to buy and export tar as a commission-based business. Shortly thereafter, it was found necessary to reformulate tar trade practices on a very different basis. The company's activities required far more than simply dealing in tar. For example, over time the company incurred obligations such as importing salt for the whole of southern Finland.[20]

3 The Tar Trade and Its Legal Characteristics before the Company Model

Finnish forests have traditionally been called *green gold*. However, the material that the forests produced was in fact pitch black: *black gold*. The reasons for tar being so profitable were many. First of all, producing tar required little financial investment. Even economic recessions had minimal effect on production itself. Second, the Crown, which owned most of the forests in Finland, allowed the peasantry to make use of the forests without charge. Burning tar, with its many stages, took several years, but it cost only time and effort – not money or financial resources.[21] Third, in Finland a large part of the country was covered by a network of lakes and rivers, which enabled transport of barrels of tar over great distances. During the sixteenth century, Sweden was almost constantly in a state of war. This required extra taxes from the peasants, and tar offered an additional source of tax revenue.[22]

During the sixteenth century, the leading tar-exporting port in Europe was situated in Danzig. The forests in Poland and Prussia had offered useful resources for tar production. However, by the 1620s suitable wood from those areas had apparently run out. At the same time, England and the Netherlands had become large-scale consumers of tar because of the burgeoning need for trading vessels. Tar was essential for sealing the wooden parts of vessels and strengthening the ropes. It also prevented rotting.[23] The tar markets were thus

19 Müller 1998, p. 19.

20 See for example "Placat om Tiäru och Beckhandelen 1654" in Sweriges Rikes commerce. politie och oeconomie uti gemen uppå Hans Kongl.Maj:ts nodigsta belfallning; Waris approx. 1940, p. 39–43; Åström 1988, p. 20.

21 Turpeinen 2010, p. 26–32.

22 Tikka 2016, p. 12–13; Aalto 2012, "Tervakaupunki" p. 50.

23 Korpiola 2018, p. 289–290; Kuisma 2006, p. 27–29, 35.

wide open to Swedish merchants, and the Dutch also knew how to exploit the situation.

The economic circumstances prior to establishment of the tar companies meant that the export of tar was limited and followed a certain codification. The city tax was the main duty which merchants needed to pay, while customs and harbour duties were also mandatory, the payments being proportional to the volume of sales. The leading tar-exporting cities were the Finnish cities of Turku, Helsinki, Vyborg and the Swedish cities of Stockholm, Västervik and Kalmar. In those cities, the markets were often in the hands of the wealthiest families, who also held leading positions in the city.[24] They bought tar barrels from peasants who had transported them to the city for sale. Primarily, the ideology of mercantilism affected the arrangement of foreign trade, the idea being that concentrating on foreign trade in a few cities would offer the best opportunities. This initiative was introduced in 1614, during the era of King Gustav II Adolphus.[25]

Swedish society and in particular the field of commerce underwent drastic changes following the 1614 initiative. Before mercantilism, trade had been controlled differently. Local farmers with small sailing vessels had conducted a significant portion of foreign trade outside cities. This kind of modest trade was so common that the Crown began to consider it ineffective. After 1614, only two Finnish cities possessed *staple rights*, i.e. the right to engage in foreign trade. The new regulation directly affected the tar trade, doubling it in one year. Three years later, the regulation was expanded to two other Finnish cities, Porvoo and Helsinki, which were also granted staple rights. Disputes between merchants were resolved in the cities at two levels. Lower court sessions were held in market places, while higher court rulings were delivered in the magistrates' court in city halls.[26] Thus commenced the golden age of exporting tar. In 1620 and 1622, all the tar exported to Western Europe was transported via Stockholm.

Not long afterwards, Vyborg became the most active tar city among the Finnish ports, and the tar trade continued to grow.[27] In 1636, a new commercial regulation was introduced prohibiting foreign ships from sailing north of the latitude of Stockholm and Turku. It also ordered those two cities to arrange

24 Hallberg 1959, p. 172; Kirby and Hinkkanen 2000, p. 144–148.

25 Möller 1954, p. 15–16.

26 Heckscher 1954, p. 73; Ranta 1975, p. 685; Müller 1998, p. 43-44; Björnsson and Magnusson 2011, p. 44–45; See also "Privilegier för Koop-Hendels Compagniet," in Samling utaf kongl. Bref, stadgar och förordningar angaende Sweriges Rikes commerce, politie och oeconomie, vol. 1 (1750), p. 663, 665–667.

27 Ruuth and Halila 1974, p. 11, 113; Waris approx. 1940, p. 34.

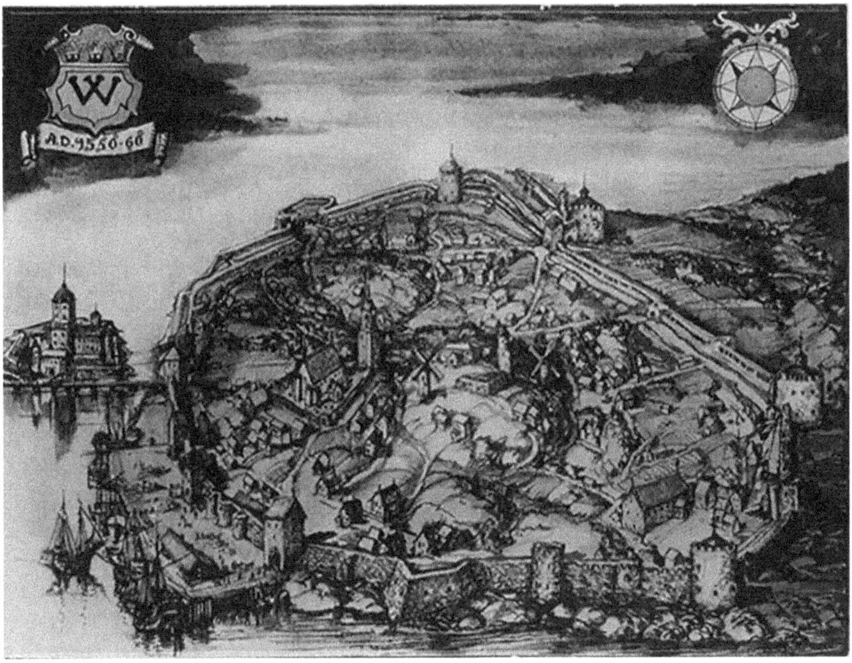

FIGURE 6 The City of Vyborg 1550–1560.

regular twice-yearly open markets, each lasting two consecutive weeks. Foreign merchants were also allowed to attend these markets. The Swedish King was now capable of controlling commerce in general and collecting specific payments, such as tolls. Tar had become a significant item of international trade, and the kingdom had raised awareness and expectations in that regards.[28]

4 Background to the First Privilege

Other countries became attracted by Sweden's treasure of tar. In particular, the Dutch and the English were involved in this rising and expanding field of commerce. Ultimately, the Netherlands, with its modern economic and commercial policy was more tempting to Sweden. As an indirect result, the Netherlands subsequently affected Sweden's domestic policy more strongly than any other foreign state at that time.[29]

28 Möller 1954, p. 18–19.
29 Israel 1989, p. 48-52; Odhner 1865, p. 79–80.

Conscious development of the production and sale of tar began with Dutch consultation. In 1629 Swedish nobleman and the commissary of Dutch commerce Konrad Falkenberg wrote to Sweden regarding local Dutch trade circumstances. This became the first known official mention of the tar trade. The commissary advised the Swedish Government to give careful consideration to adopting trade arrangements copied from the Dutch, as this would lead to greater profits.[30] Subsequently, the chancellor of Sweden recruited the Dutch merchant Johan van Swindern to investigate the production and quality of tar in southern Sweden. Van Swindern was also granted a privilege with his compatriot David Grunau to export tar from Sweden to the Netherlands. This privilege also included the obligation to teach local people proper methods for manufacturing tar. In March 1634, van Swindern applied, alone, for an exclusive privilege. Subsequently, van Swindern was the first to apply for a privilege for the first tar company.[31]

With the support of the Swedish government, van Swindern continued his successful businesses after 1634. He enjoyed a de facto monopoly, which encouraged him to continue investing, and his privilege covered the areas of Älvsborg and Gothenburg. Moreover, the local peasantry were obliged to supply him with as many wood products as he needed.[32] Although van Swindern was the target of envy, the government stood behind him. This inspired van Swindern to request a monopoly that would cover the whole of Sweden.

Van Swindern's request raised fierce debate, with the result that his application was rejected. Interestingly, however, it was in this context that a chartered company was mentioned for the first time. In his proposal, van Swindern explained that there would be no upper limit to the company's sales prices. This indicated that without large sales volumes, profit would stay low. He also explained that the monopoly would allow co-operation with Dutch merchants to remain well-organised and that, moreover, under his control the company model would also produce higher profits for Swedish merchants, who would no longer need to sell every single barrel by themselves. The Swedish Chancellor of State supported the idea of founding a company, but his justifications were different. In his view, the main rationale was the economic benefits to the peasantry. By contrast, opponents of the proposal argued for free markets and free trade.[33]

30 Wirta 2018, p. 161.

31 Original *Letter of the King 13.8.1629*, Tjärukompaniet och Förnyade tjärukomp 1648–1672; Handelskompanier, Handel och sjöfart vol. 63, Riksarkivet Stockholm (henceforth RAS); See also Fyhrvall 1880, p. 42.

32 *Privilege dated 23.3.1634*, Ämnessamlingar, Handel och sjöfart, no. 12, RAS.

33 Copy of original *Council of Ministers protocol* in Bergh 1906, p. 149.

In addition, the Swedish army argued against the establishment of a company because of van Swindern's apparent personal obsession with the occasion. Many other comments centred on the sum of money which was needed to initiate the operations of the company.[34] Among the protests, a clear concern for the peasantry nevertheless appeared. If the clerks of the company enjoyed excessive control, they might pressure the peasants to accept lower prices.[35]

Demand for Swedish tar rose considerably during the 1640s. Cooperation with the Netherlands stabilized, with changed political attitudes. At the same time, competition accelerated between England and the Netherlands over shipbuilding, in which tar played an important role. Van Swindern had fulfilled expectations. The Swedish ministers De la Gardie and Oxenstierna made a tour of inspection in Finland. After that it was clear to oblige van Swindern to improve the reduction of tar in the northern parts of the country as a counterpart in tar privilege.[36]

Van Swindern began to fulfill these hopes impressively, and his business model closely approximated to that of the future company.[37] The main tar-selling cities saw development of a certain group of merchants who focused on exporting tar. In 1643, some ten merchants sold 60–70 % of exported tar. This was controlled by giving each merchant his own quota for the number of tar barrels which could be bought from the producers. This similarly guaranteed small traders the chance to participate in the tar markets.[38]

5 The First Norland Tar Company 1648 and Its Privilege

Finally, in March 1648 attitudes stabilized and the privilege application for the company was accepted by the Council of the realm of Sweden.[39] Besides van Swindern, the founders of the Norland tar company were merchants Wolff, Liliencrantz and Westerman. In addition to van Swindern these three were respected and well known burghers in Stockholm. At the time of its establishment, around ten other merchants invested in the company. The company

34 Hallberg 1959, p. 164.

35 *Protocoll of the Council of the realm* Part 11, 255 and Part 12, 149. RAS.

36 *Ämnessamlingar, Handel och sjöfart, no.* 12, Kammarkollegio, RAS.

37 *A letter from the King 5.8.1643*, The National Archives of Finland, Helsinki, ("NAF"): "In every staple town there must be certain tar officers placed in a "Tar court": A quality controller, a tar secretary, a tar lower and a cooper. These workers will serve the tar organization."

38 Waris approx 1940, p. 71–72.

39 In Swedish "Riksråd," in Finnish "valtaneuvosto."

privilege was granted for the next twenty years. The privilege covered northern parts of Sweden, with its southern border drawn between Stockholm and Nyen. The main purpose of the privilege was to allow a certain group of reliable merchants to have the right to buy all the tar and pitch produced in the northern parts of Sweden. No one outside the company had permission to export tar. Likewise, all the tar produced had to be sold to the company. The sphere of operations covered Norland, Finland and Carelia.[40]

The tar privilege was the main legal text concerning the company. It contained nine paragraphs and was a licence to buy and export tar. The new regulation ordered those who previously had permission to export tar to sell their stocks to the new company. The privilege focused on certain details but did not cover the full extent of the company's operations. The purpose of the company was to assist in the selling of tar and pitch "in the most proper and state supporting way."[41] It also specified the conditions, geographic latitudes and rights which delineated the scope of its operations. In the privilege, the prices of tar and the level of customs duties were precisely defined. In addition, the privilege determined the geographical area of tar production and the maximum limit of output. The cities where the tar business could be conducted were Stockholm, Turku, Vyborg, Helsinki and Nyen.[42]

How could the company achieve its goals besides price control and its geographical monopoly? The privilege interfered with the operation of mayors and city councils, which were in a leading role. These organs were, due to the privilege, responsible for hiring officers to control the quality of tar and count all the barrels transported to cities. The measure used to count tar was a "läst" which comprised approximately 12 barrels of tar. In addition, customs duties were one of the main tools for the government to control operations. Customs officers were required to report annually to the highest tax authorities and the Swedish council chamber. The Finnish staple cities differed in this respect, because only certain coupons and payment orders were used. These were subsequently exchanged for cash in Stockholm. In fact, raising capital was the Swedish Crown's primary motive for the entire idea of the tar company. In

40 Samling utaf kongl. Bref, stadgar och forordningarr angaende Sweriges Rikes commerce, politie och oeconomie, vol. 2 (1747) p. 525–526.

41 "Privilegium för Tiäruhandels Compagniet" in Samling utaf kongl... (1750) p. 527.

42 By contrast, the privilege emphasized that the tar produced south of Stockholm in the provinces of Wermeland, Dahl and Wästergöteland, had to be sold in Gothenburg. Moreover, tar produced in the provinces of Wästergöteland and in Småland and Halland had to be sold in Halmstad or Småland. Tar produced in the provinces of Kalmar, Wästervik or Gotland had to be sold in Visby. See "Privilegium för tiäru handels comp 1648" in Sweriges Rikes commerce... (1750) p. 527.

the privilege, this matter drew much attention and was raised in several paragraphs.[43]

After the privilege was issued, the reaction in Finnish cities varied from displeasure to disbelief. The privilege did not only affect the tar trade, but it also changed trading habits in the northern areas of the Baltic Sea. Previously, merchants had freely bought tar from peasants and exported it to foreign merchants. In return, they imported necessary goods such as salt, spices and other items and traded them in the interior of the country. Suddenly, this traffic totally ceased. The ports became empty except for tar barrels, and the familiar partners of foreign merchants arriving to trade were unable to sell them anything. The largest reactions occurred in Vyborg. The economy of this eastern Finnish city was practically based on tar trading with north German cities. Now this trade was paralyzed, replaced by agents of the tar company. Local merchants were forced to sell their barrels to the company at almost the same price they had paid for them from the peasant producers. The controlled price markets were inflexible, and soon the Swedish government received cries of distress from the merchants and peasantry.[44]

5.1 *The Tar Privilege and Several Appeals*

The tar company provided several advantages to the Swedish Crown and the company's partners. The purchase prices of tar were low and negotiations between local merchants and the company were nonexistent. For the government, customs duties were easy to collect from just one actor: the company. Moreover, tar production was controllable, as the company was obliged to buy all the tar produced, and most importantly the monopoly maintained high sales prices to the English and Dutch. Intentions and hopes for the company were fulfilled as planned. As a result, the large number of complaints from Finnish merchants was not only undesired but also extremely irritating.

Initially, there was almost no compliance with the new ordinances. When an English merchant vessel sailed to Vyborg in the spring 1648, as it had for decades, the merchants of Vyborg sold tar to the English in the previous fashion. This recurred in the summer of the same year when a Dutch vessel appeared in the port of Vyborg. These offences earned strict reprimands from the Crown, but there were no further consequences.[45] Soon after this, in 1649, the first complaint about the actions of the company was sent to Stockholm. It was directed to the Crown and signed by every Finnish staple city. The reasons

43 "Privilegium för Tiäruhandels Compagniet" in Sweriges Rikes commerce... (1750) p. 528–530.

44 Åström 1988, p. 149; Tikka 2020, see Conlusions.

45 Waris approx 1940, p. 72.

for the complaint were the same as earlier. Even so, the answer from the Queen was foreseeable: Foreign merchants were a serious threat to the Swedish tar trade and the monopoly was a necessary defence against the risk of them capturing the entire tar trade.[46]

Dissatisfaction continued, and at the beginning of 1650 the Queen received a significant written protest. This time, the Finnish cities were appealing for the right to trade independently. Moreover, the cities complained that their reputation among foreign merchants was ruined. Furthermore, low, non-negotiable sales prices were causing displeasure. Complaints continued to occur, and as a result, a special committee was sent to Vyborg to ascertain the actual conditions and circumstances in the city. These local investigations revealed that the local agents were serving their own interests rather than those of the company. For example, the company's first agent in Vyborg, Cröell, was caught paying too little to the merchants for barrels of tar.[47]

The committee's report along with the complaints from the cities precipitated the next tar regulation, which was approved by Parliament on 23 November 1650. The regulation particularly concerned relations between Finnish and Norlandian cities and the company. Finally, after much frustrated criticism, the local merchants were granted some allowances. The most substantial change was permission to do business in Amsterdam, Lübeck, Hamburg and Danzig. The prerequisite for this business was nevertheless that the company received sufficient prior notice and that the merchants were in possession of a bill of exchange guaranteed by the city council or mayor.[48]

At the same time, Sweden had become a more stable superpower in the Baltic Sea area, which required reforms in the field of administration. The commercial, manufacturing and navigation sectors represented an important area for development. In 1651, the Commercial Collegium (*Kommerskollegium*) was granted unprecedented extra authority by the Crown. For the expanded Sweden, there was a need to be present and visible in its new provinces, and the College founded two new units in Wismar and Riga besides that of Stockholm. These new positions both strengthened and facilitated control.[49] In the same year, England established its own version of the Council for Trade, which was closely connected with the Navigation Act.[50]

---

46 Aalto 2012, "Sotakaupunki" p. 64–65.

47 *Appeal from the merchants of Helsinki*, Tjärukompaniet och Förnyade tjärukomp 1648–1672, Handelskompanier, Handel och sjöfart vol. 63, RAS.

48 "Privilegium för tiäru compagniet 1649" in Sweriges Rikes commerc.. (1750), p. 608–610.

49 "Instruction för Commercie Collegium 1651" in Sweriges Rikes commerce... (1750), p. 670.

50 Pihlajamäki 2018, p. 274–276; Israel 1995, p. 55–56.

Nevertheless, complaints against the company still continued to appear, despite or because of the government's reaction to them. The affairs of the tar company were handled during a parliamentary session in 1654, when the tar company was clearly the main target of blame for difficulties with Vyborg merchants. After the dismissal of Cröell, Mechever and Hans Schmidt, who also tended to pursue their own private business interests, held the post of company agents. Moreover, van Swindern himself was dismissed from the company for dishonesty.[51] For the next parliamentary session, the Finnish staple cities carefully prepared a new complaint, where they again applied for the right to export tar by themselves. The reasons were manifold. Firstly, Vyborg was facing an unforeseen problem: the city and its province was suffering from a shortage of salt because Vyborg merchants could no longer trade with foreign merchants. Secondly, the sales prices of tar had declined in Europe, which lowered profits. Thirdly, the company made payments in copper coins, even though customs duties needed to be paid in silver coins. Fourthly, the company granted bills with limited validity, even though merchants could not know in advance when they would need to use them. This increased the practical difficulties of trade. However, the ultimate provocation came when the company's officials failed to appear in local courts to respond to these claims.[52]

As a result of all these complaints and the report of the Committee,[53] a new commercial code for the tar trade was passed in August 1654. This allocated a certain number of shares to Finnish merchants in addition to Stockholmers, which transpired to be the most essential change in the new code. Thus these less affluent merchants finally had a possibility to be part of the hated tar company. The combined value of the shares in question was 30 000 silver coins. The share issue was valid from the end of October 1654, and cities who redeemed shares had the right to a representative on the company's board of directors. It was underlined that both profits and losses would be divided equally among old and new shareholders according to the number of shares in their possession.[54] This brought the company's character closer to that of the joint stock

51 See for example 31.1.1651 and 19.3.1653 dated resolution of parliament, Tjärukompaniet och Förnyade tjärukomp 1648–1672, Handelskompanier, Handel och sjöfart vol. 63, RAS.

52 *Complaint from Vyborg 12.5.1654*. Ämnessamlingar, Handel och sjöfart, no. 12, Kammarkollegio, RAS.

53 The report included interviews with citizens and the partners and heads of the Company. These were conducted by sending members of the trade commission to Vyborg. During these interviews, Vyborg merchants tried to convince the committee members to set aside half of the Company's shares for Finnish merchants. "Placat om tiäru och beckhandelen 1654 in Sweriges Rikes commerce... (1750) p. 778–780.

54 "Placat om tiäru och beckhandelen 1654" in Sweriges Rikes commerce... (1750) p. 778–780.

company model, because the position of the partners was recognized and specified for the first time.

In the commercial code of 1654, a few other matters were also determined. New permanent prices were set, and the size of a barrel of tar was specified. The company was also ordered to import salt and other necessary sales items to Finnish staple cities. To facilitate smoother trading, the company was ordered to offer credit. In practice, however, trade with foreign vessels in staple cities remained fully in the tar company's hands.[55]

5.2 *Later Development and Dissolution of the First Company*

The year 1654 was notable for Sweden in an economic and political sense. In that same year Queen Christina abdicated and was succeeded by her cousin Carl x Gustav in June. During the reign of Christina, the Swedish economy had suffered a recession. Her methods of governance had proven fatal, and the newly crowned King faced severe challenges. At the same time, during 1652–1654 the first Anglo-Dutch war was in progress, which negatively affected the Swedish tar trade.[56] In 1654, Parliament decided to grant greater authority to the Commercial Collegium. This meant that citizens of staple cities could no longer directly complain to the Crown about commercial matters. Rather, they could only direct their complaints to the Commercial Collegium, whose task was to consider cases individually and decide whether thereafter to present complaints to the King. Local disputes were directed to the local courts for resolution. The new commercial tar code precipitated an enormous leap in legal consciousness. The dispute process began primarily with the local courts, and after that, the next level was the Commercial Collegium, which decided whether to introduce the case to the monarch.[57]

Despite the reforms of 1654, the tar company nevertheless continued to face adversity. The political atmosphere in Sweden was fractious, and attitudes towards King Carl x Gustav were contradictory. During his reign, the country was in a nearly constant state of war, which devoured state capital.[58] Soon after, opinion became polarized towards the tar company. This occurred following the sudden death of the King during a parliamentary session in January 1660. His son, who was still under age, could not accede to the throne; instead, the Royal Regency assumed political power. The Regency was strongly against the

55 "Placat om tiäru och beckhandelen 1654" in Sweriges Rikes commerce... (1750) p. 780–782.

56 Englund 1994, p. 206–208.

57 "Placat om tiäru och beckhandelen 1654" in Samling utaf Kong... (1753) p. 782.

58 Kirby 1990, p. 217–219.

existence of the tar company and began to advocate the company's dissolution, which provoked heated debate.[59]

Above all, practical difficulties concerning trade still remained. As the Dutch and English were the tar company's main partners, the discussions had to acknowledge the situation of the partners. Company agent Appelbom, who was on duty in the Netherlands, was obliged to negotiate with local merchants about the conditions of dissolution. The Dutch offered to donate 200 000 silver coins to cover the company's debts, but the negations failed to progress further.[60] A second practical problem was the high volume of tar production. In 1659, the Commercial Collegium had already received a memorandum from the company's director, Krister Bonde, expressing his concern about high tar production. During that time, the code obliged the company to buy all the tar produced, which caused uncontrollable difficulties.[61]

The first agreement on the dissolution of the company was passed in a parliamentary session in November 1660.[62] Sweden's need for foreign credit had increased to unsustainable levels and required a rapid solution. Because the Anglo-Dutch war had practically frozen the tar trade, the government of Sweden was desperate. In February 1661, the Commercial Collegium issued a report which saved the company from dissolution at the eleventh hour. The College suggested that instead of closing down its operations, the tar company should be founded all over again, based on fairer principles. Moreover, it would have a wider-ranging investor base. A new five-paragraph statute for a reformed company was issued on 5 July 1661.[63]

The main reason for not dissolving the company completely was that the interests of the opposing parties were at such variance that refunding the tar company represented a provisional compromise. At a time of war, Sweden needed financial capital and a consensus had to be reached. Tar was seen as a trade product that could save the country. However, the complaints against the company were hindering the Commercial Collegium's efforts to further the interests of Sweden. The concerns of the Government and private citizens were nevertheless clearly at odds, which created a "laboratory" where legal issues were evaluated. It must also be taken into consideration that the tar privilege was personally granted by the Crown. When the ruler passed away, the privilege

59 Parliamentary speech in Gothenburg, spring 1660, *Riksregistraturet*, RAS; Hallberg 1959, p. 114.

60 Parliamentary speech in Gothenburg, spring 1660, *Riksregistraturet*, RAS.

61 Hallberg 1959, p. 112–113.

62 "Riksdagarnas och mötens beslut II, 26.11.1660" in Samling utaf Kong... (1753) p. 1396.

63 "Förordning om nya Tiäru-Compagniet 1661" in Samling utaf Kong... (1753) p. 42–47.

automatically expired and it had to be concluded again with the following ruler. Therefore the death of the ruler precipitated decisions.

The main problem with the previous tar privilege was its overly superficial and general definitions. The essential purpose of the privilege was to promote the tar trade "in the most useful way." However, achieving this target was not anticipated beforehand in detail. The controlling of the prices was the practical way to guide the trade. Soon envy arose between the parties. Monopolies are generally seen as unfair and arbitrary entities, which was no exception even in this case. This case was no exception. Especially in Finland, the company and its directors were viewed as arrogant and elitist – to be fair, a not unreasonable view as only a few of the wealthiest merchants enjoyed the profits. Thus, it was a natural step for the Government to move the regulation of tar in a more practical direction.

6 The Reformed Tar Company and Its New Regulations from 1661 Onwards

As noted, in 1660 the King of Sweden, Carl x Gustav, died suddenly during a Parliamentary session. The dissolution of the tar company and the founding of a new entity was partly the result of these events. In the same year, following the death of the King, Sweden signed a peace treaty with Russia. The treaty ceded parts of Poland to Sweden, and a temporary period of peace was attained. This allowed Sweden to pay greater attention to developing the country, and improvements in the field of law were also achieved. The new tar statute introduced essential reforms for Finnish cities at the expense of the company's directors. The changes focused on the trade and production of tar, and the statute's text concentrated on practical instructions.

During the summer of 1661, a novel statute for the company was negotiated and passed. At the same time, to distinguish itself from the former company, the new entity was named the "reformed company."[64] The updated statute intervened strongly in the ownership of the company. Concentration of ownership among a few of the wealthiest merchants was no longer permitted. Instead, strict limits on the level of share ownership were specified: a maximum of 1000 dalers and a minimum of 100 dalers.[65] Previous stakeholders had

64 Fyrhvall 1880, p. 54–55.

65 The Swedish monetary units were a complicated system in the early modern period. The old system based on marks, but was replaced first by copper coins and later silver dalers. Because the value of copper varied lot, it affected the value of money as well. The daler was originally worth of 28 grams of pure silver, but soon reduced to 26 grams. It was mostly used as a calculation unit and not as a practical coin. Möller 1959, appendix 1.

a preemptive right to redeem the shares. This control of investment powerfully affected the company's activities and its entire future, as the previous owners were forced to relinquish some of their shares. The shares also featured a novel method of resale. Finally, the new rules intentionally allowed the burghers of small tar cities to participate in the company.[66]

Nevertheless, the novel regulations within the statute failed to overcome the company's difficulties. For instance, thousands of tons of tar had remained unsold by the previous company. One of the conditions of the reformed privilege was that all stockpiled tar was to be transferred to the new company. Moreover, the new legislation ordered the company to redeem all existing barrels of tar owned by city merchants. This was a demanding order to implement, as the majority of the company's capital was tied up in its tar. Luckily, the payment was over the long term, but on the other hand world market prices of tar decreased[67]

The main paragraphs of the new statutes were clearly generous compared to the previous ordinance, and small-scale local merchants in provincial Finnish cities really were taken into account. The paragraphs of the statute were also focused on controlling the amount of production. First, the company had the sole privilege to manufacture pitch from tar. This was explained by the fact that only the company knew the real consumption of pitch. Secondly, overproduction was a clear problem. Consequently, the statute also emphasized concerns about the country's forests and the possibility of their over-exploitation, which was seen as a threat to the entire nation. The end of the statute featured an order regarding the procedure for handling disagreements between the tar company and the cities. Complaints were to be primarily resolved with the help of the Commercial Collegium.[68]

The resolution of 1654 had solved the main difficulties of local burghers in the staple cities, and thus formed the basis of the statute of 1661. The Regency had a strong urge to improve Sweden's economy, and while the statute was not perfect, nevertheless it was the best that could be devised at the time.

6.1 *The Reformed Tar Company at the Centre of Conflict*

The reformed tar company nevertheless soon faced adversity, as the company and the Royal Regency were headed for deadlock. The Regency insisted that company should receive more tar than it was capable of reselling. In addition, the Regency even defined the prices that the company was to pay for barrels of

66 "Förordnung om nya Tiäru-Compagniet 1661" in Samling utaf Kong... (1753) p. 43–47.

67 Samling utaf Kong... (1753) p. 160–161.

68 "Förordnung om nya Tiäru-Compagniet 1661" in Samling utaf Konj... (1753) p. 46–47.

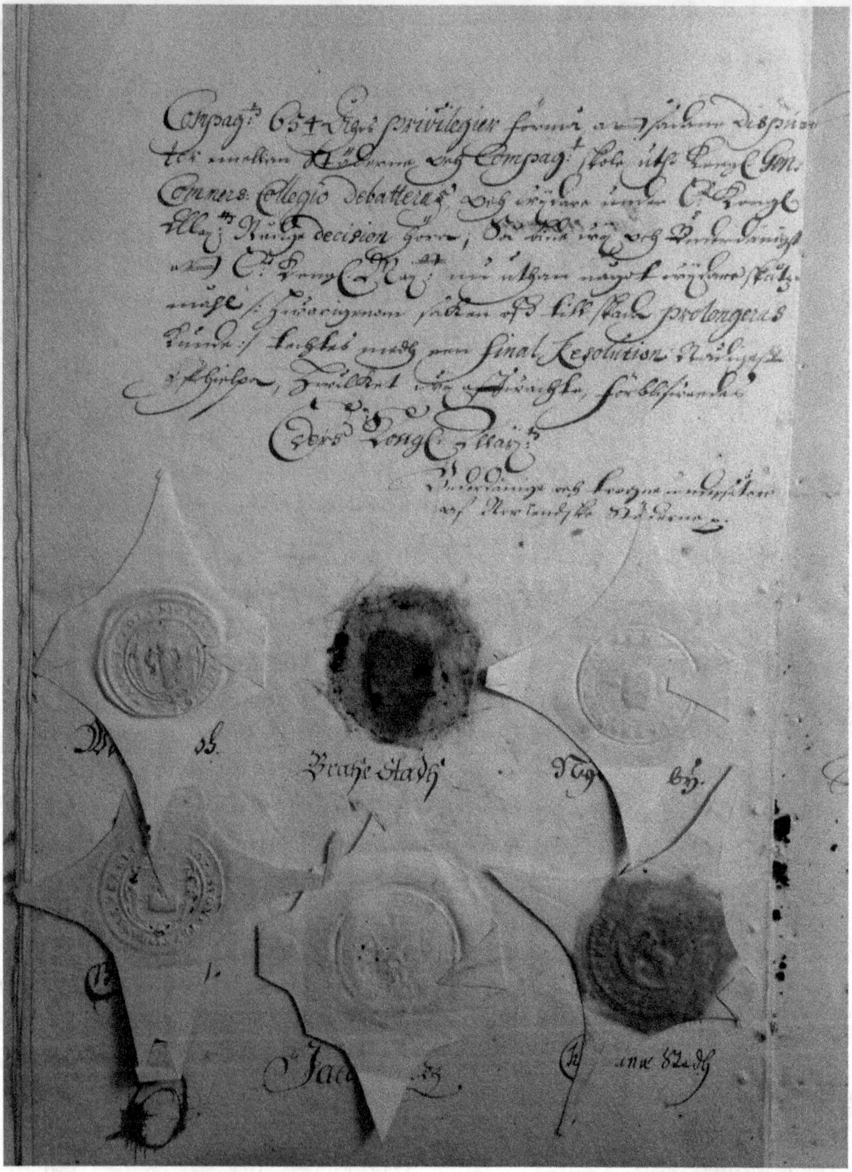

FIGURE 7 The Privilege of the Tar Company from the year 1654.

tar. Earlier, this had not been a problem because the prices in other countries were high. However, the situation had changed radically. During its first year, the reformed company was obliged to buy 23 000 mers of tar, which was the largest amount the company had ever redeemed. This imposed an enormous burden on the management of the company's finances. In addition, the former partners meanwhile demanded redemption of their shares, while simultaneously Sweden's financial affairs were also worsening.[69]

At the beginning of 1662, the directors of the tar company had already formulated a complaint concerning three matters: overly high customs duties, poor practices in dealing with bills, and the fact that tar production was exceeding consumption. The Regency responded on 21 March 1662. The only matter on which the Regency acquiesced was the lowering of customs duties: these were reduced retroactively from 1661. Instead, when it came to granting bills, an even stricter policy was launched. The Regency had become aware that some small retailers who did not deal with tar or pitch at all had been redeeming bills and it decided to prohibit this practice.[70] In June of the same year, a new reply from the Regency was published after heated debate. This time it concerned bank notes.[71] The Regency decreed that the tar company could not receive any bank notes or credit of any other kind at all. As to the complaint concerning excessive tar production, the Regency gave the company permission to produce pitch from 2000 mers of tar yearly.[72]

During the summer of 1662, measures were implemented to achieve balanced finances within the company. However, many of the shareholders of the previous tar company were no longer interested in being involved in the reformed company. In particular, many of the wealthiest shareholders were missing. This caused difficulties in raising capital and in coping with payment to tar producers. The proposed solution to this problem was a financial agreement with Dutch company Gangel & Deutz. Under this agreement, Dutch agents in Amsterdam paid the tar company's agents in advance so that they were able to buy salt and other necessary products from Amsterdam and ship them to Vyborg. This practice became the company's primary operating principle.[73]

Despite the changes, trade in Amsterdam failed to operate smoothly. The quality of tar was the next concern. Consequently, at the end of 1662 the

69 Fyhrvall 1880, p. 56; Samling utaf Kong... (1753) p. 160.

70 "Resolution för Tiäru Compagniet 1662" in Samling utaf Kong... (1753) p. 60–63.

71 In Swedish "Banco sedlar": in the 1660's the bank of Stockholm began to distribute bank notes against the currency deposited at the bank. This was revolutionary. However, due to a lack of experience, too many notes were distributed, which apparently caused great troubles for the bank. Lappalainen 2006, p. 100–101.

72 "Resolution för Tiäru Compagniet" in Samling utaf Kong... (1753) p. 75–76.

73 Hallberg 1959, p. 116–117.

Regency published a new document containing a reminder that tar barrels must be full and the quality of the tar of a better standard.[74] Furthermore, in April 1663, the problem of overproduction of tar resurfaced.[75]

The fact that Sweden had to trade with other European countries made it highly dependent on the political affairs of other nations. In May 1665, England and the Netherlands headed into war, which further worsened the tar company's weak financial situation. In the preceding winter, the tar company with its shareholders had approached both the Royal Regency and the Commercial Collegium to apply for financial support. The Regency and the College failed to reach a consensus regarding the difficulties. The College, for instance, proposed that the southern parts of Sweden should fall within the tar company's remit: however, the Regency disagreed. The solution was to raise customs duties on the purchase of tar to two dalers per mer.[76]

On 28 May 1665, the official decision on the company's petition was announced in Stockholm. The decision included, besides the abovementioned points, regulations regarding the practices of the tar trade. These familiar matters were handled in eight paragraphs. The first paragraph included a rule on regulation of producing tar: tar officers in the countryside, where tar was produced, were obliged to report all the tar produced. They also needed to ensure that the correct sums were entered into land registers.[77] The next paragraphs abandoned the extensive use of forests. The fourth paragraph stated that the company's obligation to buy tar would be cut by one-third compared to the previous year. The fifth paragraph stated that the southern parts of the country would remain outside the company's remit, but those areas were to pay higher customs duties: two dalers per mer. The last paragraph announced a new fixed price per mer.[78] In addition, the company was no longer obliged to buy tar produced before 1659. This was justified, as the problems with the older tar would have been insurmountable.[79]

---

74 "Bref om Tiäru tilwärkningen 1662" in Samling utaf Kong. (1753) p. 129.

75 "Resolution för Tiäru-Compagniet 1663" and "Brev om Tiäru tilwärkningen 1663" in Samling utaf Kong... (1753) p. 160–163.

76 Hallberg 1959, p. 118; "Resolution för Tiärucompagniet 1665" in Samling utaf Kong... (1753) p. 333–336.

77 Later, on the basis of these records it was possible to examine how much tar was produced and in which parts of the country. This was also seen as an equitable way to share primary production between the peasants.

78 The new price was determined to be no more than 10 copper daler or marks or one silver daler.

79 "Resolution för Tiäru compagniet 1665" in Samling utaf Kong... (1753) p. 333–336, 354–355.

In summary, the difficulties the reformed tar company faced during 1660–1665 were fundamental. The Finnish peasantry was accustomed to producing tar and thus generating extra income. Because of this, the decrease in tar production was extremely challenging, and no one was inclined to stop production of tar voluntarily. Finally, the Regency gave up its efforts and set an upper limit on the amount of tar that the company was obliged to buy.

7 A New Attempt with the Ordinance of 1666

Unsurprisingly, difficulties remained. An inconvenient problem faced by Sweden was stagnant trade with the Netherlands because of the second Anglo-Dutch war. The Regency and the Commercial Collegium had clearly failed to anticipate that production would once again exceed demand. The Regency began desperately to prescribe new ordinances, including several in one year, which indicated the extent of the problem. These ordinances imposed several limitations on handling currency. Borrowing money was possible only with certain written bills used outside Sweden. However, the use of bank notes was also prohibited except for selling on credit. Nearly all actions and regulations introduced by the Regency and College were guided by a chronic shortage of money. By any standards, the tar company was not on a stable development course, and the situation could not be remedied simply by new regulations.[80]

In 1666, the company's debt had reached 90 000 dalers. After two years, its foreign creditors also began to request payments with high interest. In order to ensure the company's survival, it was essential that new negotiations concerning the company's regulations should begin in that same year. This time the focus was administration, which encouraged the directors to participate in the discussions. The management of the company needed to be restructured. The primary proposal was that shareholders would elect three directors among themselves: one legal expert, one expert in foreign and one in domestic trade. A board, or more likely delegation, was nominated with sixteen members, whose task it was to guide the directors with their decisions.[81]

In fact, the shareholders thus had more influence than ever before. Their task was also to nominate the company's agents outside Sweden and in Turku, Helsinki and Vyborg. Shareholders who invested 500 dalers or more had the right to request personally from the company's office information concerning the company's businesses. If discrepancies were found, the shareholders could

80 Fyhrvall 1880, p. 59.

81 Palmsk.samlingar, a document dated 1.10.1666, RAS; Fyhrvall 1880, p. 59.

then report them to the company's assistant, who then informed the director. Company meetings were held whenever needed. The influence of each shareholder at their meetings was proportionate to the amount they had invested. For example, an investment of one thousand dalers was equal to one vote.[82]

Nevertheless, the tar company's troubles continued to increase. Its financial difficulties were obvious, and repayment of loans was a burden. Some relief was found when in March 1667 the Regency issued a decision concerning an extended privilege. The privilege included the right to sell tar outside the company, and was granted to a small number of merchants favoured by the Regency. The intention was to stimulate the tar trade with the assistance of some influential figures. This was actually partly successful. However, no far-reaching effects were achieved. Agents in Hamburg, Lubeck and Amsterdam still reported low sales volumes.[83]

The tar company's struggles were thus far from over. In 1668, the burghers sent a letter of complaint to the Regency, whose answer was published in October in Stockholm. It included paragraphs considering previously familiar issues such as use of equal measurements, money transactions and storage of tar.[84]

Discontent with the tar trade and the company's operations appeared to be endless. In 1670, several complaints arose from East Bothnian peasants and city burghers. The main issues concerned customs duties and overproduction. Moreover, the peasants were dissatisfied with how barrels of tar were measured. After several complaints of this nature the Royal Regency prepared a statement reversing its previous principle: the Commercial Collegium should henceforth address these sorts of complaints instead of the king. During July 1670, the Regency once again published new regulations. This time it concerned the measurement of a barrel of tar.[85] In conclusion, the Regency emphasized that the company still retained a monopoly over the trade in tar. This meant that neither members of the Admiralty, nor Stockholm merchants nor anyone else had permission to trade tar without a licence from the company.

82 Palmsk.samlingar, a document dated 1.10.1666, RAS.

83 Document dated 19.3.1667, Ämnessamlingar, Handel och sjöfart, vol. 12, RAS.

84 "Resolution för Tiäru-Compagniet 1668" in Samling utaf Kong... (1753) p. 716.

85 The new measure would be 48 canfuls of tar instead of the earlier 54 canfuls. With the help of county governors, the overproduction of tar should have been controllable. This was necessary not only because of the reselling problems of burghers, but also because of overuse of the forests. In a clear order to the tar company, the Regency determined that the new measure of one mer was 13 tar barrels instead the previous 12.

As could be foreseen, the reforms and the company's difficulties represented an insurmountable challenge. The company's creditors also pressed for repayment even though the company had no funds. Discussions about the company's dissolution and a new privilege began in 1671 and were met with strong opposition among burghers and the Commercial Collegium. After lengthy negotiations, the company's directors and shareholders decided that two-thirds of the company's capital would be removed and new shareholders would be sought to invest a total of 200 000 silver coins. This was designed to launch the company on a new economic path; however, this failed to produce the desired effect.[86] Instead, the burghers, who had resisted the existence of the company, finally managed to convince the Regency of the impudence and interference of the company's directors. The Commercial Collegium was thus obliged to organize investigations and a committee was established for this purpose.[87]

The committee concluded its report in 1671, finding that the directors were guilty of several offences and derelictions. Because the tar trade was in crisis and liberation of the tar trade was loudly demanded, the committee was obliged to elaborate a proposal for a new privilege.[88]

8 The Reorganized Tar Trade and the New Privilege of 1672

During 1672 Sweden experienced several changes, both internally and externally. In March, war broke out between France and the Netherlands, and Sweden intervened in this conflict by siding with France and offering troops for the southern coast of the Baltic Sea. For Sweden, with its financial problems, this decision was easy, as it received payments against the troops given to France. As a result Sweden participated in the war between 1673 and 1674.[89] Furthermore the internal political balance in Sweden changed after King Carl XI turned 18 and was crowned the lawful ruler. Prior to that, the Chancellor of Sweden, Magnus De la Gardie, had been the most powerful person in the Royal Regency. Although the situation did not immediately change, the new King began withdrawing from the previous administration, first in regard to Swedish internal policy. Nevertheless, in 1672 the young King did not interfere in the tar trade. However soon the evidence against the tar company was clear: the company's debts were high and its directors unreliable. However, the burghers'

86 Document dated 5.9.1671, Ämnessamlingar, Handel och sjöfart, vol. 12, RAS.
87 "Resolution för Tiäru-Compagniet 1670" in Samling utaf Kong… (1753) p. 815.
88 Tiäru compagniet 1648–1660, Ämnessamlingar, Handel och sjöfart, vol. 12, RAS.
89 Kirby 1990, p. 295–297.

appeal to totally liberalize the tar trade was too risky a proposal. Fear of foreigners seizing the entire Swedish tar trade was rife. Consequently, a new privilege was announced on 23 July 1672.[90]

At the same time, the entire tar company was replaced by a new "reorganised tar company." However, the new ten-year privilege differed little from the previous one. Some of the most important shareholders were the same, such as the Stockholm Magistrate Mårten Bunge, the merchant Klas Wilkens and chamber council member Barthold Ruuth. The new reorganized company began on a totally new economic basis. The previous company's loans, tar stocks and property were not considered the new company's responsibility. Consequently, the new company was entirely separated from the previous company, in contrast to the preceding privilege of 1661. A two-year period of transition was introduced.[91] During this time, the old company could sell their old tar while the new company could not sell anything. However, the new company already had the obligation to buy certain amounts of tar from local merchants. The most notable reform concerned the obligation to buy tar. The company's trading partner remained Deutz in Amsterdam.[92]

As usual, the new privilege determined sales prices, but this time it was unnecessary for the payment to be in cash. Instead, payments could be made in items whose worth was counted in monetary units of three and a half copper coins. The practice of fixed prices and amounts of tar was also retained.[93] A new phenomenon, however, was the 11th paragraph of the privilege and its mention of possible complaints. The suggested practices as to investigating and handling complaints were comprehensively explained. In general, regarding the new privilege, the King intervened in company affairs less than earlier. Moreover, the company's operations no longer needed to be based on the interests of the Crown, which also represented a change from the previous privilege.[94]

However, the existence of the company was on an uncertain footing for many reasons. The ongoing war did not facilitate the tar trade with the Netherlands, as Sweden was allied with France – the Netherlands' enemy. Instead, the export of tar to England and France increased considerably.[95] The first official

90 "Privilegium för Tiäru-Comp. 1672" in Samling utaf Kong... (1753) p. 950-952; Israel 1995, p. 796-797; Tarkiainen 2000, p. 168–171.

91 This included years 1672 and 1673.

92 "Privilegium för Tiäru-Comp. 1672" in Samling utaf Kong... (1753) p. 950–952.

93 For example, in Vyborg the annual amount of the tar for the city was 3000 mers. The price per mer was 56 copper dalers, which had to be paid immediately.

94 "Privilegium för Tiäru-Comp. 1672" in Samling utaf Kong... (1753) p. 952–955.

95 Hallberg 1959, p. 123.

move towards dissolving the company came in March 1773, during a parliamentary session. The reasons behind the proposal, initiated by the burghers, were familiar: the tar trade should be liberalized and the monopoly broken up, as it was too demanding to maintain trade connections with the Netherlands. In 1676, the King granted a new privilege on the grounds of the uncertain times. Even during wartime, some exceptions to the company's monopoly existed because of the urgent need for salt. This increased the pressure for the company's dissolution, which finally led to the liberation of the tar trade.[96]

9 The Final Attempt to Control the Tar Trade with a Company Model 1689–1712

The period between 1648 and 1676 brought remarkable changes including changes to the conditions of trade – and the idea of free trade began to dominate during the reign of King Carl XI. The previous Royal Regency had failed to meet its economic targets, which also raised the need for change. In addition, the "Great Land Reduction"[97] was launched which transferred political power from the nobility back to the monarch. Moreover, wealthy merchants lost control over minor burghers. During the 1670s and 1680s, calls for the company's dissolution accelerated, and finally, in 1682, an agreement was reached on free trade. Nevertheless, the return of a free tar trade after 35 years did not proceed smoothly. Previous routines had become ingrained and, but also the era was challenging: prices were low and burghers had neither the capital nor the ships to trade. Dutch merchants stopped sailing to Vyborg. Instead, Vyborg merchants had to sail to Amsterdam and pay high customs duties. In Stockholm, the local burghers were also in trouble, as the Dutch and English had taken over the local tar trade. It was necessary to improve the legislation once again.[98]

In January 1682, during peace negotiations in Nijmegen, dissolution documents for the company were signed. The new ordinance took effect in October the same year. This liberated the tar trade, but it nevertheless still set customs duties, which were protested strongly by the burghers.[99]

96 Samling utaf Kong. Bref, Stadgar och förordningar ungående Sweriges Rikes commerce, politie och oeconomie, vol. 4 (1760) p. 13, 16–17; Hallberg 1959, p. 127; Fyhrvall 1880, p. 68–73.

97 In the Great Reduction of 1680, the Swedish Crown recovered lands earlier granted to the nobility. This was accomplished during the reign of Carl XI and in practice the nobility lost its power to the. See Ylikangas 1986, p. 67–69; Roberts 1979, p. 7.

98 Fyhrvall 1880, p. 73; Israel 1989, p. 300–304.

99 "Resol. för Tiäru. Compagniet. 1682" in Samling utaf Kong... (1760) p. 483–485.

As a consequence of sluggish economic progress, reorganization of the monopoly was reconsidered. Previously, the word "company" had been used to denote a corporation which traded tar under a certain privilege and enjoyed a kind of monopoly in its own field. At this time, however, the character of such corporations changed, and instead of "company" the word "society" was more often used. Societies did not enjoy the same kind of monopoly as companies. Actually, the model was closer to that of a joint-stock company or cooperative.[100]

In July 1689, a new privilege was issued, which covered a larger portion of the territory of Sweden than the former privileges. However, the new privilege was partly based on the privilege of 1654, and historian Oscar Fyhrvall subsequently characterized the new era as a 26-year "industry of tar slavery."[101] The position of Sweden as a superpower in the Baltic Sea area was also consolidated around 1689. Therefore, the state once more assumed stricter control of the tar trade. The privilege eventually came to cover the whole of Sweden, except the island of Gotland.[102]

Shortly after the privilege was published, the Netherlands expressed its discontent. With the assistance of the Dutch ambassador, van Haarem, the Netherlands formulated a complaint in which it accused Sweden of breach of contract. The newly established monopoly was at the centre of these accusations. From Sweden's perspective, its actions were justified, as the name of the new entity was the tar society instead of the tar company, which clearly indicated that this was not a question of a monopoly. However, these semantics failed to calm the Dutch.[103] The tar society, however, enjoyed a wider trading area than the previous tar company. For the first time, it exercised control of the domestic tar trade, as its privilege covered the whole of Sweden. Nevertheless, the society faced the same general problems as earlier. For instance, production continued to exceed export demand, which forced control of the trade through customs duties.[104]

In January 1697, the society's four-year contract was coming to an end and the King signed a letter directed to the Commercial Collegium covering 24 specific articles concerning the society's practical operations, mainly involving amounts of tar, old tar, the responsibilities of the Commercial Collegium, smuggling or other kinds of cheating, and payments. The articles did not refer

100 "Öppit bref för Tiäru-Compagniet 1689" in Samling utaf Kong... (1760) p. 78–79, 81.

101 Fyhrvall 1880, p. 84–92.

102 "Öppit bref för Tiäru-Compagniet 1689" in Samling utaf Kong... (1760) p. 78–83.

103 Privilegibrevet, *Ämnessamlingar, Handel och sjöfart, no.* 78 , RAS; "Öppit bref för Tiäru-Compagniet 1689" in Samling utaf Kong... (1760) p. 78.

104 "Bref om Tullen på Träwärcke 1689" in Samling utaf Kong... (1760) p. 84–85.

to the society's internal actions, but prescribed rules for the society's functioning with other actors, which demonstrates that the society's internal decisions were made without the King's influence. Subsequently, the privileges became contracts between the Crown and the society.[105]

In summer 1697, the King's Chancellery signed an official contract with the society over the trade in tar. Henceforth, the society's role was more like that of an agent steering trade between producers and foreign merchants. The main reason for this change was the realization that the old system enabled smuggling between cities. The rules regarding the rights of directors and shareholders were similar to those in 1698. The contract also had a set duration: in the society's case, four years.[106] Consequently, a new contract was signed in 1702 in Bielewitz, Poland, during the Great Northern war. The content was nevertheless similar to that of the earlier contract.[107]

The tar society was dissolved in 1712 during the Great Northern War. Sweden maintained high tar prices. The English, in particularly, had begun to produce their own tar in their new colonies, mostly in North America.[108]

10 Conclusions

The tar company existed in multiple forms for 64 years. In contrast to Dutch or English companies, the central idea of the tar company was based on trade in one sales article. Conversely, the operating principle of Dutch and English companies was to dominate trade in certain geographical areas and became the major source of public finance.[109] Partly for these reasons, the tar company represents an early model of a company which was hopelessly dysfunctional. The company's own directors could not entirely define the company's internal rules, because the Crown set most of these. Moreover, Sweden had little experience of companies, and when the tar company was founded in 1648, it disrupted existing commercial activities. The privilege artificially created a new supply chain: peasant producers could sell tar only to city burghers, and city burghers could sell tar only to company agents in their own home cities. This trading path was also controlled by fixed prices and fixed sales volumes. As a result, the unfettered freedom to practice one's own occupation was destroyed.

105 "Bref om Tiäruhandelen 1697" in Samling utaf Kong... (1760) p. 631–635.
106 "Contract om Tiäruhandelen 1697" in Samling utaf Kong... (1760) p. 660–668.
107 "Contract med Interessenterne uti Tjäruhandelen 1702" in Samling utaf Kong... (1760) p. 899–909.
108 Waris approx. 1940, p. 117.
109 McLean 2004, p. 365.

During the first decades of its existence, the tar company provoked an exceptional number of complaints from producers as well as local and Dutch merchants; moreover, the structure of the company continually changed as it was dissolved and re-established. The Swedish Commercial Collegium attempted to address these complaints by introducing regulations that are more democratic. Unfortunately, the conflict between the merchants in the cities and the Swedish Crown made smooth operation of the company impossible. A monopoly was granted and revoked several times after 1648: in 1660, 1672, 1682 and 1689. The last company – or, to be precise, society – no longer enjoyed a monopoly position. It had moved a few steps closer to becoming a joint stock company as we understand the term today.

How did the company's "articles of association," its privileges, improve over the decades? The first tar company was granted a tar privilege for twenty years, and it was run by four directors, who also constituted the majority of its main investors. An eight-member board comprising minor shareholders, called assistants, formally represented individual shareholders. Their role was solely to conduct inspections and offer advice to the directors; their power was extremely limited. This pattern of management caused numerous complaints, because of which the new statute of 1654 increased the number of investors and made the leadership more democratic. The next privilege, in 1660, did not interfere in the management of the company except to specify the amount shareholders were required to invest.

However, the 1666 instruction profoundly altered the management structure. Now there were to be three directors with specific fields, and their tenure was of fixed duration. The board had 16 members with a consulting role. The privilege of 1672 included no new articles on the management. However, in 1689, the management structure was rearranged yet again. Two of the four directors were replaced every third year. Shareholders with investments of 1000 dalers exercised one vote. Those with smaller investments could gather together to share one vote. These management changes illustrated the progress from the early stages of the company. However, they probably developed from the needs of the king instead of from internal needs.

Furthermore, the Crown micromanaged control of sales at every level, using the privileges. Moreover, from the very first privilege, the amounts of tar traded and the size of the barrels were strictly controlled, as were the purchase and resale prices and customs duties. Sweden's mercantilist commercial policy ultimately proved unsustainable. Gradually, the structure of supervision evolved, as can be observed in the legislation. In 1689, there was still mention of customs duties and amounts of tar, but its character had altered. They were no longer the king's sole focus. Tar regulation had become more diverse and the scope had expanded.

Eventually, the most significant and powerful of the privileges concerned both currency and control of debts and loans. The year 1661 saw the beginning of a new phase, when the Commercial Collegium was given the main responsibility for the tar company. Sweden was heading for major financial difficulties, and economic policy required a dedicated College focused on one issue. By issuing orders concerning payments, the College governed the company's financial resources. It made mistakes and experienced failures, but was nevertheless able to maintain a tolerable balance in Sweden's financial affairs. The company evolved from being the company of a monarch to something closer to a state-owned company.

Interpreting mercantilist ideology creates challenges for historians. How can trade be separated from state and government, and is it even possible or necessary? Essentially, the state formulated the statutes which created the company's operational framework. In a sense, this meant that the state or monarch exercised full control. But did this make the tar companies state-owned companies? To answer this question requires a discussion of the differences and similarities between the concept of nation and business. In the seventeenth century, Swedish trading was highly polarized, with controlled trade in the cities and less regulated trade between peasants in the countryside. The cities could be described as outwardly regulated by the monarchy, but still part of regulated society. The lower level of the cities comprised its inhabitants, the citizens, who obeyed the rules imposed by the monarch. This tempted rulers to supervise trade through control of the cities. Nevertheless, the problem with the pattern was the citizens themselves, who were not steerable like machines. Instead, they wished to satisfy their own desires. This separates the state from trade, as the citizens rather than the government conducted trade. The tar company was designed to control these agents: peasants, traders, foreign buyers, and investors. However, it was doomed to failure. Still, the saga of the company was essential for further development.

The legal character of the tar company also exemplified changes in ideas and influences, which came from many directions. The Netherlands, England and France all affected it to some degree. Moreover, Sweden was in turn ruled by the Crown or the Royal Regency, which had opposing interests. The Regency was an arena for competing high nobility, whereas the King or Queen exercised absolute power, depending of course on their personality. The legal character of the Companies thus could not develop steadily. Rather, evolution occurred in sudden leaps and sometimes movement was even backwards. This development was fettered by constant complaints, slow tar markets, Sweden's relations with foreign powers, and by changes in mercantilist ideology. However, the apparent trigger for evolution of the legal character of the tar company was the numerous cancellations of privileges. These provided necessary pauses for new regulations to mature, and the new privilege was always able to learn something from its predecessors. After trial and error, a more serene era began when the tar trade was opened and liberalized.

Unprinted Sources

Riksarkivet Stockholm (RAS), Ämnessamlingar, Handel och sjöfart, no. 12, no. 63.

Source Editions

Samling utaf kongl. Bref, stadgar och forordningar angaende Sweriges Rikes commerce, politie och oeconomie, vol. 1 Stiernman, And. Anton von (ed.) (Stockholm: Kong. Tryckeriet, 1747).

Sweriges Rikes commerce. politie och oeconomie uti gemen uppå Hans Kongl.Maj:ts nodigsta belfallning, vol 2. Stiernman, And. Anton von (ed.) (Stockholm: Kong. tryckeriet, 1750).

Samling utaf Kong. Bref, Stadgar och förordningar angående Sweriges Rikes commerce, politie och oeconomie, vol. 3, Stiernman, And. Anton von (ed.) (Stockholm: Tryckeriet, 1753).

Samling utaf Kong. Bref, Stadgar och förordningar ungående Sweriges Rikes commerce, politie och oeconomie, vol. 4, Stiernman, And. Anton von (ed.) (Stockholm: Tryckeriet, 1760).

Literature

Aalto, Seppo. 2012. "Helsinki, tervakaupunki" in Jensen-Eriksen, Niklas. Lappalainen, Mirkka. Nurmiainen, Jouko and Siltala, Sakari (eds.), *Kansallinen kapitalismi, kansainvälinen talous* (Helsinki: Siltala).

Aalto, Seppo. 2012. *Sotakaupunki, Helsingin Vanhankaupungin historia 1550–1639* (Helsinki: Otava, 2012).

Amend-Traut, Anja. 2017. "Legal Structure of Early Enterprises – from Commenda-like Arrangements to Chartered Joint-Stock Companies" in De ruysscher et al. (eds.).

Bergh, Severin (ed.). 1906. *Handlingar rörande Sveriges historia. Svenska riksrådets protokoll 1645, 1646*, tredje serien, Part xi. (Stockholm 1906).

Björnsson, Anders & Magnusson, Lars (eds.). 2011. *Jordpäron, Svensk ekonomihistorisk läsebok* (Stockholm: Bokförlaget Atlantis).

De ruysscher, D. Cordes, A. Dauchy, S. and Pihlajamäki, H. (eds.). 2017. *The Company in Law and Practice: Did Size Matter? (Middle Ages – Nineteenth Century)*, (Leiden-Boston: Brill).

Fyhrvall, Karl Oskar. 1880. *Svenska Handelslagstiftningens historia, Tjärhandelskompanierna* (Stockholm).

Gardberg, Carl Jacob. 1981. "Kaupunkilaitos keskiajalla ja uuden ajan alussa" in Gardberg, C.J., Tommila, Päiviö and Endén, Rauno (eds.) *Suomen kaupunkilaitoksen historia* (Helsinki: Suomen kaupunkiliitto).

Gephen-Jager, Ella. Soling, Gerard van and Timmerman, Levinus (eds.). 2005. *VOC 1602–2002; 400 Years of Company Law* (Dordrecht: Kluwer).

Hallberg, Annagreta. 1959. "Tjärexport och tjärhandelskompanier" in Steinby, Torsten (ed.), *Historiska och litteraturhistoriska studier no 34*, (Helsinki: Svenska litteratursällskapet i Finland), 86–190.

Heckscher, Eli F. 1954. *An Economic History of Sweden* (Cambridge: Harvard University).

Heckscher, Eli. 1953. *Merkantilismen* (Stockholm: P.A. Norstedt & Söners Förlag).

Hofstraeten, Bram van. 2017. "Delving for Diversity in Early Modern Company Law: Mining Companies in Seventeenth-Century Liège" in De ruysscher et al. (eds.).

Israel, Jonathan I. 1989. *Dutch Primacy in World Trade, 1585–1740* (Oxford: Clarendon Press).

Israel, Jonathan. 1995. *The Dutch Republic, Its Rise, Greatness and Fall 1477–1806* (Oxford: Clarendon Press).

Kirby, David. 1990. *Northern Europe in the Early Modern Period; The Baltic World 1492–1772* (London: Longman).

Kirby, David and Hinkkanen, Merja-Liisa. 2000. *The Baltic and the North Seas* (London – New York: Routledge).

Klein, Peter Wolfgang. 1992. "A New Look at an Old Subject: Dutch Trade Policies in the Age of Mercantilism" in Groenveld, Simon & Wintle, Michael (eds.) *State and Trade, Government and the Economy in Britain and the Netherlands since the Middle Ages* (Zutphen: Walburg Press).

Korpiola, Mia & Ojala-Fulwood, Maija. 2019. "Controlling Immigrants in Sweden, ca. 1520–1620: Norms, Regulation, and Legal Practice" in Anette Baumann, Alexander Jendorff & Frank Theisen (eds.), *Religion – Migration – Integration. Studies on the Reciprocal Effects of Religiously Motivated Mobility in Pre-Modern Europe* (Tübingen: Mohrsiebeck).

Korpiola, Mia. 2018. "High and Late Medieval Scandinavia, Codified Vernacular Law and Learned Legal Influences" in Pihlajamäki, Heikki, Dubber, Markus, Godfrey, Mark (eds.), *The Oxford Handbook of European Legal History* (Oxford: Oxford University Press).

Kuisma, Markku. 2016. *Metsäteollisuuden maa; Suomi, metsät ja kansainvälinen järjestelmä 1620–1920*. (Helsinki: Suomalaisen kirjallisuuden seura).

Lappalainen, Mirkka. 2017. "Loyal Servants of the King and the Crown (1620–1680) – Stewards and Governors in Sweden before the Age of Absolutism" in Karonen, Petri and Hakanen, Marko (eds.) *Personal Agency at the Swedish Age of Greatness 1560–1720* (Helsinki: The Finnish Literature Society).

Lappalainen, Mirkka. 2006. *Maailman painavin raha; kirjoituksia 1600 – luvun Pohjolasta* (Helsinki: Werner Söderström Osakeyhtiö).

Lindkvist, Thomas & Sjöberg, Maria. 2010. *Det Svenska samhället 800–1720; Klerkernas och adelns tid* (Lund: Studentlitteratur).

Nováky, György. 1990. *Handelskompanier och kompanihandel; Svenska Afrikakompaniet 1649–1663, En studie i feodal handel* (Uppsala; Acta Universitatis Upsaliensis).

McLean, Janet. 2004. "The Transnational Corporation in History: Lessons for Today?", *Indiana Law Journal*, vol. 79, 2, 363–377.

Müller, Leos. 1998. *The Merchant Houses of Stockholm, c. 1640–1800; A Comparatively Study of Early-Modern Entrepreneurial Behaviour* (Uppsala: Uppsala University Library).

Möller, Sylvi. 1954. *Suomen tapulikaupunkien valtaporvaristo ja sen kaupankäyntimenetelmät 1600-luvun alkupuolella*, Dissertation (University of Helsinki, 1954).

Odhner, Clas Theodor. 1865. *Sveriges inre Historia under Drottning Christinas Förmyndare* (Stockholm: P.A. Norstedt & Söner).

Palmén, Ernst Gustaf. 1876. *Historisk framställning af den svensk-finska handelslagstiftningen från Gustaf Vasas regering till 1766* (Helsinki: J.C. Frenckell & Son).

Pihlajamäki, Heikki. 2018. "The Birth of Commercial law in Early Modern Sweden" in Pihlajamäki, Heikki, Cordes, Albrecht, Dauchy, Serge and De ruysscher, Dave (eds.), *Understanding the Sources of Early Modern and Modern Commercial Law: Courts, Statutes, Contracts, and Legal Scholarship* (Leiden-Boston: Brill).

Ranta, Raimo. 1975. *Turun kaupungin historia 1600–1721*, (Turku).

Roberts, Michael. 1979. *The Swedish Imperial Experience 1560–1718* (Cambridge: University Press).

Runefelt, Leif. 2001. *Hushållningens dygder. Affektlära, hushållningslära och ekonomiskt tankande under svensk stormaktstid* (Stockholm: Almqvist & Wiksell International).

Ruuth, J.W. and Halila, Aimo. 1974. *Viipurin kaupungin historia 1617–1710* (Helsinki: Torkelin säätiö).

Kari Tarkiainen. 2000. "Kustaa Vaasasta Ruotsin ajan loppuun. Kaarle IX" in *Suomen hallitsijat* (Porvoo: Weiling+Göös).

Tikka, Katja. 2016. "Kauppaa ja laivoja, Komppaniatoiminnan kehityspiirteitä 1600-luvun Itämerellä" in Tapio Bergholm (ed.), *Työ merellä, Nautica Fennica 2015–2016* (Helsinki: Suomen merimuseo).

Turpeinen, Oiva. 2010. *Mustan kullan maa; Tervan historia* (Somero: Amanita).

Waris, Heikki. approx. 1940. *Tervakauppakomppania vuosina 1648–1661* (University of Helsinki).

Wirta, Kaarle, *Dark Horses of Business, Overseas Entrepreneurship in seventeenth-Century Nordic Trade in the Indian and Atlantic Oceans*, Dissertation (Leiden University, 2018).

Ylikangas, Heikki. 1986. *Käännekohdat Suomen historiassa* (Porvoo: WSOY).

Åström, Swen-Erik. 1988. *From Tar to Timber. Studies in Northeast European forest exploitation and foreign trade 1660–1860* (Helsinki: The Finnish Society of Sciences and Letters).

CHAPTER 5

Invisibility and Information: Commercial Legal Practices at the Grass-Roots Level in a Nineteenth-Century Finnish Timber Trading Company

Ulla Ijäs

1 Introduction

In the nineteenth-century Hackman & Co was one of the largest timber exporting firms in the Northern Baltic area and one of the first multi-branch conglomerates in Finland. The firm was established in 1790 by a Bremen-born merchant, Johan Friedrich Hackman. After his death in 1807 the firm was managed and operated by his widow, children and grandchildren. Besides their entrepreneurial duties, the Hackmans participated in legislative work in the Diet of Finland.[1] The company remained a family business until 2003, when it was sold to an Italian investor and later the brand name Hackman merged with Finnish company Fiskars.

This chapter, as a case study, reflects the complex social, cultural and political environment of merchants in nineteenth-century Finland. Furthermore, it illustrates how the common practices of merchant law were understood and adopted, and how these were developed and used in everyday situations at the grass-roots level, which was my research target in the project *The Making of Commercial Law: Common Practices and National Legal Rules from the Middle Ages to the Modern Period*. This chapter, which focuses on the trading house, Hackman & Co, operating in Vyborg (Sw. *Viborg*, Fin. *Viipuri*), adopts a 'law-in-action' viewpoint. Ron Harris noted 'a considerable gap between high discourse and the actual functioning of the legal system' in the eighteenth- and nineteenth-century business world.[2] The chapter asks how legal plurality was addressed in an international business environment. How was information about legal plurality transmitted to the European periphery? How was this

1 The Diet of Finland was the legislative body of the autonomous Grand Duchy of Finland. It assembled every three to five years until 1905. The Diet did not gather in 1809–1863. The Diet of Finland consisted of estates (peasants, burghers, nobles and clergy). Only men were eligible to participate.

2 Harris 2011, p. 10.

DOI:10.1163/9789004436046_006

realized in legislative work in Finland, when the Finnish Diet finally opened in 1863? The importance of combining business and law, as Roger Cotterrell has pointed out in his research, is highlighted in this chapter. Writing legal history from below, that is, by studying a firm and the people involved in the firm and its business, we might discover the development of both business and law.[3]

Unsurprisingly, the answers to these questions are complex. Functioning transnational merchant networks and legal plurality required knowledge and a deep understanding about different legal and juridical institutions. This knowledge helped to support the interests of export merchants when legislation was modernized in Finland in the latter part of the nineteenth century. Then, in their work in the Diet, the Hackmans appeared to be quite conservative, promoting the *status quo* instead of radical modernization.

Despite recent interest in the impact of legal literature on early modern commercial legislation, we still know rather little about the actual interaction between custom and legislation and between commercial actors and legislators. In addition, the discussion focuses on medieval trade and the Law Merchant and to a lesser degree on the late early modern / modern period, when the Industrial Revolution gradually started to increase transnational trade.[4]

In the history of transnational trade, it is a long debated question whether there was a single 'Law Merchant' or *Lex Mercatoria*, originating back in the Middle Ages. Discussion covers whether the Law Merchant functioned and continued because local rulers supported it, or whether no distinct, uniform and trans-regional Law Merchant existed at all. Some scholars have demonstrated the importance of custom in the formation of commercial law. Merchants were key actors when introducing new techniques and contracts, for example, when new ordinances prohibiting mercantile practices were introduced.[5]

Several studies concern central European and, especially, north-western European and North American merchant houses or enterprises and their inputs in the development of mercantile legislation.[6] These studies, however, are not fully applicable to the European northern periphery, where economic and legal conditions were different.

3 Cotterrell 2009, p. 481–500; Harris 2011, p. 7; De ruysscher 2016, p. 158–202, esp. 161.

4 Harris 2011; Karonen 2004, p. 351.

5 De ruysscher 2012, p. 3–29; Trakman 2011, p. 309–310.

6 Flume 2015, p. 45–83; De ruysshcer 2012, footnotes 1-6; Dahlén 2014, p. 57–58.

2 The Local Context: Eastern Finland between Sweden and Russia

Hackman & Co were prominent in local business in the northern Baltic area. During the period studied, roughly from 1812 to the 1880s, Hackman & Co's hometown – Vyborg – was the second largest town in the Grand Duchy of Finland. The town was established by the Swedes in the thirteenth century.[7] In the Great Northern War, in 1721, the town and the surrounding province were taken by the Russians. From 1721 to 1812, Vyborg belonged to the Russian Baltic provinces. In Vyborg and the surrounding Vyborg province, old Swedish legislation was used side by side with Russian proclamations (*ukase*) and ordinances. Old medieval town privileges[8] were affirmed, in 1742, while in 1763, by Catherine II's order, the Swedish law of 1734 was introduced in Vyborg province since it was used in the neighboring Kymmene province, annexed by Russia in 1742 after war between Russia and Sweden. The Swedish law of 1734 was used in civil matters, but in criminal cases the old medieval laws (King Christopher's Law of the Realm and King Magnus Eriksson's Law of the Realm[9]) were still used. In 1785 administrative reforms took place in Russia. New orders concerning trade started to regulate Vyborg merchants. From then on, in Vyborg, as in all Russian provinces, the right to trade was based on individual financial ability to pay certain fees. Previously, in Vyborg, under the old Swedish system the right to trade depended on burger rights.[10]

In 1812, Vyborg and the surrounding province were incorporated into the autonomous Grand Duchy of Finland. The war between Sweden and Russia had ended three years earlier; Sweden had lost its Finnish territories to Russia; these now formed the Grand Duchy of Finland under Russian rule. In the Grand Duchy of Finland, Swedish legislation remained in force. However, because the legislative organs in Finland did not assemble until 1863, new laws were not enacted. In the Grand Duchy of Finland, '[t]he state had an important, even crucial role in determining the functional environment of business activities because of its "supremacy position"', as Petri Karonen pointed out in

7 Kallioinen 2012, p. 47–57, where he discusses towns in the medieval Baltic Sea region.

8 Vyborg town privileges from 1403 followed Swedish town privileges. From 1721 to 1812 and even later during the nineteenth century, the town government and privileges faced constant challenges from the Russian administration despite the fact that Catherine II enforced the town privileges in 1742. Ruuth 1982, p. 138; Ruuth and Kuujo 1975, p. 165-170; Ruuth 1903. p. 1906.

9 See also page 4–6.

10 About the changes in 1785, see, for example Unianova 2009, p. 3–4.

his study on Finnish business managers.[11] This meant that imperial proclamations and statutes as well as bilateral agreements with sovereign states regulated trade during the nineteenth century.

In nineteenth-century Finland, legislation could not develop in the same way as in those countries with functioning legislative institutions. Hence, in transnational trade, customs and merchants' endeavours to find bi- and multilateral agreements should be highlighted. In this chapter, I will discuss the importance of information, knowledge and transnational networks as one of the key aspects in transnational trade and development of legislative processes. I will suggest that Finland, connected with trading networks for European trade, was not, in the business context, on the periphery, despite lacking modernization in legislation. Especially when studying Hackman & Co – operating in Vyborg, which was in the Finnish context especially an international town – and the Hackmans – connected by family ties to German timber trading families – highlighting the peripheral context would be a deep misunderstanding of contemporary circumstances. Transnational ties and proximity to the Russian metropolis of St. Petersburg – Vyborg being only 150 kilometers or two days by horse, one by train or by sail from St. Petersburg – Vyborg export merchants were deeply embedded in the transnational business environment. Viewpoints of Eastern Finland are highlighted when Hackman men participated in legislative work; they were highly tolerant towards Russia and did not want to disrupt the prevailing political situation although they promoted liberal customs policies when expressing their opinions in the Diet of Finland.

In Finland, the absence of a working legislative organ for most of the nineteenth century is usually seen as the reason for slow progress in markets and legislation. Economic and social changes were reflected in legislation only in the last three decades of the nineteenth century. Old customs and law codes were very much in use and applied in the nineteenth century. Besides, imperial orders and ordinances regulated trade as well as bilateral agreements with other sovereign states. Traditional ways of arranging business – a family firm or a merchant house – were capable of fulfilling the needs of business and the economy until the latter part of the century, when industrialization started to take place in the country. Then, the discussion in the Diet of Finland focused especially on customs and monetary reforms. The law on joint-stock companies was not introduced until 1864.[12]

11 Karonen 2004, p. 350–354. With an English abstract Masters and Politicians. Business Managers as Economic and Political Actors in Finland, 1600–1920.

12 *Hans Kejserliga Majestäts Nådiga Förordning, om anonyma- eller aktie-bolag.* Gifwen i Helsingfors, den 24 Nowember 1864.

A major contribution to a wider understanding of the nineteenth-century business and legal situation in Finland is that the leading businessmen were almost invisible in the courts of law. This chapter explains that situation with network theories adapted by several business historians. They highlight the importance of stability; if trust in the network had broken, the existence of the whole network would have been at risk. In particular, taking disputes to institutional organs such as courts of law might mean that disputes became institutionalized. Instead of such institutions and legal proceedings, the merchant community trusted in negotiating and other less 'fatal' institutions than courts of law, i.e. consuls, whose negotiating skills and knowledge of common codes of conduct were trusted in dispute situations.[13]

A change can be traced appearing gradually during the nineteenth century; a new generation of educated businessmen with their liberal ideas was born in the latter part of the century. At the same time, Hackman & Co and some of their peers preferred the old guild-based privilege system. The nineteenth century was an interesting period in the history of merchant houses. Then, gradual change occurred and the old system based on guilds and privileges vanished. Industrialization, the complexity of trade and the collapse of old communal values gave room for a new type of individual entrepreneurs. This meant that not only new institutions but also new legislation concerning trade were necessary.[14]

The chapter takes the form of a case-study and is based on empirical research of business archives consisting of letters between the multi-branch Hackman & Co and their business partners. Business archives consist mainly of letters and copy letters. Merchants copied all posted letters in order to have legally valid documents whenever needed.[15] From the extensive archival document series, I picked every fifth year, from 1815 to the 1860s, for more detailed examination. In the nineteenth century, only copies of letters sent from Hackman & Co are available; the letters received series started in 1884 but I have not used these in this study.[16] Besides business letters, court records and petitions to the governing institutions concerning litigation, as well as the protocols of the Diet, are also considered in this chapter. The focus is on the first part of the

13 Makko and Müller (eds.) 2015; Brand and Müller (eds.) 2007; Kallioinen 2012, p. 98–99; Ogilvie 2011, p. 4–5, 433: Müller 2004; Müller 1988.

14 Ogilvie 2011, p. 97–112; Faundez 2016, p. 373–419; Keskinen 2012, with an English summary Private and Public Interests. Kallioinen 2012; Müller 1988.

15 Ogilvie 2011, p. 344–390; Müller 1988, p. 225, 245, 274.

16 Some volumes are destroyed; for example, 1850. Hence, I have also read complementary volumes around these destroyed materials/years.

nineteenth century, using letters and litigation, and on the latter part of the century, studying political influence.

3 The Company

In the nineteenth century, Hackman & Co was mainly a timber trading company, which owned sawmills, exported timber and imported salt and colonial goods. In 1790, together with his business partner J.S. Ignatius, J.F. Hackman established a company, which at that time was called Ignatius & Hackman. The partnership ended in 1807 when J.F. Hackman died suddenly. Both Ignatius and Hackman were consuls in Vyborg; Ignatius was the Danish consul and Hackman obtained his post as Prussian consul in 1803.

Because a partnership had no legal personality distinct from that of its members, it ended whenever one of its members died, retired or was otherwise unable to carry on business. When Hackman died, Ignatius wanted to retire and left the daily management of the firm to the widow, then 32-year-old Marie Hackman.[17] From 1811 to 1816, Marie Hackman did business under the name J.F. Hackmans Wittwe until she changed the name to Hackman & Co. Then, she wrote a circular letter (in German and in English) to all her business partners.

> The encrease [sic] of my trade and other Family relations enduce [sic] me to take into Copartnerhisp Mr. George Augspurg my proved Friend and manager of my Business these eight years past. My eldest son also soon in the age to be a useful member of the house, I change its Firm into Hackman & Co [...][18]

Hackman & Co was a typical family firm or merchant house in early modern Europe. According to Ron Harris, 'in its origins, the *compagnia* was a closed family partnership' where family members invested their capital and labour. The continental European *société generale* descended from the *compagnia*. Beside these, Harris points out a third type for organizing trade; *commenda* or *societas maris*, which gradually developed for maritime business purposes. In a *societas maris*, the partnership was limited for short-term purposes and partners had different duties and liabilities; usually one partner invested money and other contributed labour. This type of organized maritime business spread

17 Harris 2011, p. 20–21; Tigerstedt 1940, p. 191–218.

18 ELKA, Hackman & Co, B 33, Circular letter, 31st Dec. 1815.

gradually from Italy to the northern German ports and led eventually to limited partnership.[19]

J.F. Hackman, Marie Hackman, J.F. Hackman Jr. and Hackman & Co owned shares in several sawmills and ships.[20] Some of these partnerships were short-term and based on the *societas maris* type of partnership agreement. In the 1790s, J.F. Hackman owned shares in several ships together with other Vyborg merchants and ship captains, who typically were from the Low Countries. For example, the *Frouw Fredrica* was owned by J.F. Hackman (4/8), a fellow Vyborg merchant Jacob Johan Seseman (3/8) and Haye Tadsen from Amsterdam, who was also the captain of the ship with his 1/8 share. The *Frouw Fredrica* carried seal oil and timber from Vyborg and imported salt from the Mediterranean Sea.[21]

From the late 1820s, Hackman & Co was owned by Marie Hackman (1/4), George Augspurg (1/4), J.F. Hackman Jr (1/4) and Paul Wahl (1/4). After Augspurg's death in 1831 and Paul Wahl's departure in 1848, the company remained mostly in the hands of the Hackman family until the twentieth century. The family members took care of daily management; sons and sons-in-law were introduced to the business. J.F. Hackman Jr. and his sons studied business in European trading houses; they stayed around a year each in several trading houses, learning the trade in practice, and some studied in special business schools established in the mid-eighteenth century in Germany. J.F. Hackman Jr.'s eldest son Woldemar Hackman studied at one of these schools in the Bremen merchant academy. Later, he became the Spanish vice-consul in Vyborg and managed Hackman & Co until his sudden death in 1871. Victor Hackman, the third son of J.F. Hackman Jr., studied law at the Imperial Alexander University in Helsinki before starting his career in the family business. The youngest son, Wilhelm, studied at the Polytechnic Institute in Stuttgart; his engineering skills proved to be important when the family firm expanded to new branches such as the pulp and steel industries in the late nineteenth century.[22]

J.F. Hackman Jr.'s sons-in-law held important posts in the Finnish administration and participated actively in the family business. The most active in this respect were the husband of eldest daughter Emilie – Court of Appeal judge, lawyer and fellow nobleman, Baron Carl Emil Cedercreutz – and Alexandrine's

19 Amend-Traut 2016, p. 63–83; De ruysscher 2016, p. 158–202; Harris 2011, p. 19–20; Kallioinen 2012, p. 57–58.

20 Tigerstedt 1940, passim.

21 Tigerstedt 1940, p. 270–271.

22 Tigerstedt 1952, p. 39–40, 326–327, 353–354.

FIGURE 5.1
Wilhelm Hackman, ca 1875.

spouse (military) captain Carl August Ekström,[23] who took care of the family businesses in eastern Finland.

J.F. Hackman Jr. died in 1879, after which his children owned the company. However, they stayed as silent partners in the family firm. The operational management was Wilhelm Hackman and C.A. Ekström's responsibility. They answered with their personal assets for the company's liabilities. Others did not bear such liability, but, on the other hand, they could not participate in the management of the company. All profits were shared so that Wilhelm Hackman and C.A. Ekström got one-third each and others (seven in total) shared one-third.[24] When comparing this arrangement with the previous liabilities when Marie Hackman, George Augsburg, J.F. Hackman Jr. and Paul Wahl shared the company in four equal shares, they all bore similar personal liability. This arrangement was not based on law, but instead, their mutual – and most probably oral – agreements.[25]

23 Kotivuori 2005. Ekström was a so-called staff captain (штабс-капитан) and served in the imperial army in several engineering groups. In his youth, he had also worked in the Fiskars iron works.

24 Enbom 1991, p. 49.

25 The Hackman & Co archives have no records on shareholders' liabilities. The information given here is based on Örnulf Tigerstedt's company history written in the 1940s.

The firm remained a family firm during the nineteenth and twentieth century. This old model of a family firm or merchant house functioned well if the family members found it profitable and if they were willing to invest their time and energy in the company. The family firm was the most common way to organize business in larger European trading centres at the time. In Antwerp, for example, 56 per cent of firms were family firms. In family firms, business transactions as well as agreements between the partners/family members were typically unwritten and flexible.[26] Hence, when the family firm was the prevailing type for organizing trade, the need for structured legislation was less than in situations when companies included non-family associates and partners. The owners of Hackman & Co did not see it as profitable enough to become a pure joint-stock company (*aktiebolag*), which became possible in 1864 under an Imperial statute. In Finland, joint-stock companies started gradually becoming more general after the 1880s when business expanded and demanded more economic capital which investors could bring into the business.

It seems that Hackman & Co stayed in the hands of a single family because it had enough resources, i.e. financial and human capital. After J.F. Hackman

FIGURE 5.2
J. F. Hackman, ca 1865.

26 De ruysscher 2016, p. 194.

Jr's death, sons, sons-in-law and grandsons guaranteed with their commitment that the company always had competent management. They were careful in business ventures and always prioritized the company and family instead of quick profits. This circumspection becomes visible in litigation – this is almost non-existent and consists of only minor issues but never large and complex matters. Especially in the 1860s, when speculation in Finnish business was high, the Hackmans' solid and careful approach, based on valid information, was valued internationally. Long tradition in business gave them a trusted position which was not threatened by imprudent disputes in courts of law. One of the company's twentieth-century leaders expressed the family firm's values by saying that 'Truly, there are those who believe that ruthlessness can bring a permanent victory. I think that these gentlemen forgot that carefulness, patience and consideration will be the foundation for trust which will be, when time goes by, a much greater asset than all short-term victories.'[27] This attitude differs from modern business attitudes, where rapid economic victories are the primary goals in business. As Dave De ruysscher has suggested, by studying entrepreneurs' social background it might also be possible to find out more precise information on the organization of trade from the legal perspective. Family firms and modern joint-stock companies, at the time of industrialization, might reveal a change in business, courts of law and government policies.[28]

4 Local Practices

4.1 *Law*

During most of the nineteenth century in Vyborg, in principle, the law code which was followed was the Swedish law of the Realm of 1734. Besides the law of 1734, the so-called *Handelsorning*,[29] or trade ordinance, issued in 1734, defined the premises of trade. According to the law and the ordinance, trade transactions should be based on mutual agreement with flawless goods and between two men with permission to trade. The trade ordinance prescribes quite thoroughly who could hold a licence to conduct trade and how they should be trained. Most importantly, traders should have a privilege; a

27 Henry Hackman in 1965. *Hackman & Co 1790–1965* (1965). Translation from Finnish by U. Ijäs.

28 De ruysscher 2016, p. 201–202.

29 "Den 19. Dec. [1734] Allmän Förordning för dem, som här i Riket wilja fåra och drifwa handelen" in Utdrag Utur utur alle ifrån den 7. decemb. 1718/1791 utkomne publique handlingar.

merchant-to-be should seek the burghers' permission from the town magistrate and prove a commitment to the town by undertaking to live there for at least six years after swearing the burgher's oath. Furthermore, those who dedicate themselves to the wholesale trade cannot commit to the retail trade. Trade can be carried out only in towns or – if in the countryside – only on special market days. According to mercantilist policies, only staple town merchants could engage in the import and export trade.[30]

Trade was a privileged profession and merchants constituted a privileged institution in much the same way as the medieval guilds. Merchants' organization into a special society in Vyborg is unclear, although the 1734 trade ordinance required these societies in the staple towns.[31] This ordinance was remodelled in 1859 and replaced with the issue of an imperial ordinance, which follows the Swedish one but is more particular when listing the skills required of a future wholesale merchant (*grosshandlare*). For example, one requirement was to speak Russian, German, English and French but not Swedish or Finnish.[32] At the time, Swedish was the language of the administration in the Grand Duchy of Finland. This meant that those wholesale merchants who did not speak Swedish had to use lawyers or advocates in law if they wanted to proceed in court. The language the Hackmans spoke was German, but they could speak and write Swedish, while several family members knew Russian, English and French, too. Hence, language was not an issue when taking disputes to local courts of law.

The law and ordinances did not, however, state how traders, i.e., burghers, should organize their trade when joining as business partners or whenever they formed a company. This notion highlights Finland as the 'periphery' of law and jurisdiction. In continental Europe, there were such legally diversified forms of organizing trade as in France, where the *Code de commerce* in the early nineteenth century defined, and to some extent typologized, company types. A great many of these partnerships were based on oral contracts between trading partners, as was the custom in larger European towns and companies at the time.[33] The paperwork concerning Ignatius & Hackman and later Hackman & Co does not include any written documents concerning the organization of responsibilities between the partners.

30 Merchants in staple towns were allowed to engage in the import and export trade. The staple system was based on seventeenth-century Swedish legislation. In Finland, the system was abolished in 1879. Vyborg recovered its former staple rights in 1816.

31 Wolff 2014, p. 249; Nyberg 2012, p. 15–17.

32 Hans Kejserliga Majestäts Nådiga Förordning angående wilkoren för winnande af burskap å großhandel i Finland. Den 29. Junii 1850.

33 De ruysscher 2016, p. 169, 171.

In the Hackman & Co letters, particular acts and limitations concerning the export trade are discussed briefly. For example, in 1860, Hackman & Co informed their British partner Dahl in London that 'besides [the] cargoes of lathwood only are not allowed to be shipped from Finland, it being permitted to ship one fathom of lathwood every 10 strd of deals'.[34] These regulations and acts are much understudied; subject to and based on empirical evidence from the letters it is almost impossible to trace which act or imperial protocol was discussed, used and applied in each case. As the above example illustrates, in some cases, the orders were extremely particular, limiting trading to a certain type of good or amount of particular goods. If the partner could not agree with the protocol or violated it, Hackman & Co could always claim that they only followed the rules given by the sovereign majesty.

4.2 *Litigation*

The empirical data do not consist of a single example of litigation where Hackman & Co would have pleaded to a particular law code or acted either in Finland or elsewhere. In addition, the letters contain no trace of any transnational, coherent or autonomous law concerning merchants. Instead, as illustrated above, Russian imperial statues and ordinances were discussed when explaining why trading was sometimes prohibited or impossible.[35] These discussions did not cause any lengthy disagreements, let alone litigation. Typically, the language used in letters was very conciliatory and polite. For example, in 1860, when a London agent sold timber to a Hackman business partner in England at a lower price than Hackman & Co would agree, Hackman & Co wrote that the incident caused 'an unpleasantness' but threatening to take the agent to court was not an issue.[36]

The empirical evidence suggests that only occasionally did Hackman & Co need to threaten proceedings in court. One explanation for this invisibility in local courts of law might be geographical. A partner's place of residence might be unknown, as was the case in 1825, when Hackman & Co tried to force lieutenant von Fock to pay a 14 000-ruble debt to Mr. Cramer, who had mutual businesses with Hackman & Co. Unfortunately, no-one seemed to know where von Fock lived at the moment.[37] Identifying and locating the business partner

34 ELKA, Hackman & Co, B 108, 15 June 1860 to Dahl in London.

35 See for example ELKA, Hackman & Co, B 55, to Menvielle, Wetterström & Co in Malaga, 25 April 1827. This letter will be discussed later in this chapter.

36 ELKA, Hackman & Co, B 108, to Dahl in London, 14th March 1860. Agents in international trade, see Kallioinen 2012, p. 103–104.

37 ELKA, Hackman & Co, B 51, to Cramer in St. Petersburg, 16 March 1825; 27 March 1825.

was crucial: without valid information about the actual person responsible, a merchant had only a slight hope of redeeming his payments.

When studying the court protocols from the local town court (magistrates court, *Viborgs rådstuvurätt / Viipurin raastuvanoikeus*) and the Vyborg Court of Appeal (*Viborgs hovrätt / Viipurin hovioikeus*) we may establish that Hackman & Co or the members of the Hackman family were not very often represented in the court. In the lower court, not a single case involves Hackman & Co.[38] In the Vyborg Court of Appeal, some litigation concerned Hackman & Co or members of the Hackman family.[39] One of the few cases Hackman & Co was involved in was discussed in the Court of Appeal in June 1855. Then Hackman & Co, together with Paul Wahl and a District Judge (*Häradshöv(/f)dingen*), from Rautalampi parish in central Finland, appealed to the court to organize a forest inspection in Rautalampi parish in order to measure the timber which would be ready for cutting and sawing in Hackman and Wahl's sawmills.[40] The litigation illustrates the Court of Appeal's administrative role more than the actual disputes merchants were involved in.

Later the same year, the Vyborg Court of Appeal took on other litigation involving Hackman & Co. Then, a widow – Anastasia Ponomareff from Nilsiä in north-eastern Finland – was unable to provide timber promised for Hackman & Co. This was a clear breach of contract and Hackman & Co appealed to a court of law. However, the Vyborg Court of Appeal transferred the case to Iidensalmi district court, where local disputes were to be discussed and resolved.[41]

In 1865, yet another administrative appeal was dealt with in the Vyborg Court of Appeal. Hackman & Co, together with Paul Wahl & Co and some other merchant houses, applied to the Court of Appeal to reduce town taxes in

38 In the Hackman & Co archive, previous researchers have searched through the Magistrates Court protocols and find no cases that involved Hackman & Co or members of the Hackman family as defendant or claimant. Only the cases of J.F. Hackman sr.'s accidental death and the suicide of a clerk forced members of the Hackman family to the courtroom. See ELKA, Hackman & Co, Sandelin file, notes. My own research including certain sample years corroborates the fact that Hackman's participation in the local court was very low. Other merchants, usually small haberdashers and other lesser merchants, resolved their disputes in this court.

39 I have searched every fifth year since 1840. The work is time-consuming since no case diaries are available until the 1880s.

40 KA, Vyborg Court of Appeal Protocols (Viipurin hovioikeuden arkisto), Caa:17, Civil Case protocols, 1855, 11 June 1855.

41 KA, Vyborg Court of Appeal Protocols, (Viipurin hovioikeuden arkisto), Caa:17, Civil Case protocols, 1855, 16 July 1855.

Joensuu in eastern Finland, in the area where they owned sawmills. The Governor, however, refused and the Court of Appeal agreed with the Governor.[42]

If disputes did not proceed to court, we might ask why they had such tolerance, since there must have been disputes and disagreements over prices, the quality of timber, delivery terms, or payment for timber. An explanation might be that merchants governed their affairs through an informal system of justice, noted by contemporaries. In all of the cases where evidence was given, a court of law did not rely on any specific article of law.[43] There is no reference to a uniform body of transnational law on which merchants would have relied in litigation. Rather, it was a code of conduct, mutually employed, negotiated and applied in complex situations. Hence, I would agree with Leon Trakman in his conclusion that '[a]bstract notions of a self-ordering and self-perpetuating Law Merchant are romantic at best.'[44]

At the local level, in the town court, small-scale merchants and lesser businesses claimed their interests or were sued in litigation. Hackman & Co, as an export trading company, mainly did business with foreign business partners: hence their disputes were dealt with on foreign soil. Total absence in the lowest courts of law may also indicate that a large company dealt with their minor disputes outside the courtroom. This may illustrate that they were not involved in complex arguments – which would have needed outside intervention – or they solved problems by negotiating. The absence of court cases may also indicate that the legislation on which the court based its decisions was inefficient for solving complex transnational litigation.[45] Furthermore, the evidence suggests that smaller businesses were sensitive to criticism and their sense of honour demanded strengthening from (neutral) outsiders, i.e. court(s) of law. The reputation of wealthy and powerful merchants was more solid and they had either more flexible or more efficient ways of dealing with their dispute issues than the local lower courts.

Wealthy and powerful merchants focused on continuity and hence avoided open confrontation with governing bodies and, more importantly, with their business partners. As Leos Müller, for example, has shown, taking disputes to court was the ultimate act and merchants refrained from taking their disputes to the courtroom whenever possible since this might disrupt mutual trust and security and disconnect network ties. Long-term profitability and the proper functioning of the market were preferred. The main reason for export

42 KA, Vyborg Court of Appeal Protocols (Viipurin hovioikeuden arkisto), Caa:27, Civil Case protocols, 1865, 25 Feb. 1865.

43 Trakman 2011, p. 318.

44 Trakman 2011, p. 345.

45 Lambert 2017, p. 42.

merchants avoiding open confrontations in courts of law, according to Müller, was that the export merchants' networks prioritized stability, continuity and risk diminution. This explanation is accepted by economic historians studying early modern trade. According to Leos Müller, disputing from a distance was difficult. Moreover, he attributes merchants' unwillingness to proceed via courts of law to institutional weaknesses, i.e. the courts of law were inefficient and legislation outdated. He also demonstrates that the social standing of a merchant family was so important that any short-term benefits could hardly be overcome.[46] Hence, taking a dispute to a perhaps dysfunctional or inefficient court of law would be devastating for family status, business networks and social capital.

The litigation reveals that Hackman & Co were seen as a legal entity: the people behind the company are not named. Hackman & Co was obviously associated with the Hackman family; both the family and the company carried the same name and the company was owned by the family members, as illustrated above. The evidence does not suggest, however, that family *per se* would have been the main issue when discussing business disputes. The empirical data do not reveal any discussion concerning family values or individual family members as responsible agents in litigation cases. Instead, the company is discussed as a legal entity although contemporaries knew the managing director of the company and probably associated him with the company and *vice versa*.[47]

5 Information, Knowledge and Trust

As demonstrated above, wealthy merchants are underrepresented in the law courts and the code of conduct was not formally stated but, rather, implicit in the network. Common practices, as I will illustrate next, emphasized valid information, knowledge and trust based on these two factors. I will shed light on one institutional structure that was based on these features, namely the consular system. I demonstrate how this institution worked in a complex transnational business with multiple legal and juridical systems but common practices.

Historians have highlighted that information and skills are crucial for international shipping and trade. Some scholars have underlined the guild system,

46 Müller 1988, p. 21–23, 35–36, 245–246, 273, 282; Milgrom, North, Douglass and Weingast 1990, p. 1–23; Kallioinen 2012, p. 96–99.

47 Kallioinen 2012, p. 117–118 about the discussion of individual responsibilities and the responsibility of the community.

while others have pointed out that consuls and the consular system carried valid information. Sheilagh Ogilvie has emphasized that in international trade individual firms were the source of information and news. Mika Kallioinen has argued that, in the nineteenth century, the rapid and efficient transmission of information secured reputational mechanisms. Then, merchants were no longer reliant on information produced and transmitted only by merchants themselves.[48]

5.1 *Information*

As Kallioinen illustrates, information is the basic tool needed for making decisions. Furthermore, information is used to reduce the uncertainty associated with decision-making.[49] Hence, we should consider information as one of the key aspects when trying to find out how merchants dealt with disputes in a complex transnational trading system.

Although written records were crucial, several unwritten codes reflected the 'normal' way of trading. These, according to Kallioinen, 'formed an organic, multilateral, and decentralized institution'. One of the most common practices was an understanding that 'agreements must be kept' (*pacta sunt servanda*).[50] This code of conduct was highlighted in 1815, when Marie Hackman expanded her family business by introducing a new partner:

> We assure you of our utmost endeavours [sic] for your Interest in every respect, and as the Funds & Stores of the House remain the same, our joined endeavours [sic] will enable us the better to fulfill your kind orders, and assuring you that you will meet with the same honesty & punctuality [...][51]

The letter not only spread information about a change in the management but also ensured that business would be carried on as usual. Even a small change in business circumstances could result in distrust between partners, inside the network, hence harming the whole network.[52]

The above-cited letter was not the only time when Marie Hackman sent information about changes in business. She had already sent a very similar letter

48 Lambert 2017, p. 45; Kallioinen 2012, p. 69–86, 107–108, 174; Ojala 2015, p. 245; Kaukiainen 2002, p. 153–157.

49 Kallioinen 2012, p. 69.

50 Kallioinen 2012, p. 93.

51 ELKA, Hackman & Co, B 33, Circular letter, 31st Dec. 1815.

52 Hasselberg and Petterson 2006, p. 53–56, citation p. 37.

in 1807.[53] At the same time, she sent a written document affirming that she had permission to sign under the name Ignatius & Hackman and asked the Magistrates Court to verify her signature.[54] Associates in mercantile partnerships represented mutual agency. This means that every partner could sign contracts on behalf of the other partners. In this case, the magistrate's court approved the right for Marie Hackman to sign on behalf of Ignatius & Hackman. She was also accountable for the company's liabilities with her personal property, which was also the common practice at the time in other parts of Europe.[55] Information about the changes, together with Marie Hackman's signature sample, would prevent disputes over ownership of the business and hence, at the utmost, prevent disputes and disagreements reaching the law courts.

Crucial for a well-working merchant network was that circulating information was valid. The trade ordinance of 1734 stated that a tradesman or their clerk (*kiöp-swän*) or apprentice should keep records 'thoroughly and skilfully' (*mogen- och skikelighet få må tillåta*).[56] The ordinance of 1850 stated that an apprentice applying for the status of burgher should have knowledge in several fields including arithmetic, geography, languages, and so on.[57] If we think about universal transnational trading practices, it seems – based on the empirical study of Hackman & Co – that record-keeping and copying letters was a crucial way of transmitting and assuring information. Meticulously kept yearly account books and so-called *Brief Copey Buchs* (*Kopieböcker*) starting from the year 1790 reveal the importance of written records. The original contracts or credit bills have not survived but, instead, the final sums are calculated every year, at the end of March and every letter sent is copied to special copy books. Recorded information guaranteed that mutual trust in the network was hard to break. If, however, trust broke down, records and written documents would guarantee that possible court proceedings were favourable.

Information concerning good legal practices and trading customs also spread via merchant manuals. According to J.F. Hackman's inventory, compiled

53 ELKA, B 27, 28 June 1807 to Bruun in St. Petersburg. "Marie Wwe Hackman wird zeighnen Ignatius & Hackman…"; B 31, Circular 31 Dec. 1815. "…we annex our respective Signatures…"

54 KA, Vyborg Magistrate Archive (Viipurin maistraatin arkisto), Magistrate Protocols (Maistraatin pöytäkirjat), AI 149, 1 July 1807, § 10 "… Bitte die Richtigkeit der Nahmens ünterschrift gerichtlich zu verificiren."

55 De ruysscher 2016.

56 "Den 19. Dec. [1734] Allmän Förordning för dem, som här i Riket wilja fåra och drifwa handelen" In Utdrag Utur...

57 Hans Kejserliga Majestäts Nådiga Förordning angående wilkoren för winnande af burskap å großhandel i Finland. Den 29. Junii 1850.

after his death in 1807, he owned several manuals, including P.G. Ludowici's *Vollständiges Kaufmanns Lexicon*, Schuman's *Handbuch für Kaufleute* and G.R. Rohn's *Wohlerfahrere Kaufmann*. In his recent work, Dave De ruysscher studies the relationship between merchant manuals and law. He illustrates how these manuals helped to spread double-entry bookkeeping and 'proper manners'. He points out, however, that the manuals were at best an author's reflection of their own opinions and customs, not the customs of a larger trading society or any widely adopted norms.[58] The Hackman letters, when discussing disputes, contain no references to these manuals. However, they helped businessmen to discuss similar terms and, hence, facilitate resolving disputes.

Information is closely connected with knowledge, which in turn is related to learning. In the late nineteenth-century, when business became more complex, on the one hand, and on the other hand professional training became possible, the Hackman family sent their offspring to learn the trade and to gather the latest information in other trading houses in Europe, as illustrated earlier in this chapter. When Woldemar Hackman applied for burgher status in 1858, he emphasized his education at a Bremen merchant academy, where he had finished a course in 'business science'. This was in line both with the law of 1734, the trade statute (*Handelsordning*) of 1734 and the imperial statute of 1850, all of which placed value on the training and knowledge of a businessman. Understanding legal pluralism also helped the Hackmans' work in the Diet of Finland, as will be illustrated later.[59]

5.2 *Consuls*

In nineteenth-century Finland, merchants were not organized into guilds or guild-like institutions. It seems that the consular system was the institution to which merchants entrusted their disputes. Consuls were more often discussed in letters than the local magistrates (court) or Court of Appeal. Usually a consular position is understood as an honorary post or part of the diplomatic corps. Consuls' formal duties are known but less is known about the daily work they were involved in.[60] Consuls' knowledge of local and foreign measures, laws and customs was appreciated and ability to spread correct information was part of their duties.[61]

58 Tigerstedt 1952, appendix 5 (Inventory done after J.F. Hackman sr.'s death in 1807); De ruysscher 2016, p. 154–172.

59 KA, Vyborg, Magistrate Archive, Vyborg Magistrate Protocoll, AI 236, 5th June 1858, § 4; Karonen 2004, p. 347–366, see esp. 349.

60 See the entire books Makko and Müller 1985; Müller 2004.

61 Ojala 2015, p. 215. Ojala highlights the importance of information. In his view, the state diminished risks in trade by consuls.

Based on evidence from the correspondence of Hackman & Co, consuls occupied a crucial place in the network, in particular guaranteeing valid information in a situation where information was scarce, asymmetrical and costly.[62] We might assume that institutions such as the consular system helped the merchant network to work smoothly and without taking disputes to courts of law. Jari Ojala has written about the consular system in Sweden and Finland and demonstrates that a consul's post legalized a tradesman's position in their own community and in their network. This means, according to Ojala, that a merchant who obtained a consular post was also considered 'a proper' merchant outside their own community. In other words, the consular system was a way to ensure that merchants in this transnational system were qualified and knew trading patterns as well as common practices in trade. Hence, a consular post was not solely an honorary position.[63]

If we think about the 'law in action' perspective, consuls were at the very core of this action. In 1860, a long and complex process reveals the consul's duties in transnational judicial procedure. Then, a merchant-entrepreneur – Hampus Julius Oldenburg from the town of Pori (Sw. Björneborg) which is situated on the south-western coast of Finland – had faced trouble with his match factory. The factory, which employed hundreds of people in Pori and produced 100 000 matches a day, sold its products to England and its overseas colonies. Oldenburg had borrowed money from the Bank of Finland with the help of his friend, Swedish consul Conrad Hernmarck. Mr Hernmarck was a friend of Lars Gabriel von Haartman, who was the vice chairman of the Economic Division of the Finnish Senate (1841–1858) and whose nephew was married to Antoinette Hackman, a daughter of J.F. Hackman Jr. Despite support from his powerful friends, Mr. Oldenburg's businesses was about to collapse in 1860. Already in 1858, in order to overcome his financial troubles, Mr. Oldenburg started to sell company shares and promised other shareholders that the annual profit would be 15 per cent. Many well-known and established gentlemen rushed to purchase the shares even though they were not sure if they had access to company decision-making or profits; the prospects were too tempting and Mr. Oldenburg knew how to sell his visions. Oldenburg's close connection to Mr. Hernmarck, the Swedish consul and a trusted and solid businessman with good connections to the highest administration, lent a certain prestige to Oldenburg with his risky business ventures.[64]

62 Kallioinen 2012, p. 69; Ogilvie 2011, p. 255–256.

63 Ojala 2015, p. 212–223.

64 Yrjänä 2009, p. 252–257. Doctoral thesis with an English abstract The Forest Devil.

Some businessmen had bought shares with bills of exchange assigned to Hackman & Co. Then Hackman & Co got involved in the match business. At that time, the head of Hackman & Co was Woldemar Hackman, the Spanish vice consul in Vyborg. In early 1860, a Parisian banking house A. Dutfoy Kinon & Cie had approached Hackman & Co (there was no French consul in Vyborg) and asked what they should do with Mr. Oldenburg, who had sent to another Parisian banker called Bayvet a large quantity of matches in order to cover his debts of 65 000 francs. Hackman, who knew both of these Parisian bankers, wrote to Mr. Oldenburg and asked if there was some sort of misunderstanding and how Oldenburg was going to pay his debts. In July 1860, Hackman advised Bayvet that they should discuss the matter with their advocate in Paris and then, if necessary, send all documents to the Parisian *tribunal de Commerce* with the help of the Russian consul in Paris.[65] It is impossible to know, without studying the litigation in the *tribunal de Commerce*, how the court resolved the problem and whether the debtors got their money. In Finland, Oldenburg succeeded in negotiating individually with his debtors and hence the match factory survived without taking the dispute to a court of law. Here, once again, negotiation and tolerance played an important role.

Before 1864, when legislation concerning joint-stock companies was introduced, there was other similar litigation such as Oldenburg's. Businessmen could sell shares without letting the shareholders intervene in business operations. In many cases, company money and private money were mixed, which caused problems when the shareholders came to redeem their profits.[66]

The Oldenburg case is one of a few cases where special commercial courts and specialized advocates or lawyers are mentioned. However, as the letter illustrates, the court seat is in France, not in Finland, where this kind of court seat never operated. The letter written by Woldemar Hackman reveals that Mr. Hackman knew that such courts existed in France. He also trusted that the Russian consul in Paris would help in the matter.[67]

65 About the *tribunal de commerce* in Antwerp, see De ruysscher, 2016, p. 164–165.

66 ELKA, Hackman & Co, B 108, to Oldenburg in Björneborg; to Dutfoy Kinon & Cie in Paris, 14 March 1860; to Bayvet & Cie in Paris, 6 July 1860; Kyösti Järvinen. *Der Zahlungsverkehr im Außenhandel Finnlands vor der Ausbildung des einheimischen Bankwesens. Ein Beitrag zur Entwicklungsgeschichte des intenationalen Zahlungswesens*. Probleme der Weltwirtschaft. Schriften des Instituts für Seeverkehr und Weltwirtschaft and der Universität Kiel. Herausgegeben von Prof. Dr. Bernhard Harms. Jena: Gustav Fischer 1921, passim; Yrjänä 2009, p. 252–25, 285 and passim.

67 During this time, legislation concerning consuls must have been similar to Russian. In 1793, in Sweden a special consular instruction was given. Müller 2004, p. 84; Ojala 2015,

It seems that consuls eased the transnational juridical procedure. They offered a third-party consultation or opinion on the matter.[68] Especially on the periphery, where qualified advocates and lawyers were scarce, consuls might have performed their duties by resolving disputes. J.F. Hackman and J.F. Hackman Jr. were Prussian consuls in Vyborg and Woldemar Hackman the vice-consul of Spain. As consuls, they became involved in court litigation which was not directly connected to them. They gave their opinion, spread information and negotiated between the disputing parties.

Besides gathering and reporting business information to their consular 'home' country, consuls helped their fellow natives and business partners overseas despite their national background, as the Oldenburg case illustrates. However, based on the evidence gathered from the Hackman & Co letters, it is difficult to say if the French partners contacted Hackman & Co because the head of the company was a consul, or because of personal friendship or business ties. The prevailing documents in the Hackman archive only sporadically illustrate the consular services provided by consuls in Vyborg. Some common features, however, based on the empirical evidence can be identified.

In litigation, a consul's knowledge and capacity to act as a special advisor was crucial. This was highlighted in 1825, when the whole cargo of a ship coming from Sweden was 'rotten'. Hackman & Co reported the incident straight away to Consul Lang in Gothenburg and organized an inspection by Court of Appeal judges. The inspection protocol – as well as a public notary's protest – was addressed to the captain of the ship.[69] The empirical data, based on letters, does not reveal any law codes behind the procedure, nor does it give further information concerning the public notary or judges.

Despite the sporadic nature of consular duties found in the empirical data, it is still quite evident that consuls had to know local legislation and the legislation and trade ordinances of those countries they did business with. Yet, in the letters, direct links to particular legislation are very scarce. In 1827, Hackman & Co explained to their business partner in Malaga that the Trade Act sets a limit on imports and hence, in Malaga, they must ask the local consul how to

---

Ojala's chapter focuses on the Swedish consular system. According to Ojala (p 217), there was no existing consular system in Russia. This notion is somewhat contradictory with the information given in the letters. In theory, the system might have been different but in practice it seems very similar.

68 Kallioinen 2012, p. 105–106. Kallioinen discusses town councils as a third-party institution in litigation.

69 ELKA, Hackman & Co, B 52, to Capt. Gullbrandson in Uddevall, 4 Sept. 1825. In this case, the Court of Appeal in Turku, since Vyborg court of Appeal was established in 1839.

FIGURE 5.3 The City of Vyborg 1890, The house of Hackman's

proceed. This is one of a few letters that refers to any legislation or statutes.[70] Typically, merchants' actions refer to long-established common practices which are mutually agreed and followed. These practices seem to be so inbred in the merchant community that everyone knows and acknowledges them, without verbalizing these practices and patterns in letters.

In many ways, consuls' work was about preventing disputes. For instance, consuls issued certificates and documents which guaranteed that cargo did not include prohibited goods and the weight of the cargo was calculated correctly. Once in Montpellier, Hackman & Co fell into a dispute over the weight of a cargo. The local Russian consul, however, could guarantee that the cargo was calculated according to Swedish weights.[71] In Vyborg, if there was not a

70 ELKA, Hackman & Co, B 55, to Menvielle, Wetterström & Co in Malaga, 25 April 1827. In the letter, Hackman & Co refers to 'handelstraktat'. "In *Finnland* ist alle Waaren Einfuhr in *Fremden* Schiffen ausser denen des Productions Landes strang werboten und bloss *Salz* unter Schwedisch & Norwegischer Flagge laut einem besondern Handels tractate abwon ausgenommen...".

71 ELKA, Hackman & Co, B 52, to Bellaud & Co in Montpellier, 31 Aug. 1825.

suitable consul, the local magistrate could issue certificates to ships sailing out.[72] Hence, it seems that consuls' and magistrate's administrative duties overlapped in some cases.

6 Legislative Work at the National Level

The Hackmans were representatives in the Diet of Finland; first, J.F. Hackman Jr. and Woldemar Hackman represented the burgher estate in the Diet. Then, after J.F. Hackman's ennoblement in 1874, J.F. Hackman Jr. and Woldemar Hackman represented the noble estate. Wilhelm Hackman also took part in legislative work in the Banking, Finances and State Committees in the Diets 1877–1906 (except 1897).[73] In their work in the Diet, the Hackmans were conservative and, in many cases, pro-Russian instead of promoting the separation of Finland from Russia. In economic issues, the younger Hackmans promoted liberalism.

The importance of information and transnational networks became visible when merchants (burghers) alongside other estates started to gather in the Diet of Estates in Finland in 1863. Karonen has illustrated how business managers in the Grand Duchy of Finland had fairly good access to information, especially if they lived in Helsinki.[74] The Hackmans, who stayed periodically in Helsinki while taking care of their businesses there, and having close connections with the Helsinki-based business and administrative elite, could use their networks in their political work.

In the Diet, the trading elite had a direct channel to influence commercial legislation. The Hackmans, with their two-generation representative participation, were an exception among the Finnish business elite. The majority of merchants did not have this representative duty.[75] The Hackmans were also exceptionally well informed about foreign laws and customs. Their knowledge of transnational trade, along with experience gained in business and study trips abroad, gave them a privileged position when compared to the majority of Finnish burghers, who only seldom had 'in situ' experience of trade in foreign countries. During discussion in burghers' meetings, the Hackmans used information they had gathered abroad.

72 ELKA, Hackman & Co, B 40, to Uhthoff in Cadix, 25 June 1820.
73 Tigerstedt 1952, p. 39–40, 326–327.
74 Karonen 2004, p. 250–254.
75 Karonen 2004, p. 353.

In 1863, when the Diet assembled for the first time since 1808–1809, J.F. Hackman Jr. raised discussion about legislation concerning customs and duties. He suggested that the bourgeois estate (*borgarestånd*) should petition the emperor in order to lower the duties on imported salt and all export duties should be abolished for export by Finnish ships. He pleaded for the benefits to the national economy and public finances and continued that 'almost all states have either abolished or reduced their customs duties to near zero.' The bourgeois estate decided to support Hackman's petition in further discussions.[76]

In February 1864, when the bourgeois estate discussed the banking and monetary system in Finland, J. F Hackman Jr. noted that he had learnt how special bonds (*obligations*) were used in Hamburg.[77] The following month, in March 1864, J.F. Hackman Jr. pointed out in a discussion concerning merchant privileges that town burghers should protect their privileges and not allow shops or factories to be established too near a town. He wanted to maintain the ancient system of the privileged bourgeoisie. The same protectionist principle was realized in discussion about appropriation taxes in April 1864. Mr Hackman pointed out that the joint-stock company (*aktiebolag*) system was not consistent with the prevailing appropriation tax system; taxes should not be paid according to the profits made in one company but based on all company shares a businessman might own, after his total losses were reduced. Yet again, Mr. Hackman highlighted the privileges of his peers. In his speech, Hackman did not take a stand on the benefits of the joint-stock system, nor did he promote the old tax system. His remarks were purely informational although he pointed out that it would be difficult to sum up all losses and gains if a company was transnational, such as a foreign insurance company operating on Finnish soil and sea.[78]

In the Diet of 1867, Wilhelm Hackman, along with fellow merchant Rosenius from Vyborg, petitioned that a special 'merchant court' should be established in Finland. The petition was dismissed because the idea was considered out-of-date and confusing. His second petition concerned building a railway from Helsinki to St. Petersburg, which was later realized.[79] Both of these speeches were made in order to pursue the advantages of merchants.

---

76 "Borgareståndets Prokotoll vid Landtagen 1863–64", (1864) p. 191–199. The Diet Protocolls as a source, see Karonen 2004, p. 119–121.

77 "Protocoll hos Vällofliga Borgarståndet å Landtdagen I Helsingfors 1863–1864 III, (1865) p. 52, 66.

78 "Borgareståndets Prokotoll vid Landtagen 1863–64", (1865) p. 215–224, 412. The Imperial statute over joint-stock companies was issued in 1864.

79 Karonen 2004, p. 124.

Next time the Hackmans debated in the Diet was in 1877, now participating in a discussion as members of the noble estate. The discussion dealt with railways. Then Woldemar Hackman pointed out how railways were financed in Germany. He also referred to his experiences in Germany and to a book 'which I have recently read'. Later that year, when the noble estate discussed the banking system, Mr. Hackman promoted the interests of export traders.[80]

In the Diet of 1882, when the noble estate gathered, Wilhelm Hackman gave a speech about the financing situation for factories. His opinion was that creditors who made loans to Finnish factories 'should know the local legislation' and added that 'our industry is credited mostly by foreigners who do not usually study the local laws very thoroughly'.[81] Here again, he highlighted knowledge of legislation and local circumstances. Furthermore, he pointed out the transnational character of trade in Finland and pursued his own social group's interests.

Typically, the Hackmans appealed to the conservative system according to which trade was organized. They saw that the old privilege system was still valid. Here, they promoted their own social class, the town burghers. Sheilagh Ogilvie has found that the guild system might have been beneficial for those inside the institutional system, but on the whole it harmed society. Being inside the system, Hackman & Co benefited from the old institutions and hence the new liberal trading legislation would harm his and his peers' business opportunities. Ogilvie's explanation in this particular case seems valid and there is no reason to believe why the Hackmans would have promoted changes in the legal premises of trade when they could benefit from the old system. In particular, J.F. Hackman Jr. was very cautious and promoted the old privileged system.

The younger generation, in contrast, was more open to new and liberal political ideas and principles and to the benefits that liberalization would bring to society as a whole but especially for their peers, export traders. Here we can see, however, that the young Hackmans stayed at a very practical level; they were interested in how transportation of goods, for example, and jurisdiction concerning merchants should be organized. In their representative work in the Diet, the Hackmans based their opinions on their own experience and information they had gathered in practice but also from the books they had read. Their transnational contact network and their position in special committees – Wilhelm Hackman was the head of the Banking Committee in

---

80 "Protocoll fördt hos Finlands Ridderskapet och Adel vid Landtdagen år 1877", I. (1877) p. 223–224, 588, 822–823.

81 "Protocoll förda hos Finlands Ridderskap och Adel vid Landtagen år 1882, (1882) p. 286.

the Senate – enabled them to promote the interests of export traders.[82] The Hackmans' reasoning in the Diet follows the spirit of the law of 1734 and trade ordinances of 1734 and 1850. They emphasized information and knowledge but did not promote drastic changes in legislation.

7 Concluding Remarks

Adopting the 'law in action' approach and studying legal history from below offers an opportunity to find out how changes in legal culture affected grass roots-level agencies. As illustrated in this chapter, the approach highlights common practices in transnational trade. More than legal texts and their interpretations, the trade and businesspeople trusted in communal values, codes of conduct, and information, which can be negotiated and revalued. Trusting that a business partner shared the same values and acted according to similar premises was essential. Valid information was crucial for well-functioning transnational trade. The importance of information and knowledge was written into the Swedish trade ordinance and the later imperial statute, followed in practice by nineteenth-century Finnish businesspeople.

Valid information was guaranteed in several ways. Merchants could study common terms and language by reading merchant manuals. In the Hackman trading house, several German manuals were used. Furthermore, study trips and time spent learning the trade in practice in foreign trading houses ensured that young merchants had the necessary skills when they entered business.

Valid information was also guaranteed by keeping records. Every letter and monetary transaction was written down and copied into special books, from which contracts, discussions and transactions could be verified in case of dispute.

Information was spread via institutional channels as well. In this case, the consular system in particular seems a valid institution. Consuls were trusted as negotiators in disputes. Based on evidence gathered in Vyborg it is hard to say if the consular system replaced or covered other institutions such as merchants' associations, which never existed in Vyborg even though they were obliged to by law. On the other hand, the consular system was a transnational institutional system, which the merchants' associations never were. Hence, the Vyborg merchants' peripheral location might be true in a geographical sense,

82 Compare with Karonen 2004, p. 121–131, 153.

but study of information flows and networks suggests they were at the very core of European business. French bankers and the legal system, as well as German logistical innovations, were known in Vyborg and hence this information was used in legislative work as well.

In nineteenth-century Finland, the old Swedish law of 1734 faced problems caused by the new Russian rule. In principle, Swedish law set the legal limits. Russian statutes, however, replenished the system. Without studying the statutes, it is difficult to say exactly how much these affected the grass-roots level in trade. Based on empirical evidence gathered from the Hackman & Co letters, it seems that the statutes played an important role. Hackman & Co made remarks on these statutes when they restricted transportation and, for example, limited the use of ships to Finnish ones.

After performing thorough research on letters in the Hackman & Co archive, it seems that the merchant community based its actions on mutual agreements and unwritten codes of conduct. The whole network was based on trust and valid information, shared and communally accepted but not verbalized directly in letters. Disputes were so threatening to the existence of this network that they were avoided at any price. Hence, few cases were resolved by the court(s).

In the few litigation cases Hackman & Co were involved in, these were mostly minor disputes over unpaid debts or administrative issues. Hackman & Co were not sued nor did they bring suit against anyone in similar transnational litigation such as the Oldenburg case. Their knowledge was valid and trusted, since their French business partner asked advice on how to proceed with the Finnish businessman Oldenburg and his debts.

Based on the evidence gained from the Oldenburg case, it seems that those merchants involved in complex transnational disputes resolved in courts were either shady businessmen seeking rapid wins, or those financing them. Hackman & Co do not fit either category since they avoided taking their disputes to courts of law.

Information exchanged via letters includes only one or two remarks on prevailing legislation concerning shipping, for instance. Some imperial ordinances concerning the export limitations of timber are mentioned but the discussion in letters seems to stay at a more practical level. Either it is assumed that the receiving partner has full knowledge about the legal premises of the trade, or the information is spread in other ways than via letters. The ordinance of 1850, for example, requires that a merchant have knowledge about legislation concerning shipping, bankruptcy, and companies but these issues are not discussed in everyday situations. Nor did Hackman & Co, when involved in litigation, violate the prevailing legal or customary premises of trade. Hence, if any juridical questions or disputes arose, they cannot be studied from the letters. The evidence gathered from courts of law proves that Hackman & Co resolved their disputes outside the courtroom. We may assume that their juridical knowledge and information gained over several generations of being involved in the export and import trade gave them a superior position in their local community. If local disputes did not take them to court, nor did transnational disagreements either. Instead, their foreign partners trusted their negotiation skills and ability to solve problems. As consuls, they were trusted and the information they gave was considered valid even in complex transnational disputes such as the Oldenburg case.

In legislative work in the Diet of Finland, the Hackmans were quite conservative. They promoted the old privilege system and preferred to restrict trade to towns. They also saw that the new joint-stock company system and reforms in taxation were non-compatible. In particular, they pointed out the difficulties that transnational trade would bring to the local level when foreign profits and transactions should be adapting to Finnish practices.

In their legislative work, the Hackmans took care of the export traders' position in Finland. They legitimized their decisions with information they had gathered in practice and stayed at a very practical level; they were concerned how transportation should be organized, how taxation would affect international traders, and how commercial disputes should be resolved. In the latter case, they were somewhat outdated – the same way as they were when promoting the old privilege system in trade. It seems that although the Hackmans were well informed and knew foreign practices, it was hard for them to adapt their actions to the modernizing world. This might be one reason why they refused to participate in the new democratic parliament in 1906.

Despite modernization, the chapter shows that export merchants promoted traditional values and trading institutions. The old system must have been well-functioning from the viewpoint of the export merchants. Codes of conduct, dating back to the middle Ages, were still very much valid in the late nineteenth-century business environment. As businesspeople, the Hackmans were very cautious in all their opinions and highlighted valid information on which all decision-making should be based. This reasoning, as well as avoiding open confrontation in the law courts, demonstrates that the *status quo* was the most profitable and preferable situation for export merchants such as Hackman & Co. They followed the traditional family firm model and hence any disruption in prevailing circumstances was a considerable risk for their businesses.

Online Source

Kotivuori, Y., *Ylioppilasmatrikkeli 1640–1852:* Karl August Ekström. Published on-line 2005 (consulted on 7 September 2017).

Printed Sources

Borgareståndets Prokotoll vid Landtagen 1863–64 (Helsingfors: J.C. Frenckell & Son 1864).

Den 19. Dec. [1734] Allmän Förordning för dem, som här i Riket wilja fåra och drifwa handelen. In Gustaf Reinhold Modée et al. (eds), *Utdrag Utur utur alle ifrån den 7. decemb. 1718/1791 utkomne publique handlingar* (Stockholm: Lorentz Ludowig Grefinn et al. 1742–1829).

Hans Kejserliga Majestäts Nådiga Förordning angående wilkoren för winnande af burskap å großhandel i Finland. Den 29. Junii 1850.

Hans Kejserliga Majestäts Nådiga Förordning, om anonyma- eller aktie-bolag. Gifwen i Helsingfors, den 24 Nowember 1864.

Protocoll förda hos Finlands Ridderskap och Adel vid Lantdagen år 1882 (Helsingfors: FLS Tryckeri 1882).

Protocoll fördt hos Finlands Ridderskapet och Adel vid Lantdagen år 1877, I (Helsingfors: Finska Litteratursällskapets Tryckeri 1877).

Protocoll hos Vällofliga Borgarståndet å Lantdagen i Helsingfors 1863–1864 III (Helsingfors: J.C. Frenckell & Son 1865).

Manuscripts

KA Kansallisarkisto (National Archives of Finland): Vyborg Court of Appeal (Viipurin hovioikeuden arkisto), Protocols (Viipurin hovioikeuden pöytäkirjat) Caa:17 (1855); Vyborg Magistrate Archive (Viipurin maistraatin arkisto), Magistrate Protocols (Maistraatin pöytäkirjat) AI 149 (1807).

ELKA Elinkeinoelämän keskusarkisto (Central archives for Finnish Business Records): Hackman & Co, B 27, B 31, B 33, B 40, B 51, B 52, B 55, B108.

Literature

Amend-Traut, Anja. 2016. "Legal Structure of Early Enterprises – from Commenda-like Arrangements to Chartered Joint-Stock Companies (Early Modern Period)" in Pihlajamäki et al. (eds.).

Brand, Hanno & Müller, Leos (eds.). 2007. *The Dynamic of Economic Culture in the North-Sea and Baltic Region* (Hilversum: Uitgeverij Verloren).

Cotterrell, Roger. 2009. "Spectres of transnationalism: Changing Terrains of Sociology of Law" in *Journal of Law and Society* 36, no. 4, 19–36.

Dahlén, Marianne & Larsson, Mats. 2014. "Business history and legal history" in *Business History*, Vol. 56, 54–70.

De ruysscher, Dave. 2016. "Partnerships as Flexible and Open-Purpose Entities: Legal and Commercial Practice in Nineteenth-Century Antwerp (c. 1830–c. 1850)" in Pihlajamäki et al. (eds.).

De ruysscher, Dave. 2016. "How Normative Were Merchant Manuals? Of Customs, Practices, Techniques and … Good Advice (Antwerp 16th Century)" in Pihlajamäki et al. (eds.).

De ruysscher, Dave. 2012. "From usages of merchants to default rules: practices of trade, ius commune and urban law in early modern Antwerp" in *The Journal of Legal History*, 33:1, 3–29. Published online 28 Mar 2012.

Enbom, Sten. & Sandelin, C.F., *Viipurilainen kauppahuone Hackman & Co. 1880–1925* (Oy Hackman Ab, 1991).

Faundez, Julio. 2016. "Douglas North's Theory of Institutions: Lessons for Law and Development" in *The Hague Journal of the Rule of Law*, Oct. 2016, Vol. 8, 373–419.

Flume, Johannes W. 2015. "Law and Commerce: The Evolution of Codified Business Law in Europe" in *Comparative Legal History*, 45–83.

Hackman & Co 1790–1965 (Helsinki: Hackman & Co, 1965).

Harris, Ron. 2011. *Industrializing English Law. Entrepreneurship and Business Organization 1720–1844*. Political Economy of Institutions and Decisions (Cambridge: Cambridge University Press).

Hasselberg, Ylva and Petterson, T. 2006. "Företag, nätverk och innovation" in Ylva Hasselberg & Tom Petterson (eds) *'Bäste broder!' Nätverk, entreprenörskap och innovation i svenskt näringsliv* (Stockholm: Gidlunds förlag).

Järvinen, Kyösti. 1921. *Der Zahlungsverkehr im Außenhandel Finnlands vor der Ausbildung des einheimischen Bankwesens. Ein Beitrag zur Entwicklungsgeschichte des intenationalen Zahlungswesens*. (Herausgegeben von Prof. Dr. Bernhard Harms. Jena: Gustav Fischer).

Kallioinen, Mika. 2012. *The Bonds of Trade. Economic Institutions in Pre-modern Northern Europe* (Newcastle upon Tyne: Cambridge Scholars Publishing).

Karonen, Petri. 2004. *Patruunat ja poliitikot: yritysjohtajat taloudellisina ja poliittisina toimijoina Suomessa 1600–1920* (Helsinki: Finnish Literature Society).

Kaukiainen, Yrjö. 2002. "Information and Maritime History. Introduction to Forum Information and Communication in the Maritime World" in *International Journal of Maritime History*, Vol. XIV, No. 1, 153–156.

Keskinen, Jarkko. 2012. *Oma ja yhteinen etu. Kauppiaiden keskinäinen kilpailu ja yhteistyö Porin paikallisyhteisössä 1765–1845*. Annales Universitatis Turkuensis C345. (Turku: University of Turku).

Lambert, B. 2017. "Making Size Matter Less: Italian Firms and Merchant Guilds in Late Medieval Bruges" in De ruysscher, D., Cordes, A., Dauchy, S. and Pihlajamäki, H. (eds.), *The Company in Law and Pracice: Did Size Matter?* (*Middle Ages – Nineteenth Century*) (Nijhoff: Brill).

Makko, Aryo & Müller, Leos (eds.). 2015. *I främmande hamn. Den svenska och svensk-norska konsultjänsten 1700–1985* (Malmö: Universus Academic Press).

Milgrom, Paul, R., North, Douglass, C. and Weingast, R. 1990. "The Role of Institutions in the Revival of Trade: the Law Merchant, Private Judges, and the Champagne Fairs" in *Economics and politics*. Vol. 2, No. 1, 1–23.

Müller, Leos. 2004. *Consuls, Corsairs, and Commerce. The Swedish Consular Service and Long-distance Shipping, 1720–1815* (Uppsala: Uppsala Universitet).

Müller, Leos. 1988. *The Merchant House of Stockholm, c. 1640–1800. A Comparative Study of Early-Modern Entrepreneurial Behavior* (Uppsala: Uppsala University Press).

North, D. 1991. "Institutions" in *The Journal of Economic Perspectives*, Vol. 5, No. 1, 97–112.

Nyberg, Klas, & Jakobsson, H. 2012. *Storköpmän som samhällskraft. Borgerskapet och Grosshandelssocietet i Stockholm* (Stockholm: Informationsförlaget).

Ogilvie, Sheilagh. 2011. *Institutions and European Trade. Merchant Guilds, 1000–1800* (Cambridge: Cambridge University Press).

Ojala, Jari. 2015. "Från svenskt till ryskt system: det finska näringslivets samarbete med konsuler i utlandet på 1800-talet" in Makko, Aryo, & Müller, Leos (eds.), *I främmande hamn: den svenska och svensk-norska konsulstjänsten 1700–1985* (Malmö:Universus Academic Press).

Pihlajamäki, Heikki. Cordes, Albrecht. Dauchy, Serge and De ruysscher, Dave (eds.) 2016. *Understanding the Sources of Early Modern and Modern Commercial Law* (Leiden-Boston: Brill).

Ruuth, J.W. 1906. *Viborg stads historia I–II* (Helsingfors/Viborg, 1903).

Ruuth J.W. et al. 1982. *Viipurin kaupungin historia I Vuoteen 1617* (Torkkelin säätiö).

Ruuth J.W. & Kuujo, E. 1975. *Viipurin kaupungin historia III Vuodet 1710–1812* (Torkkelin säätiö).

Tigerstedt, Ö. 1940. *Kauppahuone Hackman. Erään vanhan Wiipurin kauppiassuvun vaiheet I, 1790–1879* (Helsinki: Otava).

Örnulf Tigersted, Örnulf. 1952. *Kauppahuone Hackman. Erään vanhan Wiipurin kauppiassuvun vaiheet II, 1790–1879* (Helsinki: Otava).

Trakman, Leon E. 2011. "A Plural Account of the Transnational Law Merchant" in *Transnational Legal Theory*, 2 (3), 309–345.

Ulianova, Galina. 2009. *Female Entrepreneurs in Nineteenth-Century Russia.* Perspectives in Economic and Social History. Number 2. (London: Pickering & Chatto).

Wolff, Charlotta. 2014. "Kauppa, teollisuus ja liikenne" in Kaukiainen, Yrjö, Marjomaa, Risto and Nurmiainen, Jouko (eds.) *Viipurin läänin historia V. Autonomisen Suomen rajamaa* (Karjalaisen kulttuurin edistämissäätiö).

Yrjänä, J. 2009. *Metsäpirulainen. Liikemies Erik Johan Längman (1799–1863) talousjärjestelmän murroksessa* (Helsinki: University of Helsinki).

CHAPTER 6

Commercial Law on the Periphery: University Teaching of Commercial Law in Finland, ca. 1780–1846

Jussi Sallila

1 Introduction

In this chapter,[1] I investigate how commercial law was taught at university in Finland during the late eighteenth and early nineteenth centuries. The object of the investigation is commercial law in the broad sense of the term. In the late eighteenth century, materials related to commercial matters were discussed as part of lectures on general private law, as well as specific maritime law lectures. In the early nineteenth century, commercial and economic law became an independent subject in the curriculum of the faculty of law. This chapter will focus on lecture manuscripts, as they provide the most complete picture of how commercial law was approached by jurists. Handbooks or other forms of legal literature did not include systematic treatment of commercial law. In comparison with central European countries, legal literature was undeveloped as a whole in eighteenth-century Sweden, of which Finland formed part. The role of legal literature was even more peripheral in early-nineteenth-century Finland, after the country was detached from Sweden.[2] The lack of handbooks meant that the role of university lectures and circulated lectures was greater than in countries with a flourishing legal publishing industry.

The period under scrutiny stretches from the 1780s to the 1840s and includes the great change in Finnish history brought about by the Finnish War of 1808–1809 between Russia and Sweden. As a result of the war, the common history of Sweden and Finland came to an end. The Grand Duchy of Finland became an autonomous part of the Russian Empire with a central government of its own, but the old Swedish legal system remained in force. This epochal shift coincided with transformations of society in Western Europe and the wider world

1 This chapter was written when I was employed by the project entitled the "Making of Commercial Law" at the Faculty of Law of the University of Helsinki.

2 Björne 1995, p. 62–69; Björne 1995, p. 199–203.

 | DOI:10.1163/9789004436046_007

brought about by the French Revolution and the Industrial Revolution. Developments in Finland were obviously linked to geopolitical changes – after all, the Russo-Swedish War of 1808–1809 was a minor part of the Napoleonic wars. However, from a social, economic and legal perspective, Finland did not experience revolutionary changes that were typical of Western and Central Europe; economic and cultural development was gradual in Finland.

The revolutions in politics, ideology and the economy were of great significance for the development of commercial law in the European heartland. In France, the commercial courts of Old Regime society survived the revolution by transforming themselves. Instead of being special tribunals for a privileged group of merchants, they became special jurisdictions governing commercial transactions in an objective, depersonalized sense. With the enactment of the Code de Commerce, a codification based on early modern regulations was to be applied in France.[3] In Germany, the emergence of commercial law as a distinct field of legal scholarship and codification was a nineteenth-century phenomenon. According to Schmoeckel, this was a consequence of the Industrial Revolution. Rules governing commercial transactions did exist in the early modern period, classified as part of "German private law" in academic education, but they were not conceptualized as "commercial law" before the nineteenth century.[4]

It will be argued in this chapter that while the characteristic features of the Swedish-Finnish legal tradition were not conducive to the emergence of commercial law as a specific field of law, developments in the early nineteenth century made it a possibility. Swedish law had been codified in a unitary national code with the Law of 1734. Uniformity of legal sources, along with the relative lack of special jurisdictions made the development of special private law for commerce less likely. In addition, as Sweden had never experienced full-scale reception of Roman law in the early modern period, there was no need for German-style separate teaching of national private law and general Roman law. The special privileges of towns, merchants and industrialists did influence economic activity considerably, but they were part of the constitutional order of the estate society and the general royal prerogative in the field of police regulation. The uniformity of legal sources made the Swedish and Finnish legal tradition at least proto-legalistic in character, while the interplay between national law and foreign influences facilitated a pragmatic approach in interpretation of commercially relevant rules of private law. Proto-legalist

3 Kessler 2007.
4 Schmoeckel 2008, p. 87.

and pragmatic features were accompanied by a historical focus in legal literature which underlined the continuity of the legal system and absence of revolutionary changes.

However, from the 1810s onwards the law curriculum of the Finnish university provided an institutional basis that could have served as a foundation in commercial law teaching. Following the eighteenth-century example of Uppsala University, a professorship in "economic and commercial law" (*in jure oeconomio et commerciorum, ekonomisk och handelslagfarenhet*) was established. In Uppsala, the professorship had been a mixture of law and economics, in the way that economics was understood during the Swedish "Age of Utility" of the eighteenth-century.[5]

In the 1830s and 1840s, the leading Finnish legal scholar of his generation, Johan Jakob Nordström, served as professor of economic and commercial law. In his lectures on commercial law he combined the traditional legalist, pragmatic and historical perspectives with a new "organic" vision of society. This organic vision was not unique in nineteenth-century commercial law scholarship.[6] Nordström defended the ideals of the estate society against liberal criticism, wishing to retain the distinction between urban and rural occupations. In addition, he attempted to interpret the factory privileges of industrialists as a part of the old-regime society but at the same time also as a modernizing force in the economy. Along with this organic conservatism, Nordström's lectures also included new elements of legal education. He discussed the institutions of international commerce, such as commission trade, based on contemporary German literature. While these business practices were known on a practical level, they were not regulated by Swedish or Finnish law, and Nordström was a pioneer in discussing their exact legal character. Therefore, Nordström's lectures added a new element in legal education, discussing legal aspects of transnational business networks.

2 The Finnish Economy and Culture in an Age of Transition

This chapter does not take the standard periodization of Finnish political history as its starting point. Clearly, the establishment of a separate autonomous Finnish state in 1809 was a great shift in Finnish history, and economic and

5 Liedman 1986.
6 Whitman 1987–88, p. 156, 175.

cultural historians have underlined the continuity of trends emerging in the last decades of the Swedish era.[7] Modern historians tend to be critical of teleological narratives in which late eighteenth-century developments are interpreted as "preparation" for separate Finnish statehood and culture. However, the late eighteenth century was without doubt a period of economic growth and cultural renewal in Finland. The central institution of cultural life was the university, the Royal Academy of Turku, which flourished during the late eighteenth century and gained even greater significance as Finland's intellectual centre in the Russian era.

The renewal of academic life was linked to increasing economic prosperity, Mid-eighteenth century agricultural reforms enhanced the productivity of farming. In the 1760s, foreign trade of Finnish towns received a boost as regulations benefiting the economic interests of the capital, Stockholm, were abolished. In general, Sweden's status as a minor European power meant that it could often benefit from wars between great powers through neutral shipping, although this success was subject to dramatic fluctuations. Increasing demand for Finnish lumber laid the foundations for the country's main export industry of modern times, even if the industrial development of Finland was still modest in comparison with Sweden proper, known for its major iron industry.[8] However, the economic development of Finland was hampered by the border between Sweden and Russia, which ran through Eastern Finland. The Russian conquest of 1808–1809 was followed in 1812 by the reunification of so-called Old Finland, consisting of areas conquered by Russia in the eighteenth century, with "New Finland." On the other hand, the making of Finland as a nation between Sweden and Russia was a slow process.[9] According to most economic historians, it was only around 1840 that Finland escaped the economic orbit of Sweden. For example, Swedish currency was generally used in Western parts of Finland until this period. The period between the 1780s and 1840s can be studied as a period of transition.

Founded in 1640, the Royal Academy of Turku can be said to have had a dual character until 1809. On the one hand, it was a Swedish provincial university, overshadowed by Uppsala University and later also by the Royal Academy of Sciences established in Stockholm in 1739. On the other hand, it cultivated

7 For an overview in English, see Kirby 2006, p. 68–104. Kirby treats the period between 1780 and the 1860s in one chapter and does not follow the conventional periodization of political history.

8 Kuisma 1993, p. 66–103.

9 Engman 2009.

specifically Finnish aspects of learning and culture. For most of its early history, the university had a strong theological focus, and its alumni mainly served in the Church and administrative positions. (During the eighteenth century, students from Russian-ruled Eastern Finland continued to attend the Academy of Turku, as the education of Lutheran clergymen and many civil servants was still in practice acquired on the Swedish side of the border.) In the late eighteenth century, this picture began to change. The academy had its minor share in the general flowering of Swedish natural sciences, while many contemporaries as better than Swedish universities regarded its scholarship in the humanities.[10]

3 Commercial Law Issues in the Lectures of Matthias Calonius

In the Swedish era, the Academy of Turku was not particularly prominent in legal education and scholarship. The law faculty included only one professorship, and for the most part of the eighteenth century the position was held by teachers without legal qualifications or scholarly activity. Therefore, when Matthias Calonius (1738–1817) took over the teaching of law he had to begin practically from scratch. Calonius was appointed professor of law in 1778, having taken care of teaching duties since 1771. As his professorial career continued to the 1810s, Calonius acted as a bridge between the Swedish era and the period of Finnish autonomy as part of the Russian Empire. With his background in primarily historical studies, Calonius had to learn law as he began to teach the subject, and as a scholar his main contributions were legal historical in character. In his law lectures, he relied on earlier literature of Swedish legal scholars such as Olof Rabenius as well as contemporary European natural law doctrine.[11]

Commercial law was not among the subjects Calonius lectured on during his career as a professor. Therefore, one must reconstruct his views on commercial law topics based on his lectures on civil law and maritime law. Following the system of Rabenius, Calonius identified commercial law (*jurisprudentia*

10 For a magisterial account of the history of the university, see Klinge 2010, p. 117–135, 175–197. For a recent English-language overview of legal scholarship, see Vasara-Aaltonen 2020, p. 253–257, 307–311.

11 Björne 1995, p. 131–140. Björne sets Calonius in a broader context of intellectual history of legal scholarship. For more details, see the biography Wrede 1917.

mercatoria) as part of law governing business or chrematistic activities (*jurisprudentia chrematistica*), which also included agriculture and mining as well as crafts and trades. *Jurisprudentia chrematistica* belonged to the broader category of private economic law. Swedish legal scholars had not treated commercial law systematically. Certain areas of law with distinct statutory law sources, such as maritime law and law governing bills of exchange, could be classified as subcategories of commercial law.[12]

Calonius approached commercial matters from a perspective emphasizing the importance of statutory law. This proto-legalistic approach was accompanied with historical insights, reflecting his background as a scholar of general history, as well as a pragmatic approach to legal problems. One can discern in Calonius a tendency to emphasize the practical flexibility of Swedish general private law which made it less necessary to develop specifically commercial forms of private law institutions. Similar arguments have been commonplace in Swedish and Finnish legal literature in later centuries.[13] In his discussion on the protection of *bona fide* purchasers of movables, Calonius argued that natural justice required such safeguards, and no commercial exchange was secure without it. However, as Roman law did not recognize such protection, countries tied to Roman law had had to limit its application so that commerce was not harmed.[14] Swedish law, by contrast, regulated the question in a satisfactory fashion.

Another example of criticism of approaches based on Roman law is the treatment of bills of exchange (*De cambio, nobis växel*) in lectures on civil law. While Calonius gave most of the chapter headlines only in Latin, reflecting their Roman law pedigree, in some cases he added the terms used in Swedish legislation, thereby underlining their different background. For a definition of bills of exchange, Calonius relied on the Swedish statute of Bills of Exchange enacted in 1748, quoting the Swedish-language text at length (Växelstadga 1748, Article 1). Thereafter he gave a brief account of the history of bills of exchange, pointing out that common terminology was evidence of the Italian origins of

12 Calonius 1908, p. 18–19 (Cap. I. § 34).

13 Palmgren 1944, "Utvecklingen av Finlands handelsrättsliga lagstiftning," *Vårt näringsliv och kriget: spridda studier samlade av Ekonomiska Samfundet i Finland på femtionde årsdagen av dess instiftande och tillägnade professor J.V. Tallqvist* p. 113–125, 113–115.

14 Hinc et qui caeterum juris Romani glebae se adscriptos professi sunt, varias legibus ejusdem limitationes introduxerunt, ne supra modum turbarentur commercia. Calonius, *Praelectiones in iurisprudentiam civilem*, p. 353 (Cap.XIX. § 7).

the institution. Here Calonius refers to scholarly works on bills of exchange written by the German scholars Heineccius, Siegel and Beseke. However, in his account of detailed rules on bills of exchange, Calonius refers only to the 1748 statute and does not mention foreign doctrine.

The way Calonius focused on statutory law was linked to his pragmatic approach, which distinguished him from the learned German literature that he cited. Although bills of exchange were unknown to the ancient Romans, almost all modern writers on the topic had attempted to use learned Roman concepts to define them. For Calonius, this made no sense. As bills of exchange were based on an agreement between the contracting parties and combined several contracts, it was futile to try to classify bills of exchange with the terminology of Roman law.[15] Calonius also provided a formula for bills of exchange, written in German. Bills of exchange were usually written in the language of the drawee. In Sweden, the use of bills of exchange was limited to international business contracts and documents written in the domestic language (in this context, Swedish) were therefore extremely rare.[16]

As Calonius structured his lectures on civil law based on Swedish statutory law sources as well as learned Roman and natural law doctrine, it is understandable that the pragmatic approach manifested itself in isolated remarks. The introductory chapter states that knowledge of both public and private economics is necessary in economic law, and there are general references to the works of Scottish economists Adam Smith and James Steuart. Occasionally, Calonius adds brief glosses concerning specifically commercial adaptations of private law institutions, such as agency (*mandatum*) and partnership (*societas, bolag*). His reference in this context is the practical "commercial science" textbook *Theoretisch-Praktische Darstellung der Handlung in deren mannigfaltigen Geschäften* (1792) by Johann Georg Büsch (1728–1800), principal of Hamburg commercial academy.[17]

---

15 "Otiosa itaque et inutilis est quaestio, tantum non ab omnibus juris cambialis scriptoribus agitata, ad quem contractuum nominatorum pertineat cambium, vel an sit contractus innomitaus do ut facias. Quemadmodum negotiation cambialis Romanis erat incognita; ita nec fieri potest ut in jure Romano nomen hujus contractus reperire liceat. Jura enim non feruntur de rebus incognitis." Calonius, *Praelectiones in iurisprudentiam civilem*, p. 414 (Cap. XXIII § 7).

16 "Linguam in hujus modi litteris adhibere convenit acceptanti familiarem. Hinc Germanica, Batavica, Gallica, Anglica, Italica plerumque in usu sunt. Apud nos vix unquam occurrunt litterae cambiales vel datae vel acceptatae vernacula nostra scriptae." Calonius, *Praelectiones in iurisprudentiam civilem*, p. 414–415 (Cap. XXIII § 8).

17 On Büsch, see Whitman 1917, p. 162–163, and references therein.

While the commercial law materials in the lectures have to be reconstructed from fragments, Calonius gave an independent lecture series on Swedish maritime law (*Institutiones juris nautici suecani*) in the academic year 1787–1788.[18] He repeated the lecture series in 1803, adding minor updates concerning, among other things, new commercial treaties signed by European states during the Revolutionary and Napoleonic wars. The maritime law lectures were based on European learned doctrine and Swedish Maritime Law of 1667, but they also included a general introduction in which Calonius recounted the history of commerce and navigation, as well as a brief account of the history of maritime laws. Mainly following the 1757 Danish textbook *Introductio in jus nauticum* by Henning Wedderkop, which he praised in his civil law lectures, Calonius divided the material into the law of persons (*De personis nauticis*), things (*De rebus nauticis*), contracts (*de contractibus nauticis*), shipwreck and average, maritime criminal law and maritime procedure.[19]

In the historical account, there are also signs of pride in the learned traditions of the Royal Academy of Turku and Finland. Calonius mentions that Bishop Mikael Agricola (d. 1557), a key figure of the Reformation in Finland, made the first Swedish translation of the Maritime Law of Visby, while Finnish orientalist and Swedish royal librarian Henrik Brenner (1669–1732) is cited as an authority on Persian and Russian commercial history. It is notable that the basics of commercial history and geography were a requirement for aspiring merchants whose knowledge was controlled by municipal authorities, probably also town officials trained in law.[20] The law lectures made a good impression in government circles. The Chancellor of the Royal Academy of Turku, Baron Carl Sparre (1723–1791), who also served as the Over-Governor of Stockholm and member of the Council of the realm tasked with military and naval affairs, praised the maritime law lectures by Calonius both for the usefulness of the subject matter and the systematic structure of the lectures.[21]

18 Matthias Calonius, *Praelectiones in Jus Nauticum Svecanum*, National Library of Finland, manuscript collection MS Ull.432.81.

19 Calonius, *Praelectiones in iurisprudentiam civilem*, p. 20 (Cap. 1., § 34). On Wedderkop's book, see Scherner 1977, p. 797–997, 991–994; Wrede 1917, p. 172–173.

20 Castren 1957, p. 132–146.

21 Wrede 1917, p. 172.

4 The University and Legal Education in Autonomous Finland: Increasing Resources, Meagre Results

After Finland became part of the Russian Empire following the Russo-Swedish War in 1808–1809, the university held a key position in educating the civil servants of the autonomous Finnish government. The University had a special position: it was independent of the Finnish Senate and Governor-General and directly connected to the Emperor. The direct imperial link was underlined and reinforced by the fact that from 1816 to 1894, the heirs to the throne served as Chancellors of the University.[22] Emperor Alexander I favoured the university by considerably increasing its funding. The strengthening of the university was linked to tight political control. While it was still common in the 1810s for Finnish students to study at Uppsala, a decree of 1819 made a Finnish university degree a compulsory requirement for all new civil servants. Thus, the influence of Swedish intellectual and political ideas was limited. In 1828, the university was transferred to Helsinki by Emperor Nicholas I and given the name Imperial Alexander University after Alexander I. The decision was linked to the devastation of Turku in the great fire of 1827, but the relocation of the university to the capital had been contemplated even before the fire as a means of making the university more "imperial" and less "Swedish" in spirit.[23]

After 1809, Finland's new autonomy made it necessary to increase the resources of the law faculty, given its key role in educating the civil servants of the new central government. Matthias Calonius continued to lecture at the university while serving as Procurator, the senior legal official of the Finnish government. In 1811, another chair was established at the faculty for economic and commercial law (*in jure oeconomio et commerciorum, ekonomisk och handelslagfarenhet*). At the same time, two assistant positions were established, corresponding to a new professorship and the old one, now named general Finnish jurisprudence.[24]

The expansion of the law faculty was obviously linked to Finland's new autonomous position. The establishment of a new Finnish central government increased demand for information about economic and administrative legislation, which was traditionally part of the royal prerogative and had previously been drafted by the central government boards in Stockholm. By contrast, as far as general Swedish law was concerned, judges in the two Finnish courts of

22 According to Klinge, this educational honorary position of the heir to the throne was the first of its kind in the Russian Empire. Klinge 2010, p. 234–236.

23 Klinge 2010, p. 216–229, 270–283.

24 Björne 1998, p 15.

appeal had the expertise – and social prestige – which facilitated establishment of the Judicial Department of the Senate, functioning as a supreme court.[25] This point was understood by contemporary observers. In 1819, professor of economic and commercial law Daniel Myréen wrote an article celebrating the tenth anniversary of Alexander I as ruler of Finland. In this mixture of panegyric and analysis of the first decade of the autonomous Finnish government, Myréen noted that Finnish constitutional laws and private law had not changed much during this period, but economic and administrative regulations had been reformed to a considerable extent.[26]

However, although the funding of legal education increased, another problem experienced in the Swedish era persisted. According to Calonius, people with privileged backgrounds and personal connections were favoured in appointments to public positions. For this reason, in-depth study of law was not an attractive career option, a factor contributing to low standards of legal scholarship in Sweden.[27] After 1809, personal connections played a key role in the Faculty of Law appointments at the University.

The first professor of economic and commercial law was appointed in 1812. The only applicant was Daniel Myréen (1782–1831), a Swede who had earned his doctorate in law at Uppsala University in 1810. Myréen's resumé was not particularly impressive, and his appointment depended largely on personal connections. He had served as private tutor in the family of Gustaf Mauritz Armfelt, the favourite Finnish advisor of Alexander I and, along with other duties, the Chancellor of the university.[28] The first assistant professor of economic and commercial law was Wilhelm Gabriel Lagus (1786–1859), a Finn who also received his legal education in Uppsala, where he was awarded a doctorate in 1818. He had already stood for the economic and commercial law professorship

25 Tyynilä 1992, p. 46–47.

26 "Kort öfwersigt af de fördelar Finland wunnit genom sin lyckliga förening med Ryska Riket under Kejsar Alexanders spira" Åbo Allmänna Tidning 1819, nr 125, 126, 129, 130 and 136: "Grundlagarne och privat rätten hafwa således under detta decennium undergått få förändringar, men deremot har Landets administrativa och Ekonomiska Lagstiftning blifwit dels förändrad dels wunnit en betydelig tillökning." (Åbo Allmänna Tidning 126/1819, published on 28 October, 1819.)

27 "Ubi munera conferuntur in ignavos, juris imperitos etc. vel ob natalium aliquam praerogativam, vel patronum potentiam, vel varias indigniores adhuc commendationes, vel contra solutum pretium, et sic porro, ibi adsuescunt juvenes ad sollicitanda variis his iniquis modis publica munera, avocatum a litterarum studiis: quid quod contemnere et tanquam supervacuam despicere incipiunt omnuis generis eruditionem suis principiis innixam." Calonius, *Praelectiones in iurisprudentiam civilem*, 28 (Cap I. 46 (45)).

28 Wrede 1917, p. 400–401.

while Myréen served as acting professor of general jurisprudence from 1815 to 1818 after the retirement of Calonius. Like Myréen, Lagus benefited from personal connections. He belonged to the influential family circle of Bishop (later Archbishop) Jacob Tengström, whose daughter he married in 1816. The bishop had played a key role in the pacification of Finland during the war of 1808–1809 and served as Vice-Chancellor of the University.[29]

Contributions by Myréen and Lagus were relatively meagre, especially in commercial law in the strict sense of the word. The dissertations defended under Myréen were concerned with laws governing taxation and monetary policy, questions of public economic law. On the basis of his lectures on cameral jurisprudence (*Cameral Lagfarenheten*), Sakari Heikkinen sees Myréen as a representative of state-centred cameralist economics.[30] Lagus had defended a dissertation on bills of exchange in 1813. Following the tradition of the Uppsala chair of economic and commercial law, the thesis was written in Swedish and not Latin. The *respondens* who presented the dissertation of Lagus was old Count Alexander Armfelt (1794–1876), the 19-year son of Gustaf Mauritz Armfelt who later served the Emperors as long-time Minister State-Secretary for Finland.[31]

While the historical and economic introduction is slightly more extensive than the one given by Calonius in his lectures, the treatment of legal questions is neither very brief nor particularly detailed. Although the dissertation was presented as the first volume of a larger study, a second part was never published. Calonius and Myréen were quite critical of the dissertation, and it is obvious that Lagus had written it merely to obtain an appointment at the law faculty. His main scholarly interests were in antiquarian historical studies.[32]

The manuscript collections of the National Library of Finland do not include new lecture notes on commercial law or other aspects of private economic law composed in the 1810s or the 1820s. The old lecture notes by Calonius were still being circulated. As far as maritime law lectures are concerned, there is a volume of annotations dated 1810 and written entirely in Swedish.[33]

---

29 Väisänen 2005, p. 677–678.

30 Heikkinen, Heinonen, Kuusterä and Pekkarinen 2000, p. 54–58.

31 Lagus 1876, p. 8–9.

32 Wrede 1917, p. 403.

33 *Matth. Calonius: Föreläsningar öfver sjölagen* (*anteckningar*), National Library of Finland, manuscript collection MS Bö. III.22. The differences in handwriting suggest that two or more people were involved in this vernacular reproduction, but the manuscript does not include any information on their identity.

Although the dating would suggest the annotations were based on contemporary lectures held in 1810, this seems unlikely. In his account of Calonius' academic activities in 1810, when he also served as Procurator, Wrede does not mention any maritime law lectures.[34] The contents of the manuscript largely correspond with earlier lectures and have not been significantly modified with respect to Finland's new position as part of the Russian Empire. However, the introductory account of the history of commerce and navigation includes some inaccurate information; e.g., Indians are credited with innovation of the compass. The manuscript collection also includes a copy of maritime law lectures, dated 1827 and signed by Carl Evert Ekelund (1791–1843), then assistant professor at the Law Faculty. Even this manuscript is a reproduction of Calonius' lectures. It is clear that Ekelund had the 1810 annotation manuscript at his disposal, as he refers to it when he does not reproduce the glosses of Calonius in his copy.[35]

Taken together, the decades following 1809 were not particularly fruitful for Finnish legal education and scholarship, despite the increased resources allocated to the university. One of the reasons for the decline was clearly the increasing number of positions in the new central Finnish government, for which only a basic law degree was necessary. The number of students pursuing higher degrees in law plummeted in the 1810s.[36] Public discussion of legal questions and economic policy was hampered by strict press censorship.[37] Given the challenges of consolidating Finland as an independent administrative unit, it is understandable that the law professors focused on matters of public economic law.

5 Teaching Commercial Law in Helsinki: Johan Jakob Nordström

The structure of the Law Faculty was changed with new statutes regulating the university and enacted after the relocation to Helsinki in 1828. A new professorship was established in Roman and Russian Law. The professorship of general Finnish jurisprudence was not affected by the change, while the professorship

34 Wrede 2017, p. 395.

35 *Professoren Math. Calonius Förelasningar öfver Sjö-Lagen, afskrifven af Carl Evert Ekelund, Juris Cand. och Adjunct vid Kejser. Academien i Åbo. År 1827*, National Library of Finland, manuscript collection MS Bö. I.16.

36 Castrén 1951, p. 422.

37 Castrén 1951, p. 206–264; Björne 1998, p. 25–26.

FIGURE 6.1
Matthias Calonius (1737–1817) served as member of the Supreme Court of Sweden in Stockholm from 1793 to 1800. This portrait dates from this period.

of economic and commercial law was renamed as concerning international and public law and economics (*folk- och statsrätt samt nationalekonomi*). As Björkqvist has shown, the drafters of the new university statutes discussed the position of economics intensively, with some arguing that this discipline ought to be part of the Faculty of Philosophy or a new separate faculty of political sciences (*statsvetenkaperna*).[38] In the end, teaching of economics remained a part of legal education. While the new name of the chair underlined the importance of economics, commercial law was still part of the teaching duties. Indeed, it was during this period that commercial law teaching began in earnest.

Johan Jakob Nordström (1801–1874) was the leading legal scholar in Finland during the 1830s and early 1840s. He was appointed as assistant professor of economic and commercial law in 1826, and became professor of international and public law and economics in 1833. His major academic works, published in the 1830s, were concerned with the history of Swedish law and the Swedish social order. While his studies were soon outdated as scholars using newly founded archival sources shed new light on Swedish legal history, Nordström had gained a favourable reputation in Sweden. In 1846, he resigned from the

38 Björkqvist 1986, p. 94–95.

university, acquired Swedish citizenship and was appointed head of the State Archives in Stockholm.

Nordström did not have any pupils in Finland. He is even said to have discouraged talented students from choosing law as their field of study.[39] This attitude probably reflected the bitter criticism of the Russian Empire and the elites in charge of the autonomous Finnish government Nordström recorded in his diary.[40] In his view, the appointment policy of the government favoured young men with good family connections regardless of their talent or academic merits. Calonius had voiced similar criticism in his day, and the opinion was shared by leading opposition intellectuals in early nineteenth-century Finland such as Adolf Ivar Arvidsson and Johan Vilhelm Snellman. However, unlike Arvidsson and Snellman, Nordström was not a supporter of Finnish nationalism. The nationalist cause was centred upon the Finnish language and empowerment of the Finnish-speaking majority of the country. The son of a turner in Turku, Nordström had a middling Swedish-speaking family background which alienated him both from Swedish-speaking elites and the emerging nationalist movement.

Although Nordström is thus a somewhat isolated figure in Finnish intellectual history, his role as a law professor in the 1830s and 1840s was important for the later development of Finnish legal thought.[41] His lectures on Finnish public law were the first of their kind, raising consciousness of Finland's constitutional laws at a time when detailed knowledge about them was sketchy even among leading statesmen, not to speak of the wider public.[42] In commercial law, too, Nordström made a major contribution. During his time as professor, the Finnish government was actively working to reduce the country's dependence on Swedish trade and consolidating Finland as an economic and administrative unit.[43] Through the monetary reform of 1840 and new customs regulations, Finland's special economic relationship with Sweden was terminated. The domestic economy was developed with major road and canal infrastructure projects, and the government also invested in technical

39 Ehnström 1874, p. 75.

40 A collection of these diary notes was published in 1940, see Blomstedt 1940, p. 121–152.

41 In earlier scholarship, Lindman has investigated Nordström's political philosophy and participation in political life in both Sweden and Finland, Lindman 1948. R.A. Wrede analyzed his pioneering lectures in Finnish public law. See more Wrede 1930, p. 58–62.

42 Wrede 1930.

43 Kirby 2006, p. 109–110.

and commercial education.[44] Despite Nordström's oppositional mindset, his lectures on economics, commercial law and maritime law can be analyzed as part of these efforts towards economic modernization.

Nordström had made his first major foreign trip in 1835, spending most of his time in Germany, where he attended the lectures of academic luminaries, including von Savigny, Thibaut, Gans, and von Ranke. After his return, he gave lectures first in political economy in spring 1836. The first lectures on "commercial and industrial[45] law" (*Handels- och Närings-Lagfarenheten*) took place in the autumn term of 1837, followed by lectures on bills of exchange in spring 1838 and maritime law in autumn 1838. Nordström repeated his lecture cycle in the early 1840s. In the academic year 1841–1842, he lectured on political economy and commercial jurisprudence, continuing with lectures on commercial law and maritime law in the following year.[46]

The manuscript, including Nordström's commercial law lecture notes, is the product of two separate lecture cycles, and the order of the extant manuscript is not chronological. The manuscript has the appearance of a patchwork, with different parts written and rewritten at different times. However, one can reconstruct the order of the original 1837 lectures with the help of student annotations of Nordström's private lectures on commercial jurisprudence, dated in spring 1839.[47] In addition to the public lectures that were part of professorial duties, professors also gave private lectures for extra income. The student annotations were made by Carl Adolf Öhrnberg (1810–1877), later judicial burgomaster of Helsinki, and they are preserved at the National Library of Finland.[48]

44 Kuusterä and Tarkka 2011; on technical education, see Nykänen 2015, p. 8–25.

45 Johan Jakob Nordström, "Handels- och Närings-Lagfarenheten 1837". Johan Jakob Nordström, Handskrifter Vol. I 761–1014. In this context, "industrial" activity (näring) encompasses both handicrafts and more modern forms of industrial production.

46 See the announcements of the annual programme of the University, published in Helsingfors Morgonblad (23 September 1841, 29 September 1842.).

47 "Anteckningar i Handels Lagfarenheten" [1839], National Library of Finland, Manuscript collection Bö.IV.11.

48 The lecture annotations were given to the library by Öhrnberg's son in 1902. The commercial law lecture annotations are dated to the spring of 1839 in the news item "Gåfva till universitetsbiblioteket." *Helsingfors-Posten* 9 December, 1902, p. 2. The manuscript collection includes another short collection of annotations of the lectures written by a different hand; "Anteckningar i Handels Lagfarenheten under Prof Nordströms privata föreläsningar Wåren 1839 nr 2". National Library of Finland, Manuscript collection Bö.II.37.

The content of the annotations mainly corresponds with that of Nordström's manuscript for public lectures, but they do not include references to the foreign literature that Nordström used in his own manuscript. There are also very few mentions of the legislation of foreign countries in Öhrnberg's annotations. As far as the subject matter is concerned, lectures on bills of exchange are not included in the annotations. Another volume in the National Library collections contains annotations for maritime law lectures but without exact dates.[49]

The extant lecture notes of the commercial law lecture series of 1837 are combined with notes titled "Credit, Money, and Credit Legislation," dated May 1842.[50] These lectures were drafted after the monetary reform of 1840, which necessitated revising the regulations governing the Bank of Finland.[51] Nordström discussed the new regulations and provided an early version of his studies on the use of commercial accounts as evidence in courts of law, published as two doctoral dissertations in 1844.[52] The lectures on the law of bills of exchange are also combined with the commercial law lectures,[53] while the maritime law lectures are preserved in a separate volume.[54]

6 The Foundations of State Authority in Regulating the Economy: Historical Arguments and "Organic" Conservatism

Nordström's approach to commercial law built on the Swedish-Finnish legal tradition. Like Calonius, Nordström had a background in historical studies. His

49 "Anteckningar i Sjö Lagen". National Library of Finland, Manuscript Collection Bö.II.27. The volume does not include information on who made the notes, but it was given to the library by Öhrnberg's son.

50 "Om Credit, Penningar och Creditlagarne" (date of the first page 8 May, 1842) Nordström, Handels- och Närings-Lagfarenheten 1837, p. 911–962.

51 References to decrees issued in 1840, ibid. 951–952. On the monetary reform of 1840, see Kuusterä and Tarkka 2011, p. 203.

52 *Ett och annat om handelsböckers* beviskraft (1844) and *Ytterligare ett och annat om handelsböckers beviskraft och om creditpapper* (1844).

53 "Föreläsningar öfver Wexelrätten" (date of first page 24 April, 1838.) Nordström, Handels- och Närings-Lagfarenheten 1837, p. 963–1014.

54 Johan Jakob Nordström, "Sjörätten, commenterad. 1838". Johan Jakob Nordström, Handskrifter Vol. II. 1–96. National Library of Finland, Manuscript collection MS Bö.I.3. [Cited hereafter as Nordström, Sjörätten 1838.]

first academic works were concerned with medieval Swedish legal history. The professorial thesis that he defended in 1832, titled "Description of Municipal Legislation in Finland," was also primarily a historical investigation, but it also included discussion of the foundations of economic policy.[55] Nordström's 1837 lectures also include extensive accounts of legal history and are obviously based on his earlier work.[56]

In his introduction, Nordström discussed the general principles of economic and commercial law and the foundations of state authority to administrate the economy. Nordström saw the state as an organism, not merely a mechanism protecting the rights of individual citizens. As for the theoretical foundations of the regulatory authority, Nordström mainly followed the 1829 economics textbook of Uppsala law professor Lars Georg Rabenius. While Rabenius represented a state-centred approach to economics, in his introductory remarks Nordström also cites the books of Julius von Soden (1754–1831), a German writer known as a populariser of Smithian economics. Nordström defended the mercantilist regulation of commerce and the economic division of labour between towns and rural areas on which the Swedish and Finnish economic order was based, approaching the question from both historical and philosophical perspectives.

The general introduction was followed by an account of the regulations of urban occupations in the Commercial Section of the Law of 1734 and other legislation. These rules of public law set the requirements for burgher rights and the rights and duties related to urban occupations. Nordström follows the proto-legalist tradition: throughout his lecture manuscript, citations of Swedish statutory law are the most important legal source and practically the only source of domestic law. However, Nordström's organic conservatism manifested itself in his judgments. Nordström started with a description of laws governing handicrafts. While he was aware of the criticism of trade guilds, his own view of them was positive and he did not welcome the exceptions to the monopoly rights of urban trade guilds. For example, although new towns founded in the late eighteenth and early nineteenth centuries had been given freedom from traditional guilds and their regulations, this was not proof of guilds becoming obsolete.[57]

Nordström's defence of the guild system was consistent with his organic conservatism. It is interesting to note that the Swiss historian and economist

55 The study was published in two parts in Latin *De municipiorum in Fennia constitutione* and also in Swedish (Skildring af Municipal-författning i Finland) in the same year.

56 This point is underlined by Lindman 1948, p. 38–46.

57 Anteckningar i Handels Lagfarenheten 1839, p. 105–113.

FIGURE 6.2
Johan Jacob Nordström.

Jean Charles Leonard Simonde de Sismondi (1773–1842) had recommended the re-establishment of guilds in countries where they had been abolished.[58] According to Lindman, Sismondi was one of the major inspirations for Nordström's economic and political thought, even if evidence of this influence mostly dates from the period after Nordström's emigration to Sweden.[59]

After his treatment on handicrafts, Nordström turned to "manufactures" and "factories." These newer forms of industrial production had emerged from handicrafts, as the word manufacturing itself showed. Manufacturers produced similar products as traditional craftsmen but on a larger scale. However, enterprise of this kind required greater technical and scientific knowledge as well as greater capital investment, and the larger scale of production emphasized the need for exports. For all these reasons, greater freedom was required in industrial production than in handicrafts. The regulation of industrial production of manufactures was based on the privileges of the manufacturing industry issued by the Swedish Crown in 1739. Administration of privileges was

58 Romani 2005, p. 28.
59 Lindman 1948, p. 65.

the task of the hallmark courts (*hallrätter*) established in Stockholm and other major towns. The hallmark courts oversaw a system in which special private law and procedural arrangements facilitated debt collection and made it possible to use the manufacturing workers' labour in a more efficient and less costly fashion than in the traditional guild system. In the beginning of his treatment of manufacturing law, Nordström argued that "all industrialists of the country" made up a "corporation."[60] Oversight of the internal relations of the members of the corporation was entrusted to the special jurisdiction of hallmark courts.[61] In this way, Nordström tried to reconcile his vision of organic society with the needs of the modern economy. The hallmark courts were organs of municipal government but their role depended upon the government and the imperial prerogative on which manufacturing privileges were based. Apparently, in Nordström's view manufacturers ideally constituted a trade guild writ large, operating on a national scale.

Because of the necessity for greater capital investment in manufacturing, Nordström thought that the question of entrepreneurial finance was best discussed in the context of manufacturing, even though the same legal rules applied in other contexts. The lecture notes thus include an account of the law governing companies and partnerships. As domestic legislation was not detailed in this area, Nordström explained the characteristics of different forms of enterprise, referring to provisions of the French Code de commerce and the textbook of Carl Joseph Anton Mittermaier (1787–1867), *Grundsätze des gemeinen deutschen Privatrechts: mit Einschluß des Handels-, Wechsel- und Seerechts*.[62] Nordström also described finance through debenture loans (*förlagslån*). Other legal institutions connected to manufacturing industry included monopoly rights, patents, and export subsidies.[63]

The combination of commercial law with law governing other urban economic activities was not without parallels in foreign legal literature. As Scherner has shown, eighteenth-century scholars of non-Roman German private law (*deutsches Privatrecht*) began to structure their textbooks on the basis of separate social contexts (*Lebenskreis*), and not the conceptual framework of Roman private law. In this literature, one can find textbooks on commercial law

60 Anteckningar i Handels Lagfarenheten 1839, p. 123–126.

61 Anteckningar i Handels Lagfarenheten 1839, p. 211–212.

62 According to the book catalogue published by the Stockholm Auction Chamber in 1874, Nordström owned the 1830 edition of Mittermaier's work. Förteckning öfver framl. riksarkivarien och cancellers-sekreteraren vid rikets universiteter dr J.J. Nordströms efterlemnade boksamling… Stockholm 1874 73. Available at: https://www.doria.fi/handle/10024/127796.

63 Handels- och Närings-Lagfarenheten 1837, p. 799–805.

treated in the same urban context as the law of handicrafts. However, towards the end of the eighteenth century scholars of German private law tended to focus on the more genuinely non-Roman aspects of their field.[64] Given that teaching of Swedish and Finnish law was not based on similar Roman/national divisions as in Germany and other Central European countries, the structure of lectures could be based more easily on pragmatic grounds.

7 Commercial Law and World Commerce: Pragmatic Reception of Foreign Legal Doctrine

After his extensive presentation of handicraft and manufacturing law, Nordström turned to commercial law in the strict sense of the term. Given that important parts of the Commercial Section of the Law of 1734 were part of the uniform private law of Sweden, determining the scope of specific commercial law could be difficult. A case in point was the contract of sale, at the same time the most basic contract type in general private law as well as the foundation of commerce as an occupation. Following Lars Georg Rabenius, Nordström distinguished sales completed in a non-occupational, householding role (*husbehofshandel, emtio venditio naturalis*) from sales conducted in the course of commerce as a business activity (*Näringshandel, emtio venditio negotiatoria, artificialis*).[65] While the Law of 1734 allowed non-occupational sales in the countryside, commerce as an occupation had for long time past been an urban occupation. Commerce had emerged through the increasing division of labour. It was the great driving wheel that kept circulation going. The essence of commerce as an occupation was the "mediating principle." World commerce made it necessary for merchants to acquire diverse knowledge and engage in risky ventures.

Although the contract of sale was the foundation of commerce, Nordström did not begin his account of commercial law in the strict sense by analysing it. Instead, he began with a discussion of legal aspects of relationships in which two or more interested parties were involved in the same business enterprise. The focus on these specifically commercial legal relationships was probably linked to the international nature of world commerce, as Nordström had to rely extensively on foreign legal literature while discussing these questions.

64 Scherner 1972, p. 471–472.
65 Handels- och Närings-Lagfarenheten 1837, p. 826.

Such relationships were often international, and naturally they could only be established through contract. The terms of the contract regulated the relationship if they were specifically agreed and defined. In the absence of clear contract terms, the matter was to be judged by general legal principles. As far as different kinds of partnerships or companies were concerned, the same legal principles were to be applied in all kinds of economic activity, and Nordström had already discussed them with respect to manufacturing.[66]

The situation was different with respect to agency contracts. Calonius had noted the specifically commercial forms of agency in his civil law lectures in a brief gloss, using the German terms *Einkaufs-Commission* (purchasing commission), *Verkaufs-Commission* (sales commission) and *Speditions-Commission* (freight forwarding). As Sweden and Finland belonged to the German-dominated Baltic Sea area, development of forms of commercial agency followed the German pattern.[67] In the commission trade (*kommissionshandel*), the commission agent (*kommissionär*) sells or buys goods in his own name for the account of the principal (*kommittent*).[68]

Nordström noted in his lectures that as Swedish-Finnish legislation offered no specific rules concerning the legal relationship between the parties to the commission trade, interpretation should be based on general principles and the rules governing general agency in the Law of 1734 (Commercial Section, chapter 18). In addition, considering that the commission agent never became the owner of the goods traded, his position was that of a depositary and the relevant rules (Commercial Section, chapter 12) were also applicable.[69] In practice, Nordström found the general principles of commission trade largely from Mittermaier's textbook. It was a convenient introduction to general principles of commercial law in German-dominated areas such as the Baltic Sea

66 Handels- och Närings-Lagfarenheten 1837, p. 828–832.

67 See Scherner 2012, col. 1987–1991.

68 N.B. The conceptualization of commercial agency is different in key aspects of English and continental law, and linguistically related terms such as "commission" and "factorage" have different meanings in English and continental legal language.

69 Handels- och Närings-Lagfarenheten 1837, p. 828: "Rättsförhållandet emellan Committenten och Commissionären är väl i våra lagar icke särskildt bestämdt. Måste derföre bestämmas efter allmänna grunder, och närmast ur synpunkten af mandats eller ombudsmannaför[hållandet], H.B. XVIII." [accompanied with the gloss: "Derjemte och då Commissionären aldrig blir ägare af de för Committentens räkning förvärfvade, eller honom från [den sednare] tillsända varor, utan blott depositarius, kommer ock häruti lagen om inlagsfä till användning.]

region. Mittermaier pointed to differences in particular legislation in his footnotes, but his main text was brief and suited pedagogical purposes well.

In the early nineteenth century, the commission trade was a normal form for organizing international trade and typical of the business network in which Finnish merchants participated. In the context of early modern commercial practices, Amend-Traut has argued that there are "qualified indications that the large trading companies and their numerous smaller imitations overall played a significantly smaller role" than the commission trade did.[70] Mittermaier points out that it was usual for the commission agent to reside in a different location than the principal, but this was not an essential characteristic of the institution.[71] These networks have been investigated by Finnish economic historians focusing on the efficiency of business organization.[72] In this literature, the terms describing the relationship between foreign merchants and their Finnish intermediaries are often imprecise from the perspective of a modern legal historian. This may reflect different usage in research traditions, but probably also lack of clarity in the original sources of commercial legal practice.

For example, in his study of the Finnish book trade, a business sector in which Finland was a peripheral market for Swedish and German publishers, Hakapää uses the concept of *kommissionär* (Finnish: *komissionääri*) for two different types of organizing book sales. The first type conforms with the commission trade as it is understood in modern law: the commission agent sells the books in his own name for the account of the principal and could return unsold books to him. Over the course of the nineteenth century, foreign publisher-booksellers pushed for a new distribution model in which the ownership of books was transferred to an intermediary, with no right to return the books. However, Hakapää uses the term *kommissionär* for the intermediary in this later model, too.[73]

It seems likely that such a shift in distribution model and the allocation of commercial risks occurred without a clear change in terms used in the drafting of contracts. Both Mittermaier and Nordström stressed that the commission agent did not become the owner of the traded goods, even if he became a

70 Amend-Traut 2017, p. 82.
71 Mittermaier 1830, p. 969–970.
72 Ojala p. 1999.
73 Hakapää 2008, p. 49–51, 294.

surety of the purchaser's solvency by agreeing a *del credere* commission with the principal for an additional fee. Accordingly, as the owner of the goods, the principal retained his usual right to separate his property from the insolvent estate of the commission agent.

In his definition of forwarding agency (*spedition*) contracts, Nordström largely followed Mittermaier's analysis, stating that the relationship between the contracting parties included aspects of deposit, agency, and employment contracts. Which aspect of the contract should be considered as the determining characteristic depended upon the individual contract concerned. Whether the contracting party of the freight forwarder was the sender or the recipient was also relevant.[74] However, unlike Mittermaier, Nordström does not compare the position of the freight forwarder to that of *negotiorum gestor* or cite the relevant section of the Law of 1734. Nordström's analysis of the legal issues of forwarding agency focuses on application of the rules concerning the depositary's duty of care of the goods being forwarded, as well as his right of retention.

Following his account of the commission trade, Nordström described the rules concerning commercial representatives called *factors* or *disponents*. These were representatives of merchants or trading companies, conducting the business of their master in the master's name in a certain location, based on a *procura* or general mandate. Factor relationships were a part of managing local branches of a transregional or international business.[75] The legal relationship in question was that of master and servant. From the perspective of potential business counterparts, the most important question concerned the scope of the mandate. This was determined by the *procura*, which had to be made known to business counterparts. (According to Nordström, in Finland this publicity also required recording of the *procura* in court, presumably in the location of the branch establishment. He based this requirement on an analogy of the 1748 statute on bills of exchange.) Even if the *factor* did not follow secret guidelines given to him, but not recorded in the procura, contract parties could insist on performance by the master.[76]

74 Handels- och Närings-Lagfarenheten 1837 p. 830: "hans förhållande till Committenten ligger alltså så väl depositum, som mandat; äfvenså löneaftal, och beror det af det träffade aftalet, hvilkendera sidan företrädesvis skall blifva den bestämmande" Cf. Mittermaier 1830, p. 974–975, §. 499: Speditionshandel.

75 Lammel 2008, p. 1479–1482.

76 Handels- och Närings-Lagfarenheten 1837, p. 831.

Nordström's account of *factors* is almost a word-for-word translation of Mittermaier's textbook.[77] At the end of the section he also referred to the corresponding provisions of the Prussian codification (ALR), some of which Mittermaier mentioned in his footnotes. However, unlike Mittermaier, Nordström added a remark in which he compared the relationship between the *factor* and his master to that between a shipmaster and a shipowner.[78] In so doing, he probably sought to make the powers of the relatively unknown commercial representative understood through the more familiar rules of the maritime code. Given that the powers of commercial representatives were not determined by Swedish or Finnish legislation before the late nineteenth century, it seems likely that conducting business with representatives of foreign merchants or firms could give rise to problems of interpretation.

Considering that Nordström saw mediation of economic exchange as the essence of commerce, it is not surprising that he also discussed the role of brokers and the broker ordinances that were in force in Finland. These rules were not very important in practice, as brokers were rare in Finland. In small towns, with little commerce and industry, and no clear differentiation between wholesale and retail trades, there was no need for specialized persons facilitating transactions similar to major commercial centres of foreign countries.[79]

8 Commercial Law and the Swedish-Finnish Legal Tradition: The Contract of Sale

After his account of the legal relationships of commercial agency and other mainly foreign institutions of commercial law, Nordström turned to questions with more domestic legal sources. This part of the lecture manuscript includes the most detailed legal analysis and references to foreign legislation and previous Swedish and Finnish doctrine. First, there is a part which is apparently a preliminary version of a dissertation (*praeliminärafhandling*) on sale and exchange contracts, the foundation of all economic exchange. (No such dissertation was ever published.) Nordström focused on the sale of movables and discussed two main questions: first, whether ownership was transferred

77 Mittermaier p. 948–949, §. 483. Factor.
78 Handels- och Närings-Lagfarenheten 1837, p. 831.
79 Handels- och Närings-Lagfarenheten 1837, p. 831–832.

though the mere contract, or was a *traditio* of the item of sale required. Secondly, he analysed the relationship between a *bona fide* purchaser and the previous owner of goods. This part of the lecture manuscript could build on old research and comparisons to foreign legislation.[80] There are also short mentions of such sources in the student annotations, which usually do not include any references to literature or foreign law. Thus, while discussing the sale of things not yet in existence, Nordström used the distinction between the *emptio rei speratae* and the *emptio spei*, referring to both Roman law and modern European civil codes, as the difference was not clear in Swedish (Finnish) legal sources.[81] On the other hand, on other issues Nordström could cite established Swedish-Finnish jurisprudence from Claes Rålamb to David Nehrman, Olof Rabenius and Matthias Calonius as support for his interpretations.

However, previous debates in Sweden and Finland had been conducted as part of general private law, and also later research has approached these questions as a matter of private law. More specifically commercial questions discussed by Nordström were concerned with the different commercial sale and purchase practices in which the normal rules of transfer of risk did not apply. These included a variety of conditional contracts. In his private law lectures, Calonius had stated that the potential variation of conditions attached to sale was infinite, and his examples were taken from either learned law or Swedish legislation. Nordström described trial purchases (*prof-köp*), suspended purchases (*köp på sicht*) and optional purchase (*köp på premie*), using partly German-based Swedish terminology.[82] Nordström's account may have been based on Mittermaier's textbook, but in this case there are no references to literature.

Another typically commercial practice was to conduct sale and purchase on credit (*köp på tid eller borgen*). The continuing use of credit was characteristic of commerce pursued as an occupation, and there were sources of eighteenth-century Swedish legislation which made keeping accounts compulsory for merchants. What the requirements of proper bookkeeping were was not so certain. In addition, the question of how accounts could be used as evidence in courts of law was a difficult question in the 1830s and 1840s. Nordström presented an early version of his 1844 dissertations on the topic as part of his lectures.[83]

80 Handels- och Närings-Lagfarenheten 1837, p. 833–856.

81 Anteckningar i Handels Lagfarenheten 1839, p. 258–259.

82 Handels- och Närings-Lagfarenheten 1837, p. 859–860. Anteckningar i Handels Lagfarenheten 1839, p. 306–308. Mittermaier 1830, p. 989–991.

83 Handels- och Närings-Lagfarenheten 1837, p. 861–865.

At the end of his 1837 lecture series, Nordström explained the public law governing commerce, such as regulations concerning fairs in the countryside, the different trading rights of the towns, with varying degrees of participation in foreign trade, as well as the rights of foreign merchants. The basic rules were included in the Commercial Section of the Law of 1734 and other legislation.[84]

9 Lectures on Bills of Exchange and Maritime Law: Problem-Based Approach to Commercial Law Questions

Compared with commercial law lectures, Nordström's lectures on the law of bills of exchange and maritime law were more compact. There is no sign of the patchwork of different kinds of legal materials lumped together. The main reasons for this coherence are the existence of domestic legislation as a source of law and the ease with which maritime law and bills of exchange could be treated as special legal issues. While outdated in many aspects, seventeenth- and eighteenth century domestic legislation helped to structure the lectures. On the other hand, modern foreign codifications and learned doctrine provided guidance for interpretation of difficult questions not regulated by Swedish and Finnish law.

Nordström's lectures on bills of exchange were quite detailed.[85] The most important legal source was naturally the 1748 statute on bills of exchange. However, the old statute did not regulate all questions that were relevant in early nineteenth-century practice. In addition, Finland's position between Russia and Sweden had caused some further difficulties. Due to lacunae in domestic legislation, Nordström referred extensively to foreign – mainly French and Prussian – legislation, and cited several foreign learned authorities, especially Mittermaier and Martens. In these cases, foreign law was used as support for interpretation. For example, use of accessory guarantees for bills of exchange through surety or *aval* (*avallum*) was legal in Finland, even though the 1748 statute did not contain any rules about it. Nordström used foreign legislation and doctrine to clarify legal questions related to the use of *aval*.[86]

In addition, use of both Swedish and Russian currencies in Finland made currency exchange a more complicated question in international business relations. Nordström argued that while the Swedish 1748 statute was based on the assumption that bills of exchange were paid in the currency of the location

84 Handels- och Närings-Lagfarenheten 1837, p. 866–895.
85 Handels- och Närings-Lagfarenheten 1837, p. 969–1014.
86 Handels- och Närings-Lagfarenheten 1837, p. 1003.

of payment, this was not an essential characteristic. Advocates in Finland had argued successfully in courts that bills of exchange to be paid in Hamburg currency in Finland were not proper bills of exchange, and should therefore not be enforced in the speedy fashion regulated by the law. According to Nordström, this successful insinuation by lawyers was evidence that judges did not have proper knowledge of the nature of bills of exchange.[87] Unfortunately, Nordström does not give any exact references to this case law he thought misguided. However, critical discussion of Finnish legal practice is not a common characteristic of Nordström's lecture manuscript, which makes the notes concerning bills of exchange striking.

The lectures on maritime law had many common characteristics with those on bills of exchange. In this case, the main legal sources were the 1667 Maritime Code, the 1748 regulations concerning shipmasters and crew (*Reglementet för Coopvardie-Skeppare och Skepps-folk*) and the Average statute (Haveristadga) of 1750. As far as public law regulation of shipping was concerned, decrees enacted in Finland after 1809 had somewhat modified the old Swedish system. As maritime law was essentially a matter of international exchange, comparisons to foreign legislation and the use of major European authors was natural. Nordström focused on French and Prussian legislation, and his main scholarly authorities were (again) Mittermaier, Jean-Marie Pardessus (1772–1853) and – concerning bottomry loans and maritime insurance – Wilhelm Benecke (1776–1837).

Nordström's approach to lectures in maritime law could be described as problem-based. He did not follow the order of the 1667 Maritime Code. He began his lectures by explaining the rules concerning shipowners and shipping companies – after all, construction of the vessel was the starting point for all maritime activities that the law regulated.[88] This section also included material which was probably useful for a handbook-style use of lecture notes: repetition of how rules of general private law operated with respect to ships. Such practice notes are more extensive in student annotations, possibly made in private lectures supplementing public ones. For example, Nordström explained that while legislation did not require a written contract for the sale of a ship, according to established customs (*gammal usance och sedvänja*) the sale was to be made in writing. In addition, protectionist regulations favouring domestic shipping required that transfer of ownership was recorded by the authorities, and a written sales contract had to be presented as evidence.[89]

87 Handels- och Närings-Lagfarenheten 1837, p. 1008.
88 Sjörätten 1838, p. 2–10.
89 Anteckningar i Sjö Lagen, p. 34–35.

10 Nordström's Legacy – the Limits and Possibilities of Finnish Commercial Law

The commercial law lectures of Johan Jakob Nordström show that it was still difficult to determine the scope of commercial law as a separate field of Swedish or Finnish law. Most of the subject matter belonged either to public law regulations governing the economy and maintained the sharp divide between urban and rural economic activity. Nordström's basic philosophy on commerce was like his view on economic regulation in general. The right to pursue commerce as an occupation was a positive right, not a natural one. Because of this staunch defence of mercantilist regulations and organic view of society, Nordström's ideas soon became obsolete in the latter part of the nineteenth century, as freedom of enterprise was accepted in both Sweden and in Finland.

During his years in Sweden, Nordström moved in a more liberal direction in economic policy matters, but in political questions such as reform of the legislature, the former opposition intellectual became known as an arch-conservative in Sweden. However, despite these shifts of opinion, in more strictly legal issues Nordström's thought showed more continuity. As I have pointed out in another context, Nordström insisted upon a distinction between rural and urban spheres when he contributed to Swedish legislative drafting work in the 1850s. He advocated separate rules for insolvent entrepreneurs in bankruptcy legislation, even though this would have run against the principle of equality before the law.[90]

On the other hand, the law of sales had previously been developed as part of general private law, and it was in private law literature that the doctrine was developed further in the late nineteenth and twentieth century. In this sense, the view expressed, among others, by Gunnar Palmgren is valid: Swedish and Finnish general private law was flexible enough for regulating commercial exchange and there was no great need for a special private law of merchants to act as an avenue for modernization of private law.[91]

While much of Nordström's lecture material was either tied to the order of society and division of labour or a part of general Swedish-Finnish jurisprudence, one can discern a more specifically commercial aspect of his lectures that had potential influence in the later development of Finnish law. In his discussion of forms of commercial agency, Nordström was describing the basic legal characteristics of international business practice. The kinds of commercial contracts he discussed in his lectures were those without any domestic legislation, and general private law rules of the Law of 1734 offered only limited

90 Sallila 2015, p. 187–189.

91 Palmgren 1944, "Utvecklingen av Finlands handelsrättsliga lagstiftning".

guidance in interpretation. Indeed, in the case of the commission trade, Finnish law still operates on the same basis as in Nordström's time. Developments in securities markets have raised the desirability of legislation once more to the agenda.[92]

In areas of commercial law with statutory sources, such as maritime law and the law of bills of exchange, law professors such as Nordström could draft lectures with the help of modern European legislation and textbooks and thus provide additional information for their students. Nordström's discussion of forms of commercial agency is an example of pragmatic reception of legal ideas that was probably useful in legal practice concerning international business relations. In the 1830s and 1840s, modernization of the Finnish economy was gathering pace. With his experience of foreign travel and influences from foreign literature, he could disseminate ideas about modern commercial legal practices in a country whose position in the European market was marginal and which was only starting to develop its own national economy between Sweden and Russia. It is worth noting that, while Nordström put great emphasis on Swedish cultural traditions and was a specialist of Swedish legal history, in commercial law he had to look for ideas in the legal countries in Central and Western Europe with more sophisticated legal cultures. The late-nineteenth and early-twentieth-century Finnish scholars of commercial law had a similar starting point. Their books and articles also relied extensively on foreign legislation and literature.

Unprinted Sources

National Library of Finland

Matthias Calonius, *Praelectiones in Jus Nauticum Svecanum*, National Library of Finland, manuscript collection Ull.432.81.

Matth. Calonius: Föreläsningar öfver sjölagen (anteckningar), National Library of Finland, manuscript collection Bö. III.22.

Professoren Math. Calonius Förelasningar öfver Sjö-Lagen, afskrifven af Carl Evert Ekelund, Juris Cand. och Adjunct vid Kejser. Academien i Åbo. År 1827, National Library of Finland, manuscript collection Bö. I.16.

"Anteckningar i Handels Lagfarenheten" [1839], National Library of Finland, Manuscript collection Bö.IV.11.

"Anteckningar i Handels Lagfarenheten under Prof Nordströms privata föreläsningar Wåren 1839 nr 2", National Library of Finland, Manuscript collection Bö.II.37.

"Anteckningar i Sjö Lagen", National Library of Finland, Manuscript Collection Bö.II.27.

92 Harju 2016, 30–115.

Johan Jakob Nordström, "Handels- och Närings-Lagfarenheten 1837", Johan Jakob Nordström, Handskrifter Vol. I 761–1014. National Library of Finland, Manuscript collection Bö.I.2.

Johan Jakob Nordström, "Sjörätten, commenterad. 1838", Johan Jakob Nordström, Handskrifter Vol. II. 1–96. National Library of Finland, Manuscript collection Bö.I.3.

Literature

Amend-Traut, Anja. 2017. "Legal Structure of Early Enterprises – from Commenda-like Arrangements to Chartered Joint-Stock Companies (Early Modern Period)" in De ruysscher, D., Cordes, A., Dauchy, S. and Pihlajamäki, H. (eds.), *The Company in Law and Practice: Did Size Matter? (Middle Ages-Nineteenth Century)* (Leiden and Boston: Brill).

Björkqvist, Heimer, 1986. *Den nationalekonomiska vetenskapens utveckling i Finland intill år 1918* (Åbo: Åbo Akademi).

Björne, Lars. 1995. "Patrioter och institutionalister. Den nordiska rättsvetenskapens historia I. Tiden före år 1815" in *Rättshistoriskt bibliotek*, vol. 52 (Lund: Institutet för rättshistrorisk forskning) 199–203.

Björne, Lars. 1998. "Brytningstiden. Den nordiska rättsvetenskapens historia II. 1815–1870" in *Rättshistoriskt bibliotek*, vol. 58 (Lund: Institutet för rättshistrorisk forskning).

Blomstedt, Kaarlo. 1940. "Vuosisadan takaisia oloja ja mielialoja. J.J. Nordströmin muistiinpanoja" Historiallinen Arkisto XLVII.

Calonius, Matthias. 1908. *Praelectiones in iurisprudentiam civilem* in Wilhelm Chydenius, Wilhelm and Väinö Nordström (eds.) (Helsingforsiae: [Edlund]).

Castrén, Liisa. 1951. *Adolf Ivar Arwidsson isänmaallisena herättäjänä* (Helsinki: Suomen historiallinen seura).

Castrén, Matti. J. 1957. "Kauppiaanuran alku 1800-luvun alkupuolella Helsingissä" in *Historiallinen Aikakauskirja* 56, 132–147.

Ehrström, G. 1874. "Minnesord öfver Johan Jakob Nordström" in *Tidskrift utgiven av Juridiska Föreningen i Finland* vol. 10, 68–80.

Engman, Max. 2009. *Ett långt farväl. Finland mellan Sverige och Ryssland efter 1809* (Stockholm: Atlantis).

Hakapää, Jyrki. 2008. *Kirjan tie lukijalle. Kirjakauppojen vakiintuminen Suomessa 1740–1860* (Helsinki: Suomalaisen Kirjallisuuden Seura).

Harju, Ilkka. 2013. "Komissiokaupan laintasoinen siviilioikeudellinen sääntelytarve arvopaperimarkkinoilla" in *Liikejuridiikka* 3, 60–115.

Heikkinen, Sakari, Heinonen, Visa, Kuusterä, Antti and Pekkarinen, Jukka. 2000. *The History of Finnish Economic Thought 1809–1917* (Helsinki: Societas scientiarum Fennica).

Kessler, Amalia, D. 2007. A *Revolution in Commerce: The Parisian Merchant Court and the Rise of Commercial Society in Eighteenth-Century France* (New Haven: Yale University Press).

Kirby, David. 2006. *A Concise History of Finland* (Oxford: Oxford University Press).

Klinge, Matti. 2010. *A European University. The University of Helsinki 1640–2010* (Keuruu).

Kuisma, Markku. 1993. *Metsäteollisuuden maa. Suomi, metsät ja kansainvälinen järjestelmä 1620–1920* (Helsinki: Suomen Historiallinen Seura).

Kuusterä, Antti and Tarkka, Juha. 2011. *Bank of Finland 200 years 1. Imperial cashier to central bank* (Helsinki: Otava); Eng. translation of Suomen Pankki 200 vuotta 1. Keisarin kassasta keskuspankiksi.

Lagus, W. 1876. *Minnesord öfver Minister-Statssekreteraren m.m. Grefve Alexander Armfelt, framsagda vid Kejserl. Alex. Universitetets Sorgefest den 27 Apr. 1876.*

Lammel, Siegbert. 2008. "Faktorei" *Handwörterbuch zur Deutschen Rechtsgeschichte*, 2nd. edition, vol. 1, in Cordes, A., Lück, H., Werkmüller, D. and Schmidt-Wiegand, R. (eds.) (Berlin: Erich Schmidt).

Liedman, Sven-Eric, 1986. *Den synliga handen. Anders Berch och ekonomiämnena vid 1700-talets svenska universitet* (Stockholm: Arbetarkultur).

Lindman, Sven. 1948. *Johan Jacob Nordström: hans samhällssyn och politiska personlighet. 1, Tiden intill 1854* (Åbo: Åbo Akademi).

Mittermaier, C.J.A. 1830. *Grundsätze des gemeinen deutschen Privatrechts: mit Einschluß des Handels-, Wechsel- und Seerechts* II (4th. ed.) (Landshut: Krüll).

[Myréen, D.,] "Kort öfwersigt af de fördelar Finland wunnit genom sin lyckliga förening med Ryska Riket under Kejsar Alexanders spira" in *Åbo Allmänna Tidning 1819*, no 125, 126, 129, 130 and 136.

Nordström, Johan, Jacob. 1832. "*Skildring af Municipal-författningen i Finland*": akademisk afhandling (Helsingfors).

Nordström, Johan, Jacob. 1844. *Ett och annat om handelsböckers beviskraft* (Helsingfors).

Nordström, Johan, Jacob. 1844. *Ytterligare ett och annat om handelsböckers beviskraft och om creditpapper* (Helsingfors).

Nykänen, Panu. 2015. "Tieto ja talous. Teollisuutta tukevan tutkimuksellisen tiedon jakelua Suomessa kahden vuosisadan aikana" *Kasvatus & Aika*, 9 (1).

Ojala, Jari. 1999. *Tehokasta liiketoimintaa Pohjanmaan pikkukaupungeissa. Purjemerenkulun kannattavuus ja tuottavuus 1700–1800-luvulla* (Helsinki: Suomen Historiallinen Seura).

Palmgren, Gunnar. 1944. "Utvecklingen av Finlands handelsrättsliga lagstiftning" *Vårt näringsliv och kriget: spridda studier samlade av Ekonomiska Samfundet i Finland på femtionde årsdagen av dess instiftande och tillägnade professor J.V. Tallqvist* (Helsingfors: Schildts).

Romani, Roberto. 2005. "The Republican Foundations of Sismondi's Nouveaux principes d'économie politique" in *History of European Ideas* 31, 17–33.

Sallila, Jussi. 2015. *Insolvency, Commercial Utility and Principles of Justice. The Making of Bankruptcy Law in Sweden and Finland, ca. 1680–1868*, Dissertation (Helsinki: University of Helsinki).

Scherner, Karl-Otto. 1977. "Die Wissenschaft des Handelsrechts" in Helmut Coing (ed.), *Handbuch der Quellen und Literatur der neueren europäischen Privatrechtsgeschichte*, vol 2, part 2 (Munich: C.H., Beck).

Scherner, Karl-Otto. 1972. "Anfänge einer deutschen Handelsrechtswissenschaft im 18. Jahrhundert" in *Zeitschrift für das gesamte Handelsrecht und Wirtschaftsrecht* vol. 136, 465–489.

Scherner, Karl-Otto. 2012. "Kommissionsgeschäft" in Cordes, A., Lück, H., Werkmüller, D. and Bertelsmeier-Kierst, C. (eds.), *Handwörterbuch zur deutschen Rechtsgeschichte*. 2nd ed. vol 2 (Berlin: Erich Schmidt).

Schmoeckel, Mathias. 2008. *Rechtsgeschichte der Wirtschaft. Seit dem 19. Jahrhundert* (Tübingen: Mohr Siebeck).

Tyynilä, Markku. 1992. *Senaatti. Tutkimus hallituskonselji-senaatista 1809–1918* (Helsinki; VAPK-kustannus).

Vasara-Aaltonen, Marianne. 2020. *Learning Law and Travelling Europe: Study Journeys and the Developing Swedish Legal Profession, c. 1630–1800* (Leiden-Boston: Brill).

Väisänen, Maija. 2005. "Lagus, Wilhelm Gabriel (1786–1859)" in *Suomen Kansallisbiografia* vol. 5.

Whitman, James, Q. 1987–88. "Commercial Law and the American Volk: A Note on Llewellyn's German Sources for the Uniform Commercial Code" in *Yale Law Journal* 97.

Wrede, Rabbe Axel. 1917. *Matthias Calonius* (Helsingfors: Söderström).

Wrede, Rabbe Axel. 1930. "Johan Jakob Nordström såsom statsrättsläräre" in *Tidskrift utgiven av Juridiska Föreningen i Finland* vol. 66, 291–336.

Primary Sources

Förteckning öfver framl. riksarkivarien och cancellers-sekreteraren vid rikets universiteter dr J.J. Nordströms efterlemnade boksamling [...] (Stockholm: Stockholms Bokauktions-kammare, 1874).

CHAPTER 7

The Making of Modern Scholarship of Commercial Law in Nineteenth- and Twentieth-Century Finland: Models and Adaptations

Heikki Pihlajamäki

1 The Growth of Commercial Law as a Discipline: International Models

The identity of commercial law has always been unclear. What legal institutions or bundles of norms actually belong to it? How should commercial law be distinguished from other fields of private law? And not only private law, for commercial law is one of the branches of law most difficult to place within the dichotomy of private and public law. Pollock and Maitland, then, identified commercial law via a law of proof:

> The law merchant […] seems to have been rather a special law for mercantile transactions than a special law for merchants. It would we think have been found chiefly to consist of what would now be called rules of evidence, rules about the proof to be given of sales and other contracts, rules as to the legal value of the tally and the God's penny […][1]

In 1915, Arthur Nussbaum stated that "commercial law is no longer a law of commerce, but just a collection of quite distinct materials."[2] A leading Finnish commercial lawyer has recently pointed out that many of his colleagues actually do things that have little to do with commercial law, by any definition, but rather with fields such as general contract law, labour law or competition law.[3] Even after almost 150 years of existence as an academic discipline, commercial law is still lacking a theory and identity.[4]

Theory and identity have everything to do with the creation of a discipline. This article seeks to place the birth of Finnish commercial law, with the help of comparative legal history, in an international context. Section two of the article

---

1 Pollock and Maitland 1898, p. 467.

2 Nussbaum 1915.

3 Mäntysaari 2014, p. 347–367, 353.

4 Druey 2009, p. 607–616; Fleischer 2007, p. 50–76.

 | DOI:10.1163/9789004436046_008

delves into the different European models of understanding and systematizing norms applied to merchant relations in the early modern period. Section three deals with the nineteenth- and twentieth-century development of commercial law as an academic discipline, focusing in particular on nineteenth-century Finland and, for comparison, certain other European countries. The fourth and final section draws conclusions based on the findings presented in the article.

2 Commercial Law Scholarship in the Making: the Early Modern Period

Talking about commercial law as a branch of legal literature before the nineteenth century is, strictly speaking, anachronistic. Commercial law as a branch of law was a nineteenth-century invention – as was the whole systematization of law into modern disciplines – but the sources of commercial law cannot be properly understood if detached from its early roots.[5] To understand the different ways commercial law grew as a distinct discipline in different parts of the Western world in the nineteenth century, it is necessary to look deeper into its history. Despite the fact that northern Italy lost its leading position in European commerce after the Middle Ages, early modern Italian legal scholarship enormously influenced the development of commercial law in other parts of Europe. The best examples are Benvenuto Stracca (1509–1578; *De mercatura*, 1553), Sigismundo Scaccia (1564–1634; *Tractatus de commerciis et cambio*, 1618) and Casaregis (1670–1737; *Discursis legales et commercio*, 1707). Stracca in particular is known as a practitioner who for the first time presented the body of commercial law known as the law merchant in its entirety, combining a Romanist tradition originating in the Middle Ages with a profound knowledge of commercial and court practice. For Stracca, the law merchant was a combination of rules pertaining to merchants that did not include the norms pertaining to exchange.[6]

Special legal norms pertaining to commercial relations – legal arrangements concerning contractual relations affecting merchants, commercial enterprises, insurance matters, conflict resolution and regulation issues, and bankruptcy – emerged as different from other parts of the law, such as contract norms based on Roman law, in many Western European regions already in the early modern period. In other regions, general law pertaining to contracts and procedure continued governing mercantile situations.[7] Some of the norms that originally

5 See Hilaire 1986, p. 85.
6 Hilaire 1986, p. 65–66.
7 De ruysscher 2014, p. 19.

applied to merchant relations only now regulated all contractual relations. Examples abound. The good faith of the possessor of stolen goods was originally protected amongst market merchants only, but in the sixteenth century the rule came to be applied more generally in continental law.[8] This type of change in meanings was not particular to just commercial law. In the early modern period, many medieval legal concepts acquired new meaning.

In the Middle Ages, commercial law in Europe was institutionalized in two basic models. In the southern part of the continent (along the Iberian, Dalmatian and Adriatic coasts), merchant courts, in which merchants themselves served as judges, resolved commercial cases. In north-western Europe, commercial cases were tried in normal urban and princely courts, in which merchants' privileges often safeguarded them against seizure and arrest, or guaranteed them quicker proceedings. In the south, the merchants made the rules themselves, whereas in the north the urban or princely privileges were essential to shaping the *ius mercatorum.* Both in southern and northern Europe, the earliest forms of commercial law concerned the relationship between merchants and those involved in maritime transport. In the case of producers, transporters and merchants, exceptions were made to the general legal rules. It was also typical from early on that merchants were allowed to solve their cases via arbitrage procedure.[9]

Despite the fact that arbitration procedures were quite common, the early modern state gradually took increasing control over commerce and merchants' affairs. In the early modern period, European commercial courts appeared in three forms. The southern model of *consulados*, typical of Spain (Burgos 1494, Bilbao 1511, Seville 1543), was based on the relative independence of merchants, who chose to serve as judges in their courts, although often in conjunction with professional lawyers or experienced lay judges. However, the importance of political power-holders was great also here as regards both the founding of the consular courts as well as putting commercial customs into writing. In the northern model, such as practiced in the Netherlands or England, no special merchant courts emerged, although merchants could have a say in commercial adjudication. The successful French model, based on the commercial courts (*juridictions consulaires*) founded in the mid-seventeenth century, was a compromise between the southern and northern models. As in the case of Burgos, French merchants chose the judge from amongst themselves, but the commercial courts had jurisdiction only up to a certain value amount in the case. If the value exceeded that amount, the case fell under a royal court's jurisdiction.

8 De ruysscher 2014, p. 23.

9 De ruysscher 2014, p. 26–27, 30.

Researchers have pointed out the importance of state formation as one of the main reasons behind the difference between southern and Eastern Europe. In the northern part of Europe, the strengthening modern state sought control over all forms of legal decision-making, commercial adjudication included.[10]

In recent years, historians – mainly economic historians – have intensely debated the interplay between commerce, state and urban institutions, and private ordering. In his study of Jewish merchants trading in the eleventh and twelfth centuries between Italy and the Maghrebi region of North Africa, Avril Greif underlined the importance of merchants' own cultural beliefs and social norms for arranging commerce independently of the influence of political rulers.[11] Jeremy Edwards and Sheilagh Ogilvie have questioned Greif's results, however, pointing out that the commercial transactions of the Maghrebi traders were in fact subject to formals rules enforceable by secular or religious courts.[12] To similar effect, scholars have also noted that medieval merchant guilds operating abroad always functioned with the license of their home government and their host abroad.[13] Oscar Gelderblom, in this study of late medieval and early modern Dutch cities, drew interesting conclusions that fall somewhere between these two positions. He claims that strong towns, such as Bruges, Antwerp and Amsterdam, developed flexible legal institutions able to accommodate foreign merchants and their commercial customs within the same local system.[14]

The discussion surrounding the material norms employed in commercial conflict resolution has been subject to debate as well. To put it briefly, the narrative of medieval *lex mercatoria*, with European merchants having a common law merchant in the Middle Ages and to an extent in the early modern period also, became popular after Lewin Goldschmidt had invented it in the 1880s. The idea of *lex mercatoria* received a strong boost in 1983, when Harold Berman adapted it for his influential *Law and Revolution*. Subsequently, legal historians have gradually dismantled the theory and demonstrated that a common law merchant never existed for all of Europe, neither in a procedural nor in a substantive meaning of the term.

How did Swedish (and Finnish) law of the early modern period relate to the European histories of commercial law? Was there something that could be called commercial law in early modern Sweden? As I have explained

10 De ruysscher 2014, p. 34–35.

11 Greif 1989, p. 857–882.

12 Edwards and Ogilvie 2012, p. 421–444.

13 Gelderblom and Grafe 2010, p. 477–511, 487–493.

14 Gelderblom 2013.

elsewhere,[15] special rules governing relations between merchants had begun to be codified in the Middle Ages, and in the city laws of Birka and Wisby, which included large provisions regarding maritime commercial law. The Town Law of King Magnus Eriksson of 1352 was based on a similar idea: as part of a comprehensive code of law, it also included rules concerning the commercial activities of town-dwellers. Obviously, their needs differed from those of rural people, who could get by with general rules of private law, applicable to all situations of life.[16]

A commercial regulation applying to the whole realm had gradually emerged by the seventeenth century. Norms and regulations, which later became commercial law, pertained mostly to two branches of regulation. First, a vast regulatory framework necessary for mercantilist policies was part of "cameral" or "police" regulation.[17] Second, a large number of special rules on private law for merchants were categorized under maritime law. Maritime transportation, maritime insurance, and maritime corporations had little to do with the legal needs of other merchants operating domestically. In Sweden, no sensible entity such as a law common to all merchants existed. Most of Sweden's international commerce was done by sea, whereas simple domestic commerce could function quite well with general rules of private law.

Legal literature, however, was scarce in all fields, and even fewer authors concerned themselves with commercial questions. One of the few who did, Johannes Loccenius, who was of German origin, touched upon them in his *De iure maritime & navali* (1652), which contained chapters on maritime insurance, transportation contracts and companies and one on procedural questions regarding litigation arising from maritime contracts and commercial contracts. Loccenius referred to German, Dutch and other European sources, such as Pedro de Santarem's (Pedro Santerna Lusitano) *Tractatus de assecurationes*, Hugo Grotius and Vinnius, as well as to the Amsterdam and Antwerp statutes.[18] Maritime law of the early modern period included everything having to do with seafaring, which, in other words, was subject to the systematizing

15 Pihlajamäki 2018.

16 See Reddie 1842, p. 391–392. Reddie's study is a work of comparative legal history, which traces the development of maritime commercial law in many jurisdictions, including Rome, Sweden, England and Denmark. It belongs to the same genre as the first wave of comparative legal history studies, or "universal legal histories" (*Universalrechtsgeschichte*), which emerged in the first part of the nineteenth century and include Eduard Gans's *Das Erbrecht in weltgeschichtlicher Entwicklung* (1824–35) and, for instance, Karl Mittermaier's many articles on criminal and procedural laws.

17 For more on these regulations, see Kotkas 2014, p. 59–68, 131–150.

18 Loccenius 1652, p. 18, 22, 29, 52, 55, 57, among others.

principle. Some of the rules included in the maritime law of Loccenius were of a kind that had no direct connection to merchants or commerce, such as maritime defence, privileges pertaining to shipbuilding, freedom of navigation, shipwrecks and fishing rights, as well as extensive sections dedicated to piracy (II:3), navigational security, property rights to ship, hereditary rights to ship, delicts and procedure.[19] Some of the subjects were closely related to commercial activities. These subjects included staple rights and rights pertaining to bottomry (*foenus nauticum*), jettison (*iactus*), contribution (*contributio*) and contracts and other obligations. Thus, Loccenius went through the whole legal system from the point of view seafaring, and commercial activities were only part of the larger picture. The same can be said of Jacob Albrekt Flintberg's (1751–1804) approach. His *Anmärkningar till Sveriges rikes sjölag* concerned only maritime law, although the work included an introduction to bankruptcy procedure as well.[20]

In general terms, David Nehrman (1695–1769) was even more important because his work encompassed the earlier seventeenth-century developments in all major fields of law and his studies continued to dominate the field until almost the start of the nineteenth century. In his *Inledning til then Swenska Jurisprudentiam Civilem* of 1729 (Introduction to Swedish Civil Law), Nehrman explained the Swedish system of company law – which was equal to *societas*.[21] Otherwise, Nehrman did not touch upon commercial matters. This lack of interest on Nehrman's part is quite telling of the fact that domestic commerce did well within the general rules of contract law and there was very little need for any special commercial law as such.[22] As far as foreign commerce was concerned, commercial law was part of maritime law, which included many kinds of legal norms other than just the law merchant. This was the situation when commercial law as a modern discipline started to emerge in the nineteenth century.

To sum up so far: commercial regulations developed in Sweden already in the Middle Ages, and some seventeenth- and eighteenth-century Swedish authors showed interest in commercial matters. However, it would be an exaggeration to speak of Swedish commercial law as an academic specialization in any sense of the word in the early modern period.

19 Loccenius 1652.
20 Flintberg 1794.
21 Nehrman 1729, p. 210–229.
22 See also Palmgren 1944, p. 113–125.

3 Creating Commercial Law as a Modern Legal Discipline: Europe, Sweden, Finland

When can we talk about a distinct legal discipline in the modern sense of the word? Clearly, it would at least be when three prerequisites have been fulfilled. First, a discipline needs to have people who specialize in the subject and identify with it, usually by giving it a name: "environmental law," "labour law," or "commercial law." Second, at the next stage a discipline will typically become institutionalized. It will have professorial chairs, learned societies and eventually journals. It will be taught as a separate subject at universities. Third, if we are dealing with continental law, it will also have a "general theory," or rules that are common to the whole field.

I will start with the first prerequisite, specialization and identification. In the seventeenth and eighteenth centuries, as mentioned already, commercial law as a separate entity did not exist in Sweden. Instead, rules pertaining to commerce were categorized under "police," the legal nature of which was not quite clear in the first place, or under maritime law, the significance of which was clear enough for the northern state.

This was the situation when Sweden lost its eastern half, Finland, to the Russian Empire in 1809 as a result of the Napoleonic Wars. During the second half of the nineteenth century, the economic and political situation described above, which Finland had shared with its former mother country, Sweden, began to change. However, these changes effected no fundamental changes in the law until the latter half of the century – neither in Finland nor in Sweden.[23] We now turn our attention to Finland. The police as a legal category was being dismantled, and the rules that had thitherto comprised it had to find new homes in the emerging modern branches of law. A wave of liberalization swept through Finland. The legal reforms started in 1856, when the liberal-minded Czar Alexander II, presented a programme of social and economic reforms during his visit to the Grand Duchy. The Emperor demanded the adoption of three measures: (1) the developing industries needed a functioning infrastructure of railways, roads and channels; (2) the living conditions of the rural poor needed to be improved; and (3) economic legislation needed liberalization.[24] When the Diet (the Grand Duchy's legislative body) reconvened in 1862, after a recess of more than half a century, a list of the most urgent measures was immediately drawn up and the reforms carried out on a piece-by-piece basis throughout the 1860s and 1870s. Freedom of contract saw the light of day through a series of

23 See Jussi Sallila's article on J.J. Nordström in this volume. Nordström was originally a Finnish legal scholar who spent the latter part of his career in Sweden, p. 158–186.

24 Kekkonen 1998, p. 120.

legislative acts (Hirelings Act 1865, Industry Act 1868, Marriage Act 1868). The sphere of legally competent persons widened, and the predictability of exchange increased through the Mortgage Act (1868), Warranty Act (1868) and Prescription Act (1873). To make the accumulation of capital possible, new banking laws and company legislation were needed (Private Banks Act 1866, Act on Limited Companies 1864). Freedom of industry became more or less the rule, after several partial reforms, through the Industry Act of 1879.[25]

Works on legal themes, which later came to form part of commercial law, started to appear in Sweden and Finland, and modern legal scholarship, following the German models of the historical school and conceptual jurisprudence, was born in the last decades of the nineteenth century. Examples include J.N. Lang's work on historical-comparative patent law (1880)[26] and K.H.L. Hammarskjöld's study on Swedish transportation law (1886).[27] Both works were clearly inspired by the practical needs of developing business life in both countries. Lang described how the breakdown of the *ancient regime* with its system of privileges contributed to a growing need to protect innovation. The author confirmed the connection between the degree of industrialization and the need for protection through copyright law: "Precisely those countries, which have been the first to recognize the law of copyright, namely England, North America, France, and Belgium, are also the leaders of industrial development."[28] Although it was thus the most industrialized nations that also needed copyright and patent law the most, such institutions were not unnecessary in Finland either, despite its much lower degree of industrialization. Patent law was needed not only for reasons of national economy and in order to encourage innovation, but also to protect the nation's honour: Finland, of course, should not be a "parasite plant, which earned its main income by exploiting what the innovative spirit and industriousness of other nations had created."[29] Neither of these authors was concerned, however, with copyright law or transportation law a as part of anything resembling commercial law, although Hammarskjöld at some length describes the solutions found in the commercial codes of other countries.[30]

25 Kekkonen 1998, p. 28–29.

26 Lang 1880. Lang (1847–1905) was professor of economic law and economics at the University of Helsinki. His main work was *Finlands sjörätt* [Finnish maritime law] Lang 1890.

27 Hammarskjöld 1886.

28 Lang 1880, p. 108. "Just de länder, som tidigast erkänt uppfinnarerätten, nemligen England, Nordamerika, Frankrike och Belgien befinna sig äfven i den industriela utvecklingens spets."

29 Lang 1880, p. 170 "...likasom en parasitvext som hemta sin hufvudsakliga näring af hvad uppfinningsanden och näringsfliten hos andra nationer skapat."

30 Hammarskjöld 1886, p. 165–172.

A couple of decades later, enthusiasm for commercial law was already up in the air. George Granfelt began his work on current account (Ital. *conto corrente*) as a legal institution in a somewhat passionate manner. It was, "[i]n our days [...] especially commercial law," which was "prepared [...] to follow the quick progress of the economy pulsating lively." Granfelt saw, nevertheless, commercial law not as a fully separate branch of law, but as an "intermediary station" ("*mellanstation*") between customary law and general civil law. Elsewhere, commercial law was an "experimental field, a platform for new findings," and it did not exist in Finland. Legal innovations had been introduced in Finnish commercial practice as well, but not enough to warrant a whole new field of commercial law: "[...] also in our country the business life demonstrates a capability of creating legal institutions, which with increasing pressure knock on the closed door [of general civil law]."[31] Granfelt wrote large articles on other aspects of commercial law as well, such as security contracts and transportation law.[32]

In Finland, the first legal scholar who clearly started specializing in commercial law and identifying with it was Lauri Cederberg (1881–1943). In 1924, Cederberg became the first professor of commercial law in Finland, and in fact, the chair was the first of its kind in the Nordic countries. The funding of the chair came from Alfred Kordelin, an important entrepreneur, who had donated the funds in his will.[33] This was a time of growing interest in the economic development of the new Finnish nation. Economic education was held in newfound esteem, the best example of which being the founding of the Helsinki University of Economics in 1911. Åbo Akademi University, the only exclusively Swedish-language university in Finland, was founded in 1918, and from the start a chair in "commercial, industrial, and social law" was created there.[34]

One of the first tasks for the new professor was to define the field of commercial law. Having studied in Bonn and Berlin, Cederberg was well aware of the latest trends. He had already addressed the question in his writings of whether commercial law should be codified. Cederberg did not think that it should, although it was clear that both the Finnish law of obligations and

31 "Icke förty visar sig näringslifvet äfven hos oss mäktigt att skapa rättsinstitut, som med dag för dag alt större eftertryck klappa på den stängda porten [...]". G. Granfelt, *Om kontokurranten* (Helsinki: Helsingfors Centraltryckeri, 1899), p. 1–2.

32 "Om Spedition," *Tidskrift utgifven av Juridiska Föreningen i Finland* 1905, p. 136–222; "Om försäkringsaftalets uppkomst och utveckling," *Tidskrift utgifven av Juridiska Föreningen i Finland* 1908, p. 1–112.

33 Sundström 1997, p. 1143–1152.

34 However, the first chair holder, A.W. Gadolin, managed to change the name of the professorship to that of "private law and general jurisprudence."

FIGURE 7.1 The University of Helsinki ca 1860.
(called the Imperial Alexander University 1809–1917)

commerce were in desperate need of reform. The partial statutory reforms that had subsequently been made to patch up the provisions of the Swedish Law of the Realm of 1734 were not satisfactory. A reform was, or so thought Cederberg, clearly in the interests of Finnish commerce. However, Cederberg thought that Finnish commercial law was not yet at a stage in which it could be codified. Commercial law had simply not been sufficiently worked out in existing scholarship. A codification put into effect too soon, therefore, would necessarily need to be overly based on foreign models and would run the risk of losing touch with the Finnish legal system.[35]

Interestingly, Cederberg used comparative legal history to argue that in most cases, commercial law had been separated from the rest of civil law not so much for "legal" reasons as for purely historical reasons. French commercial law was codified in the Napoleonic series of codes of 1808, but, as Cederberg correctly remarked, the roots of such codification lay firmly in the commercial ordinances of Louis XIV between the years 1673 and 1681. Because of the Napoleonic conquests, the model of separate commercial law spread to Belgium,

35 Cederberg 1919, p. 12, 41–42.

Luxemburg, Greece, Turkey and Serbia, among other places. The influence of the French commercial code explained the separation of commercial law in Spain and Portugal as well, and the Spanish legal influence in turn in many "non-European" countries. The lack of political unity likewise accounted for separate commercial law in Germany: if anywhere, it was possible to achieve agreement in the field of commercial law.[36] Finland's situation was different, though, because Finnish commercial law was not yet as developed as elsewhere. Instead of aiming for a codification of commercial law, Finnish authorities aimed for partial reforms and Scandinavian cooperation. Similarly, and again on comparative grounds, Cederberg argued that separate commercial courts were not the solution for Finland.[37]

Cederberg was in favour of codifying the Finnish law of obligations – although not all of civil law – and he thought that commercial law should be included in the code. This, however, did not lead him to the conclusion that commercial law could not exist as a separate system (and thus, a branch of law). Cederberg, writing in 1925, had read his German authorities and quoted Lewin Goldschmidt, according to whom even an uncodified commercial law could be "just as extensive and even more extensive than an uncodified one."[38] The essence of mercantile activity was the constant need to draw up contracts, in contrast to, for instance farmers, who only occasionally prepared such a contract. The "severity of commercial law" ("*die Strenge des Handelsrechts*") meant that the merchant was judged more severely than were ordinary people when informing his commercial partners. They were to perform their contractual duties more carefully than ordinary persons, which showed, for instance, in that even a slight delay in performing one's duties could lead to the dissolution of a contract. The swiftness of commerce demanded that the rules of commercial law be detailed, clear and easy to interpret. On the other hand, a certain amount of flexibility was also needed. A host of special norms regarding commercial relations – such as those concerning copyright, companies and insurances – called for a separation of commercial law from private law. Referring to Jakob Friedrich Behrend, Cederberg distinguished commercial law from general civil law in that commercial law was, by its very nature, transnational. Whereas civil law was always attached to a particular state, every institution of law merchant was at the same time an institution of global law (*Weltrechtsinsitutut*).[39]

36 Cederberg 1919, p. 44–45.

37 Cederberg 1919, "Tarvitaanko Suomessa erikoissäännöksiä kauppa-asioiden prosessuaalisesta käsittelystä".

38 Cederberg 1925.

39 Cederberg 1925, p. 8–9. See Behrend 1886, p. 12.

Cederberg rejected, however, Lewin Goldschmidt's theory of commercial law. According to Goldschmidt, commercial law dealt with transactions that mediated the transfer of goods from producers to consumers. However, and here Cederberg follows Wieland, many institutions of commercial law had little or nothing to do with mediating goods – such as rules regarding the publishing of real estate conveyance books or the right to pursue a trade. Philipp Heck's ideas suited Cederberg better. According to the father of the "Jurisprudence of Interests" (*Interessenjurisprudenz*),[40] commercial law was a law of large companies ("*das Recht des rechtsgeschäftlichen Massenbetriebs*"). The distinctive feature of commercial was that it regulated "several, repetitive, and mutually dependant legal transactions." For Heck, these mass relations had become the norm determining the legal content of commercial dealings whenever the parties had not specifically agreed otherwise. Limited companies were needed to handle the risks necessarily involved in mass transactions.[41]

Unquestionably, Heck was a modern legal scholar. He did not believe in the historical explanations given for commercial law, but departed in terms of more modern understandings of commercial law. He had inherited this perspective from Rudolph von Ihering, who had completely discredited the historical legitimation of law and instead highlighted the functional consequences of law and legal decisions.[42]

For Heck, the *Massenbetrieb*, or large company, was the decisive modern phenomenon, which explained and legitimized the need for commercial law. It was clear to him that commercial enterprises were "entangled in completely different kinds of numerous and complex legal relations than a hundred years ago."[43] Private legal relations were the relations that held modern society together: they were "the bonds that, as the division of labour advanced, kept the private economic elements of the social construction together."[44] As culture advanced, the uses of commercial law expanded.[45]

The growth of commerce was the obvious feature behind large-scale commerce, but there was much more. Division of labour characterized the modern

40 On Heck, see Falk 1995, p. 275.

41 Heck 1902, p. 438–466.

42 Ihering 1887.

43 "Es bedarf nicht der näheren Ausführung, dass heute ganz anderen Kreise der Gewerbetreibenden in zahlreiche und komplizierte Rechtsbeziehung verstrikt sind, als vor 100 Jahren." Heck 1902, p. 464.

44 "Privatrechtlichte Rechtsgeschäfte und aus ihnen hervorgehende Rechtsbeziehungen sind ja die Bande, durch welche bei fortgeschrittener Arbeitstheilung die privatwirtschaftlichen Elemente des sozialen Baus zusammengehalten werden."

45 "Deshalb wird die vertretene Deutung des Handelsrechts dadurch bestätigt, dass ihr Anwendungsgewicht bei fortschreitender Cultur sich ausdehnt."

commercial world as well: If private law in general had become more commercial in nature – which was generally acknowledged at the time – this did not render commercial law useless. On the contrary, the growing number of commercial enterprises gave rise to constantly new situations requiring legal regulations. This was the case not only domestically, but even more so internationally. The need to develop commercial law was "especially intensive" because of the expansion of the law of bills of exchange, i.e. the law of sea and land transport. Large businesses were, according to Heck, suffered most as a result of inadequate national legal orders. Heck saw national insularity as a problem and the (at least potentially) international nature of commercial law as a future promise and his field of law in particular as a "pioneer of progress" ("*Pionier des Fortschritts*").[46]

Heck did not feel the need to justify with examples his claims regarding the needs of commercial life. The huge changes that the German economic structure had experienced in the last couple of decades were obvious enough. Businesses had grown immensely. In 1882, 26% of those employed in crafts and other industries worked in plants with more than 50 employees. In 1907, 45% of all workers did so. Whereas in 1882, 7% worked in businesses with over a 1000 employees, 14% did so in the year 1907. Some industries were more concentrated than others, with mining, engineering and textile and chemical industries leading the way. Already since the eighteenth century, factory entrepreneurs (unlike artisans) had been considered merchants by law, and therefore they were obliged to submit their annual inventories and profit-and-loss accounts and to organize their bookkeeping according to the legal requirements for merchants. By the early twentieth century, producers had also increasingly taken over both the domestic and export trading of their products: electrical and chemical industries are typical examples as well as the sewing machine and bicycle industries.[47]

Heck's emphasis on the international nature of commercial law stood in clear contrast with the efforts to codify commercial law. France had codified commercial law in 1808 and Germany already during the *Deutscher Bund* in 1861, and again as one of the first legal measures after unification in 1871 as well as in 1897. If commercial law was to be developed as an international endeavour, how could it be codified? Cederberg took up the question of codification as well. In the Nordic countries, the codification of civil law had been debated since the 1820s. The mighty Napoleonic civil code stood in the background, and the international codification trends and discussions could not

46 Heck 1902, p. 466.

47 Kocka 1978, p. 492–589, 544, 556, 562; Kocka and Siegrist 1979. p. 55–117, 79–84.

be ignored in Scandinavia either. Because of Finland's annexation to imperial Russia as a result of the Napoleonic Wars, the question of codification received a different colouring in Finland. In the 1820s, Russia entered into a process of codifying its laws, and the project included all parts of the Empire. Finland was no exception. Yet leading Finnish jurists – on whose help Russians absolutely depended – refused to cooperate. This was because they feared that the codification process would not stop short of collecting and modernizing all Finnish laws that been issued after the promulgation of the Swedish Law of the Realm of 1734; they feared that the codification process would bring with it a Russification of the Grand Duchy's laws. In both Sweden and Finland, codification as an issue had more or less died out by the mid-nineteenth century, and legal scholars assumed the leading role in modernizing laws according to foreign, mostly German, models.[48]

Cederberg voiced sympathy for the idea of a limited codification with respect to the law of obligation, the planning of which had already been undertaken as a common Nordic project. Cederberg, after carefully weighing the pros and cons, assumed a positive attitude towards a common commercial code. However, he did not think that Finnish commercial law was yet, at the time of his writing, ripe for codification. This was his view even though he thought that, in principle, commercial law should not be viewed as separate from private law.[49] Here, Cederberg's views changed when he assumed the Chair of Commercial Law at the University of Helsinki. In 1925, Cederberg still thought that as far as statutory law was concerned, the unity of commercial and private law should be maintained. From this perspective, it did not follow, "of course," that commercial law should not be treated as a separate system in legal scholarship.[50]

The reason for this argument is clear and it is similar to Heck's argument regarding the international nature of commercial law. For Cederberg, however, internationalization was directed towards the neighbouring Nordic countries. Otherwise, he was not extremely enthusiastic about the international dimension of commercial law. A danger existed, wrote Cederberg, that if unification were to be successful at the level of statutory law, legal practice would

48 Elsewhere, I have explained the reasons for why the Nordic countries never codified their civil laws. See Pihlajamäki 2015, p. 135–152. The law of obligations was issued in 1928 (*Oikeustoimilaki*).

49 Cederberg 1919. Here, Cederberg followed the solution adopted in the Swiss Civil Code of 1883, which did not distinguish between general private law and commercial law (*Einheitsgesetzgebung*); Becker 2004, p. 104.

50 Cederberg 1925, p. 3.

nevertheless turn out quite differently. This would be the case because no international judicial authority existed to level out the differences.[51]

Cederberg criticized Heck for his concept of *Massenbetrieb*, which could not capture the phenomenon of commercial law adequately. Instead, Cederberg wished to base his concept of commercial law on the concept of enterprise (*företag, yritys, Betrieb*). This conception of commercial law had already by Cederberg's time rather deep roots in German legal scholarship. Wilhelm Endemann, in his *Das Deutsche Handelsrecht* of 1865, had already departed from this concept, though.[52] Julius von Gierke, Heinrich Lehmann[53] and Karl Wieland[54] continued the same tradition.[55] As Schmoeckel has remarked, one advantage of building commercial law around the concept of an enterprise was that it made it possible to take aspects of labour law into consideration.[56] It was also obvious from the point of view of a Finnish legal scholar like Cederberg that such an understanding fit the Finnish economic reality much better than did the concept of a large enterprise – which did not at all dominate the Finnish economic scene in the early twentieth century.

Roughly, at the same time, that is, in the decades preceding the First World War, the Finnish economy grew quite quickly. Between the years 1860 and 1913, the number of those working in the industrial and handicraft sector grew almost five-fold, from 31 000 to 148 000. As the population grew 1.7 times larger, the proportion of industrial and handicraft workers as a percentage of the whole working force grew from 4% in 1860 to 10% in 1910. The growth in the years 1890–1910 was especially vigorous. Although the rise was significant, Finland was still in 1910 a remarkably agrarian country.[57] This was certainly the case in relation to Germany, but the agrarian nature of the Finnish economy was clear in relation to Denmark, Norway and Sweden, too.[58] Finland's economy was different from both that of Germany and the other Scandinavian countries in that Finnish industrialization depended predominantly on a single industry, the sawmill industry, and its derivatives.[59]

51 Cederberg 1919, p. 34.
52 Endemann 1865, p. 74.
53 Lehmann 1913, p. 1–46.
54 Wieland 1921.
55 The history has been summarized in many works. See, for instance, Nörr 1994; Dilcher and Lauda 1979; Schmoeckel 2008, p. 116.
56 Schmoeckel 2009, p. 117.
57 Rasila 1982, p. 55; Kuusterä and Tarkka 2011, p. 313–319.
58 Hildebrand 1978, p. 624. 590–628, 624.
59 Hildebrand 1978, p. 624; Rasila 1982, p. 88.

A "user's perspective" to commercial law involves the need to consider law firms as well. They acted as important intermediaries between a law consisting of abstract norms and legal scholarship on the one hand, and the practical life of commerce on the other. Some lawyers began to specialize in providing counseling services to commercial enterprises from the 1860s onwards, and the first law firms specializing in commercial law appeared in Helsinki in the following decades. Of these firms, Castrén & Snellman (1888) and Dittmar & Indrenius (1899) still exist.[60] In fact, advocacy as a full-time profession emerged in part because of the drastic economic changes of the late nineteenth century. Modern advocacy and modern commercial law were in demand because of the rapid legislative reforms enacted in the Grand Duchy in the 1860s and 1870s. Traditional domestic commerce had not required specialized legal help of any kind. The normative framework had been simple, and if legal problems occurred, they could most likely be solved without the expertise of legal professionals. The situation was rapidly changing towards the late nineteenth century, however. Enterprises engaged in international commerce needed to prepare themselves proactively, put their contractual framework in order and make sure their apparatus corresponded to the exigencies of modern law.

The law firms operated, furthermore, within a growing network of economic operators, the increasing activity of which is shown in the way these non-legal economic operators organized themselves at the national level. The Finnish Organization of Creditors (Suomen Luotonantajayhdistys – Finska Kreditgivareföreningen) was founded in 1905, the Finnish Association of Forwarding Agents (Suomen Speditööriyhdistys – Finska Speditörföreningen) in 1906, the Helsinki Association of Commercial Agents (Helsingin Agenttiyhdistys – Helsingfors Agentförening) in 1911 and the Helsinki Stock Exchange in 1912.

4 Conclusion: Centres, Peripheries, Transplants and Importers

When trying to come to grips with the differences between societies, comparative social scientists and historians have long employed the terms centre and periphery – usually in order to highlight the Western world's superiority as compared to other parts of the world. The theoretical development of such a perspective began, however, only in the 1970s when social and political historians assumed a critical stance towards the Western countries as the self-evident centre of global development. The abuse of those living in colonized parts of the world by the Western powers became a self-evident part of these

60 See Pihlajamäki 2009, p. 106.

discussions. Immanuel Wallerstein's "world system" became the best-known example of the practical uses of the concepts centre and periphery.[61]

In the theory of comparative law or legal history, the concepts have not been developed much at all. (A widely read article by Douglas Osler talks about similar things, though, without employing the terminology.[62]) Traditional European legal history, from Wieacker to Bellomo, has really been interested in the "centre" only, if it is defined as the traditional core area of *ius commune*: Italy, France, Germany and the Netherlands. As Osler explains, each of these regions have their periods of prominence in the traditional story, though otherwise remaining in the margins. Thus, Italy predominated during the Middle Ages, France during the period of humanism, followed by the Netherlands and then Germany in the nineteenth century. The rest of Europe barely existed at all during the periods in question, at least not the Nordic countries.

In recent works by Nordic legal historians, the Nordic region often figures as a periphery in relation to the centre. It is the centre that provides the influences, while the periphery adapts to them. My own work on Finnish evidence law in the nineteenth century, Elsa Trolle Önnerfors' study of early modern Swedish law in wills, and Mia Korpiola's book on early modern Swedish marriage laws provide examples of this dynamic.[63] All of these works show how ideas originally produced in the centre are transferred to the periphery. However, the reception is not passive. The legal transplants or objects of reception – the terminology is endless – change during the process of transference, and the product may sometimes look quite different than it did at the starting point.

Sometimes the comparative constellations are more complex than in the three cases mentioned above. My recent book on law in the seventeenth century presents a case in point. In Livonia, conquered by the Swedes in the 1620s, Livonian law was clearly peripheral in relation to the *gemeines Recht*, the German version of the *ius commune*, but it is much more difficult to determine whether it was peripheral in relation to Swedish law as well. A complex set of legal, cultural and political factors became intermingled in this instance.[64]

It is thus worthwhile to keep in mind that the division into centres and peripheries is not fixed once and for all. There may be cases in which one region is peripheral in relation to another in a certain respect, but central insofar as other issues are considered. Returning to the problem of commercial law, and

61 Champion 1995, p. 2–9.

62 Osler 1997, p. 393–410.

63 Pihlajamäki 1997; Korpiola 2009; Trolle Önnerfors 2014.

64 See Pihlajamäki 2017: *A Case of Legal Pluralism in Early Modern Europe*.

allowing for the reservations expressed above, German nineteenth-century legal scholarship can well be regarded as representing the centre, the scholarly products of which were copied not only in Finland but in other parts of the world as well. In this respect, Finland was a periphery not a centre because the influences moved from Germany to Finland, and never vice versa.

Cederberg's opinions regarding commercial law, however, did not develop in a vacuum. The practical needs for commercial law had developed during the preceding decades, as the Finnish commercial scene experienced tremendous changes beginning in the 1880s. A new legal framework was needed. Cederberg, as the main importer of the modern doctrine of commercial law to Finland, did not primarily turn to Sweden, which at later stages of Finnish history became a major source of influence for Finnish scholars. In Cederberg's time, Swedish scholarship on commercial law still did not offer much of a framework. Thus, Cederberg turned his attention to Germany since it was at the forefront of global legal scholarship at that time. He did not, however, adopt the German teachings passively. Instead, as importers of legal doctrines always do, Cederberg weighed the various different possibilities offered by the globally supreme German legal doctrine. He read widely, picking and choosing as he did so, and then applied his readings to Finnish circumstances. In doing so, he acted much in the same way that other successful importers of legal doctrines had done previously – and were doing precisely at the same time as Cederberg was engaged in constructing the foundations of Finnish scholarship on commercial law.[65]

Literature

Becker, Ansgar. 2004. *Die Entwicklung des Kaufmannsbegriffs im Sinne eines übergeordneten Abgrenzungskriteriums für den persönlichen Anwendungsbereich handelsrechtlihcher Vorschriften* (Münster: LIT).

Behrend, J.F. 1886. *Lehrbuch des Handelsrechts* (Berlin: Guttentag).

Cederberg, Lauri. 1925. *Kauppaoikeuden suhde muuhun siviilioikeuteen* (Porvoo: WSOY).

Cederberg, Lauri. 1919. *Näkökohtia Suomen velvoite- ja kauppaoikeuden kodifioimiskysymyksessä* (Helsinki: Valtioneuvoston kirjapaino).

Cederberg, Lauri. 1918. "Tarvitaanko Suomessa erikoissäännöksiä kauppa-asioiden prosessuaalisesta käsittelystä" in *Lakimies* 1.

65 For an early example of an importer of legal ideas, see my article on Olaus Petri, the principal Swedish theologian and legal thinker of the sixteenth century; Pihlajamäki 2004, p. 29–38. For an example from the modern period and the introduction of German public law doctrines to Finland, see Pihlajamäki 2011, p. 267–277.

Champion, Timothy, C. (ed.) 1995. *Centre and Periphery: Comparative Studies in Archaeology* (London: Routledge).

De ruysscher, Dave. 2014. *Gediscplineerde vrijheid: Een geschiedenis van het handels- en economisch recht* (Antwerp: Maklu).

Dilcher, Gerhard and Lauda, R. 1979. "Das Unternehmen als Gegenstand und Anknüpfungspunkt rechtlicher Regelungen in Deutschland 1860–1920" in Horn, N. et al. (eds.).

Druey, J.N. 2009. "The practitioner and the professor – is there a theory of commercial law?" in Tison, M., De Wulf, H., Van Der Elst, C. and Steennot, R. (eds.) *Perspectives in Company Law and Financial Regulation: Essays in Honour of Eddy Wymeersch* (Cambridge: Cambridge University Press) 607–616.

Edwards, Jeremy and Ogilvie, Sheilagh. 2012. "Contract Enforcement, Institutions and Social Capital: The Maghrebi Traders Reappraised" in *Economic History Review* vol. 65, 421–444.

Endemann, Wilhelm. 1865. *Das Deutsche Handelsrecht: systematisch dargestellt*, Erste Atbtheilung (Heidelberg).

Falk, Ulrich. 1995. "Heck, Phlipp, 1858–1943" in Stolleis, M. (ed.), *Juristen: ein biographisches Lexikon* (München: Beck).

Fleischer, Holger. 2007. "Gesellschafts- und Kapitalmarktrecht als wissenschaftliche Disziplin – Das Proprium der Rechtswissenschaft" in C. Engel and W. Schön (eds.), *Das Proprium der Rechtswissenschaft* (Tübingen: Mohr-Siebeck).

Flintberg, Jacob, Albrecht. 1794. *Anmärkningar till Sweriges rikes sjö-lag* (Stockholm).

Gelderblom, Oscar. 2013. *Cities of Commerce: The Institutional Foundations of International Trade in the Low Countries, 1250–1650* (Princeton: Princeton University Press).

Gelderblom, Oscar and Grafe, Regina. 2010. "The Rise, Persistence, and Decline of Merchant Guilds: Re-thinking the Comparative Study of Commercial Institutions in Pre-modern Europe" in *Journal of Interdisciplinary History* vol. 40, 477–511.

Granfelt, G., *Om kontokurranten* (Helsinki: Helsingfors Centraltryckeri, 1899).

Granfelt, Georg Fredrik. 1908. "Om försäkringsaftalets uppkomst och utveckling", *Tidskrift utgifven av Juridiska Föreningen i Finland.*

Granfelt, Georg Fredrik. 1905. "Om Spedition" *Tidskrift utgifven av Juridiska Föreningen i Finland.*

Greif, Avner. 1989. "Reputation and Coalitions in the Medieval Trade: Evidence on the Maghribi Traders" in *Journal of Economic History* vol. 4, 857–882.

Haarmann, Pirkko-Liisa. 2012. "Cederbergin kauppaoikeus – yhäkö pätevä?" in *Lakimies 7–8*, 973–986.

Hammarskjöld, Hjalmar, L. 1886. *Om fraktaftalet och dess viktigaste rättsföljder* (Uppsala: Almqvist & Wiksell).

Heck, Philip. 1902. "Weshalb besteht ein von dem bürgerlichen Rechte gesondertes Handelsprivatrecht?" in *Archiv für civilistischen Praxis* 92, 438–466.

Hilaire, Jean. 1986. *Introduction au droit commercial* (Paris: Presses universitaires de France).

Hildebrand, Karl-Gustaf. 1978. "Labour and Capital in the Scandinavian Countries in the Nineteenth and Twentieth Centuries" in *The Cambridge Economic History of Europe VII, The Industrial Economies: Capital, Labour, and Enterprise* (Cambridge: Cambridge University Press) 590–628.

Horn, Norbert and Kocka Jürgen (eds.). 1979. *Recht und Entwicklung der Großunternehmen im 19. und fruhen 20. Jahrhundert: Wirtschafts-, sozial und rechtshistorische Untersuchungen im Deutschland, Frankreich, England und den USA* (Göttingen: Vandenchoeck & Ruprecht).

Ihering, Rudolf, von. 1887. *Der Zweck im Recht* (Leipzig: Breitkopf & Härtel).

Kekkonen, Jukka. 1998. *Suomalaisen oikeuskulttuurin suuri linja* (Helsinki: Suomalainen Lakimiesyhdistys).

Kocka, Jürgen. 1978. "Entrepreneurs and Managers in German Industrialization" in *The Cambridge Economic History of Europe: VII: The Industrial Economies: Capital, Labour, and Enterprise* (Cambridge: Cambridge University Press).

Kocka, Jürgen and Siegrist, Hannes. 1979. "Die hundert größten deutschen Industrieunternehmen im späten 19. und frühen 20. Jahrhundert: Expansion, Diversifikation und Integration im internationalen Vergleich" in Horn, N. et al. (eds.).

Korpiola, Mia. 2009. *Between Betrothal and Bedding: The Making of Marriage in Sweden, ca. 1200–1610* (Leiden: Brill).

Kotkas, Toomas. 2014. *Royal Police Ordinances in Early Modern Sweden: The Emergence of Voluntaristic Understanding of Law* (Leiden: Brill).

Kuusterä, Antti and Tarkka, Juha. 2011. *Bank of Finland 200 years I: Imperial cashier to central bank* (Helsinki: Otava).

Lang, Joel Napoleon. 1880. *Om grunderna for uppfinnareskydd genom lag* (Helsinki: Frenckell).

Lang, Joel Napoleon. 1890. *Finlands sjörätt* (Helsinki: WSOY).

Lehmann, Heinrich. 1913. "Grundlinien des deutschen Industrierechts" in *Festschrift für Ernst Zitelmann* (München) 1–46.

Loccenius, J. 1652. *De iure maritime & navali* (Stockholm).

Loccenius, J. 1652. *De iure maritime & navali libri tres* (Stockholm).

Mäntysaari, Petri. 2014. "Kauppaoikeuden teoriasta" in *Lakimies* vol. 3, 347–367.

Nehrman, David. 1729. *Inledning til then Swenska Jurisprudentiam Civilem* (Lund: Ludwig Decreaux).

Nussbaum, Arthur. 1915. "Die Auflösung des Handelsrechtsbegriffs" *Zeitschrift für das gesamte Handelsrecht* vol. 76.

Nörr, K.W. 1994. "Das Unternehmen in der Wirtschafts- und Rechtsordnung 1880 bi 1930: ein Beitrag zur Morfologie der organisierten Wirtschaft" in Coing, H. et al., *Staat und Unternehmen aus der Sicht des Rechts* (Tübingen: Mohr-Siebeck).

Osler, Douglas. 1997. "The Myth of European Legal History" in *Rechtshistorisches Journal* vol. 16, 393–410.

Palmgren, Gunnar. 1944. "Utvecklingen av Finlands handelsrättsliga lagstiftning," in *Vårt näringsliv och kriget. Spridda studier* — tillägnade professor J.V. Tallqvist (Helsinki).

Pihlajamäki, Heikki. 1997. *Evidence, Crime, and the Legal Profession: The Emergence of Free Evaluation of Evidence in Nineteenth-Century Finland* (Lund: Institutet för rättshistorisk forskning).

Pihlajamäki, Heikki. 2004. "Gründer, Bewahrer oder Vermittler? Die nationalen und internationalen Elemente im Rechtsdenken des Olaus Petri" in Eckert, J. and Modéer, K.Å. (eds.) *Juristische Fakultäten und Juristenausbildung im Ostseeraum* (Stockholm: Institutet för rättshistorisk forskning).

Pihlajamäki, Heikki. 2009. *Kansan ja esivallan välissä: suomalaisen asianajajakunnan historia* (Helsinki: Suomen Asianajajaliitto).

Pihlajamäki, Heikki. 2011. "Translating German Administrative Law: The Case of Finland" in *Rechtsgeschichte* 19, 267–277.

Pihlajamäki, Heikki. 2015. "Private Law Codification, Modernization and Nationalism: A View from Critical Legal History" in *Critical Analysis of Law* vol. 2:1, 135–152.

Pihlajamäki, Heikki. 2017. *Conquest and the Law in Swedish Livonia (ca. 1630–1710): A Case of Legal Pluralism in Early Modern Europe* (Leiden-Boston: Brill).

Pihlajamäki, Heikki. 2018. "The Birth of Commercial Law in Early Modern Sweden: Sources and Historiography" in Pihlajamäki, H. Cordes, A. Dauchy S. and De ruysscher, D., (eds.) *Understanding the Sources of Early Modern and Modern Commercial Law: Courts, Statutes, Contracts, and Legal Scholarship* (Brill: Leiden).

Pollock, Frederic and Maitland, Frederic, William. 1898. *The History of English Law before the Time of Edward I:1* (Cambridge: Cambridge University Press).

Rasila, V. 1982. "Ensimmäinen teollistumiskausi" in Ahvenainen, J., Pihkala, E. and V. Rasila (eds.) *Suomen taloushistoria 2: teollistuva Suomi* (Helsinki: Tammi).

Reddie, James. 1842. *An Historical View of the Law of Maritime Commerce* (Edinburgh and London: William Blackwood and Sons).

Schmoeckel, Mathias. 2008. *Rechtsgeschichte der Wirtschaft seit dem. Jahrhundert 19* (Tübingen: Mohr-Siebeck).

Sundström, Mia. 1997. "Lauri Cederberg" in *Kansallisbiografia* (Helsinki: Suomalaisen Kirjallisuuden Seura).

Trolle Önnerfors, Elsa. 2014. *Justitia et prudentia: Rättsbildning genom tillämpning, Svea hovrätt och testamentsmålen 1640–1690* (Stockholm: Institutet för rättshistorisk forskning).

Wieland, Karl. 1921. *Handelsrecht, Erster Band: Das kaufmännische Unternehmen und die Handelsgesellschaften* (Leipzig).

CHAPTER 8

Sweden and Finland: A Lively Laboratory for Commercial Laws and Practices

Stefania Gialdroni

Commercial law *history* acquired the "dignity" of a specific field of study only at the end of the nineteenth century, mainly thanks to the influence of Levin Goldschmidt and his *Universalgeschichte des Handelsrechts* (1891), which was read and appreciated far beyond the boundaries of Germany.[1] Despite the fact that almost 130 years have passed since the publication of Goldschmidt's best-known work, commercial law history still seems to struggle to affirm its place in the framework of legal historical studies.

The practice-oriented, often informal, equity based mercantile transactions and procedures beat back scholars engaged in more rooted fields of study such as civil law, canon law or even criminal law history and frighten off those who are willing to explore them, because archival research is particularly frustrating. On the other hand, the inherent transdisciplinary nature of commercial law history – always at the edge of economic history and open to all kinds of issues related to social history in the widest sense (religion, language, travel, etc.) –, should be seen as a great richness, that fits contemporary legal historiography perfectly.

The international project "The Making of Commercial Law: Common Practices and National Legal Rules from the Early Modern to the Modern Period" has had the double effect of stressing the importance of a technical approach to the history of commercial law without losing the transdisciplinary charm of this field of study. In the course of four years, five conferences were organized: two were devoted (in 2014 and 2017, both in Helsinki) to the historiography of commercial law; one to the role played by the small, medium-sized and large companies in law and economic practice (Brussels, 2015); one to the relationship between colonial history and commercial practices (Helsinki and Fiskars, 2016); and one to the link between merchant travel, language, and the "migration of laws" (Frankfurt am Main, 2016). The papers presented at those conferences

1 Goldschmidt 1891. The text was translated into Italian by Vittorio Pouchain and Antonio Scialoja: *Storia universale del diritto commerciale* (Turin: UTET, 1913). In general, therefore, it was read in German.

 | DOI:10.1163/9789004436046_009

led to nonconformist publications; for example, putting the role played by the big chartered companies in the development of business law into perspective,[2] pointing out the differences between the various historiographical traditions,[3] analyzing the routes followed by technical legal terms and the impact of those "journeys" on the development of commercial law.[4]

The present publication too has been developed in the framework of this ambitious project. Its aim is to contrast the traditional European heartland-centered approach to the history of commercial law, by finally placing the role played by the "periphery" of Europe, and in particular the Nordic countries, in the spotlight. For the very first time, not only the development of commercial law in Sweden and Finland (whose history is inextricably linked) has been deepened through a collective work trawling a vast number of unpublished documents, but also, all this valuable material has been made available in English, at last making it accessible to those scholars who do not speak Scandinavian languages. The point of view of the periphery has the great advantage of being intrinsically and inevitably comparative and therefore of interest to a wide range of scholars. Comparison is, in fact, the *fil-rouge* that connects all the essays in this book. They can be divided into two groups: those dealing with commercial law practice (especially company law) and those focusing on more theoretical issues, and in particular on the teaching of commercial law at Finnish universities.

The overview on company law in Sweden and Finland between the seventeenth and the nineteenth century provided by the contributions by Dave De ruysscher, Katja Tikka and Ulla Ijäs can be better understood thanks to Marko Lamberg's article (focused on the presence of foreign merchants in Stockholm from the fifteenth to the seventeenth century), which provides the necessary premises to understand the mutual influence between mercantile practices in Scandinavia and the rest of Europe. In Stockholm, German-speaking merchants were the largest and most powerful group of foreigners, certainly thanks to the vitality of the Hanseatic League, at least in the late Middle Ages. Furthermore, court protocols and other sources mention the occasional presence in Stockholm of other Scandinavians, Estonians, Russians and even Italians and Frenchmen. Nevertheless, the most numerous groups living for longer periods in Stockholm (other than German-speaking people) were Dutchmen and Scotsmen. Thus, the picture that emerges at hand of legislation (in particular the

2 De ryusscher et al. (eds.) 2017.

3 Stressing, for example, that in France and the Low Countries commercial law has been "mostly the territory of economic historians" rather then of legal historians (as it has been otherwise the case in England, Italy and Germany): Pihlajamäki et al. (eds.) 2018, p. 1.

4 Gialdroni et al. (eds.) 2020.

Town Law) and of case law (in particular the cases discussed in the Town Court), is that of a lively international harbor town and market place that profited from the presence of foreign merchants and their know-how.

This influence becomes evident in the analysis provided by Dave De ruysscher, which is devoted to the chartered companies in Sweden at the beginning of the seventeenth century. His work bases itself upon the drafts and charters of several Swedish companies, to examine the role played by the most important chartered companies of the period (the Dutch East and West India Companies and the English East India Company) and their influence on the development of trading companies in Sweden. Nevertheless, Dutch merchants appear to be more present and powerful than their English counterparts are, because they took part in the plans for such companies as well as in the very drafting of their charters. In addition, their impact is noticeable also at a linguistic level. For example, in the 1615 charter of the Stockholm Company, the investor was called *participant* (as in the Dutch East India Company) and the debenture that the *participant* received upon investment was called *action* (from the Dutch *actie*). A Dutch influence that is confirmed in Katja Tikka's contribution, which is devoted to the Swedish Tar Company, founded in Stockholm in 1648. From the very first mention of the tar trade in Sweden (1629), in fact, the direct involvement of Dutch merchants is uncontestable. Johan van Swindern, a Dutchman, was not only recruited by the Swedish government to investigate the production and quality of tar in the southern part of the country, but was also the first to apply for a privilege to set up the first Tar Company, enjoying *de facto* a monopoly of this trade. Four honored and well-known bourgeois men, including van Swindern, founded the Norland Tar Company eventually in 1648. The privilege, provided by the Council of the realm, granted the monopoly of the tar trade in Norland, Finland and Carelia as well as all export activities to the company. The troubled history of the Tar Company continued though, with ups and downs, for 64 years. As Tikka herself stresses, the big Dutch and English chartered companies of the seventeenth century were usually granted a monopoly of trade in a certain geographic area and were not limited to one single good.[5] This led to the creation of a strict connection between trade and colonization, a link that is completely absent in the Swedish Tar Company.

Changing time (nineteenth century) and place (Finland), Ulla Ijäs, with her analysis of Hackman & Co. (one of the largest timber-exporting firms in the Northern Baltic area), confirms the international dimension of trading companies in the Nordic countries, even in the framework of a family enterprise.

5 See for example the incorporation charter of the English East India Company, dated 31 December 1600: 43 Eliz. I, published in Shaw 1887, p. 1–15.

Hackman & Co. was, in fact, founded by a German merchant in 1790 and remained a family business until 2003. Because of the peculiar situation of Finland under Russian rule, its legislative organs did not meet until 1863, creating a gap in the country's legislation. According to Ijäs, this gap did not result, as one might think, in an isolation/decay of Finnish business, because it was "filled" by the merchants' expertise and (stable and reliable) international networks, as demonstrated by the Hackman family. Based upon analysis of Hackman's letters, which are the main source of this essay, it is clearly shown that several family members could speak German, Swedish, Russian, English and French. This demonstrates the outstanding capacity the family and businesses like them had to build international networks and prosperous family businesses in a country that had no legislation regarding partnerships or joint-stock companies. However, it has to be stressed that the Finnish merchants were not alone. In fact, even though the 1807 French *Code de commerce* ruled company law in France, many other countries in Europe were still finding their way towards business regulation throughout the mid- nineteenth century. That was certainly the case in the United Kingdom, where the fundamental Joint Stock Companies Act (which is considered the cornerstone of modern company legislation) was only approved in 1856. From the point of view of company regulations, therefore, Finland was not particularly backward or outlying.

An overview on "the development of commercial law in Sweden and Finland," though, cannot avoid the issue of the role played by scholars in commercial law matters. This gap is filled by two articles devoted to the teaching of commercial law at Finnish universities, which provide an interesting insight into the academic world. Taken together, they cover a timeframe of three centuries (18th–20th cent.), showing the long path that led to the recognition of commercial law as an autonomous discipline.

As Jussi Salilla explains, even though "commercial and economic law" was identified as an independent subject in Finnish law faculties in the early nineteenth century, in fact, no handbooks or other forms of legal literature appear to have been produced, so that analysis has, necessarily, to be based on lecture manuscripts. A comparison with the overwhelming central European commercial law and legal literature becomes therefore inevitable. In this context, it comes as no surprise that Johan Jakob Nordström – the leading Finnish scholar of his generation, who taught "commercial and economic law" in Helsinki in the 1830s and 1840s –, introduced in his course the legal aspects of international business on the basis of contemporary German literature. Nineteenth century Germany attracted, in fact, legal scholars from all over Europe and Nordström himself attended the lectures of Savigny, Thibaut, Gans, and von Ranke during his first major foreign trip in 1835. More surprising is, on the other hand, the independent way of thinking of scholars such as Matthias Calonius. His originality is probably ascribable to the fact that, even though he was appointed professor of law at the Royal Academy of Turku in 1778, he had a background in historical studies and his regard was therefore quite free from the awe in which Roman law was held. He dealt with commercial law in the framework of his courses on civil and maritime law, relying on Swedish legal literature and European (especially German) natural law doctrine. What is particularly interesting, from a continental perspective, is his criticism of Roman law in commercial law matters (e.g. bills of exchange or the role of *bona fide* in the protection of purchasers) in favor of Swedish statutory law.

The essay by Heikki Pihlajamäki on one hand completes the analysis began by Salilla and on the other goes much further. In fact, going to great lengths to clarify what we should understand with regards to the expression "distinct legal discipline," he uses two tools: history and comparison. This approach provides Pihlajamäki the opportunity of outlining an extremely synthetic though convincing overview of the history of commercial law: from the medieval merchant courts of southern Europe to the *juridictions consulaires* of mid-seventeenth century France, from Italy to Maghreb, from Benvenuto Stracca to Johannes Loccenius (one of the few Swedish authors who touched upon commercial questions in the seventeenth century). In general, the author underlines the lack of interest of Swedish lawyers in commercial matters, which is explained by the fact that general rules of contract law were sufficient for domestic commerce, while international commerce was considered a part of maritime law. Pihlajamäki then analyses the long process that led to the creation, in 1924, of the first chair of commercial law in Finland (and in the Nordic countries), assigned to Lauri Cederberg, who had studied in Germany and used comparative legal history to approach commercial matters. The essay ends with a reflection on the concepts of center and periphery, of transplant and importer, based on the assumption that traditional European legal history has always considered Italy, France, Germany and the Netherlands as "the center": "the rest of Europe" – writes Pihlajamäki – "hardly exists at all, at least not the Nordic countries." What is particularly interesting is that, after having provided several examples of legal transplants from the center of Europe to its northern periphery, Pihlajamäki affirms that the reception was not passive. In addition, this observation brings us neatly back to Dave De ruysscher's definition of seventeenth century Sweden as a test ground for company law related issues.

This survey of commercial law history in Sweden and Finland is surprising for several reasons. First of all, for the absence of a well-established university network in those countries until very recent times; secondly, for the appointment of non-jurists as professors of law, like in the case of Matthias Calonius in eighteenth century Turku; thirdly, for the minor role played by guild-like organizations of merchants, in the sense of lobby groups of merchants who played specific and official roles in the political structures of the state.

From all these perspectives, the situation in other parts of Europe was very different. Let us take as an example two geographical areas – the Italian peninsula and England –, that (even considering the significant and well-known differences in their legal history), share a tradition of legal studies, which dates back to the twelfth century. At that time, Irnerius *studendo coepit docere* in Bologna and Vacarius (perhaps a pupil of Irnerius) followed the archbishop of Canterbury Theobald in England. Two masters who based their teaching on Roman law: Irnerius literally re-constructing the Justinian books and then providing them with glosses, and Vacarius writing for his students his famous anthology known as *Liber pauperum*, which certainly circulated at Oxford at the end of the twelfth century.[6] After quite similar beginnings, the education of lawyers took very different paths in Italy and England. Nevertheless, Roman law – so strong, powerful, overwhelming on the continent –, maintained an important role in England in education at least until the eighteenth century, and was the only legal science studied in English universities after Henry VIII's suppression of the teaching of canon law in the 1530s.

Studying law soon became the privileged path to access a political or even an ecclesiastical career in medieval Europe. For this reason, the well-organized and lively Italian universities attracted students from all over the continent (in Bologna they were organized in the *Universitas scholarium ultramontanorum*) and especially from Germany (*Natio Germanorum*). Even when, in the Modern period, Italy fell behind and the most important centers of new academic trends became France, or the Netherlands, or Germany, Italian law schools continued to maintain high standards. Moreover, legal literature developed at an extraordinary rate from the twelfth century onwards, and even though commercial law remained of no interest to learned doctors for a long time, it was, nevertheless, in Italy that the first systematic "handbook" on commercial law was published in 1553: the *Tractatus de mercatura seu mercatore* by Benvenuto Stracca.[7] In this context, it would have been unusual to appoint a law professor who did not have a degree in law.

6 Cortese 2000, p. 233.

7 Stracca 1553. On Stracca and on the development of commercial law literature in the Modern period, see: Birocchi 2002, 246 ff.

Furthermore, as a consequence of that "principle of association," so typical of the Italian *comuni* according to Francesco Calasso,[8] Italian merchants built up guilds, within the context of the peculiar economic growth of the medieval city-states. In the *comuni*, the guilds played a specific political role in the organization of the state, as they had their own statutes and tribunals. In addition, for example in Florence, one had to be a member of one of the city guilds (or *arti*) in order to be elected as a member of the *Priorato*, the most important political authority of the Florentine Republic.[9] A central role that slowly diminished in the Modern period thanks to the establishment of the nation state and the concentration of powers in the hands of a *princeps*. The importance of the guilds, their political role, their privileges, are features that can be found, to a certain extent, in medieval England too;[10] and they continued to play an important role in the development of commercial law in the Modern period, considering that the commercial corporations of the the sixteenth century can be seen, in some way, as heirs of those medieval organizations. Otherwise, the merchants described in this book – even when they are powerful, well connected and successful – seem not to act as official representatives of any guild-like organization (especially not at a political level).

Another point of interest is, from the point of view of countries based on the *ius commune* system,[11] the absence of any reference to canon law in the Scandinavian context, even before the Lutheran Reformation, considering how strong the interferences of canon law in commercial law have been for centuries, especially with reference to the problem of usury.[12] Even though, it is usually believed that commercial law developed, from the Middle Ages onwards, quite independently of Roman law, providing new tools (such as the bill

8 Calasso 1949, p. 93–105. Calasso used the expression *principio associativo* or, more often, *moto associativo*: "(…) quel moto associativo che riteniamo anche noi come l'anima del secolo che si rinnova": p. 97.

9 The very complex institutional dynamics of Florence between the fourteenth and the fifteenth century are well described in: Guidi 1981.

10 Still ultimate the book by Gross 1890.

11 For an in-depth analysis the complex dynamics of the *ius commune* system and a critical approach to nineteenth and twentieth century historiography, see: Conte 2009. For an overview of the *ius commune system* and the role played by universities in the late Middle Ages, see the recent English translation of Mario Ascheri's classical *I diritti del medioevo italiano* (2000) 2013: *The Laws of Late Medieval Italy. Foundations for a European Legal System* (1000–1500).

12 Legal literature on the history of usury is notoriously overwhelming. For an interesting summary of the problem with reference to commercial laws and practices see: Favali 2004, p. 89–106. An in-depth and very updated analysis of the topic can be found in the essay by Mayenburg 2020.

of exchange), new contracts (such as the *commenda* or the maritime insurance) and new forms for the organization of trade (such as the *compagnia*),[13] in all countries where the system of *ius commune* was widespread, the background of Roman-canon law could not be ignored, even within the framework of commercial law.

In conclusion: when, in the Modern period, the role of Italy (or better, of the Mediterranean) as an economic center began to fade, the new dynamics of the transoceanic trade left the country at the periphery of a world that was changing its very dimensions as early as the the sixteenth century.[14] Even though northern Europe too had been involved in fundamental economic activities for the whole late Middle Ages, thanks to the role played by the Hanseatic League from the Baltic to the North Sea,[15] the "heartland" of commercial law began its "migration" to new commercial centers: to the Netherlands, to England and (now we can say) up to Scandinavia. As the papers of this book demonstrate, Sweden and Finland were at the crossroads of cultures and commercial interests, allowing us to re-examine them as lively laboratories for commercial laws and practices rather than dismissing them as a negligible periphery.

Literature

Ascheri, Mario. 2013. *The Laws of Late Medieval Italy. Foundations for a European Legal* System (1000–1500) (Leiden-Boston: Brill), Eng. translation of: *I diritti del medioevo italiano* (2000).

Birocchi, Italo. 2002. *Alla ricerca dell'ordine: fonti e cultura giuridica nell'età moderna* (Turin: Giappichelli).

Calasso, Francesco. 1949. *Gli ordinamenti giuridici del Rinascimento medievale* (2nd ed., Milan: Giuffrè).

Conte, Emanuele. 2009. *Diritto comune* (Bologna: Il Mulino).

Cordes, Albrecht. 1998. *Spätmittelalterlicher Gesellschaftshandel im Hanseraum* (Cologne: Böhlau).

Cortese, Ennio. 2000. *Le grandi linee della storia giuridica medievale* (Rome: Il Cigno).

13 For a survey of commercial contracts in the Middle Ages, see: Sarti 2016, p. 107–108.

14 A good summary of this huge topic, completed by a very interesting (and carefully selected) international bibliography, can be found in: Fusaro 2008.

15 For an updated overview of the topic and of the relevant bibliography, see: Wubs-Mrozewicz and Jenks 2013. See also the classical work by Cordes 1998.

De ruysscher, D., Cordes, A., Dauchy, S. and Pihlajamäki, H. (eds.) 2017. *The Company in Law and Practice: Did Size Matter?* (Middle Ages – Nineteenth Century) (Leiden-Boston: Brill).

Favali, Lyda. 2004. *Qirād islamico, commenda medievale e strategie culturali dell'Occidente* (Turin: Giappichelli).

Fusaro, Maria. 2008. *Reti commerciali e traffici globali in età moderna* (Rome-Bari: Laterza).

Gialdroni, S., Cordes, A., Dauchy, S., De ruysscher D. and Pihlajamäki, P. (eds.) 2020. *Migrating Words, Migrating Merchants, Migrating Law. Trading Routes and the Development of Commercial Law* (Leiden-Boston: Brill).

Goldschmidt, Levin. 1913. *Universalgeschichte des Handelsrechts* (Stuttgart: Ferdinand Enke, 1891), It. trans. V. Pouchain and A. Scialoja, *Storia universale del diritto commerciale* (Turin: UTET).

Gross, Charles. 1890. *The Gild Merchant. A Contribution to British Municipal History,* vol. 1–2 (Oxford: Clarendon Press).

Guidi, G. 1981. *Il governo della città-Repubblica di Firenze nel primo Quattrocento*, voll. 1–3 (Florence: Olschki).

Mayenburg, David von. 2020. ""Wörter für Wucher": Ius commune and the 16th Century Debate on the Legitimacy of South German Trading Houses" in Gialdroni, S. et al. (eds.).

Pihlajamäki, H., Cordes, A., Dauchy S. and De ruysscher D. (eds.). 2018. *Understanding the Sources of Early Modern and Modern Commercial Law. Courts, Statutes, Contracts and Legal Scholarship* (Leiden-Boston: Brill).

Sarti, N. 2016. "Il medioevo dei diritti" in *Tempi del diritto. Età medievale, moderna, contemporanea*, (ed.) P. Alvazzi del Frate et al. (Turin: Giappichelli), 53–112.

Shaw, John (ed.) 1887. *Charters relating to the East India Company from 1600 to 1761* (Madras: Govt. Press).

Stracca, Benvenuto. 2013. *De mercatura seu mercatore tractatus* (Venetiis: Paolo Manuzio, 1553).

Wubs-Mrozewicz Justyna and Jenks Stuart (eds.). 2013. *The Hanse in Medieval and Early Modern Europe* (Leiden: Brill).

Index

www.ingramcontent.com/pod-product-compliance
Lightning Source LLC
LaVergne TN
LVHW010642300926
849161LV00005B/1020
* 9 7 8 9 0 0 4 3 9 3 1 9 6 *